Water Distribution Conflict : India-China and Pakistan

WATER DISTRIBUTION CONFLICT
India-China and Pakistan

Dr. Amitabh Bhatt

PRASHANT PUBLISHING HOUSE
DELHI-110094

Published by :
PRASHANT PUBLISHING HOUSE
C-34, 28 Foota Road, Gali-3,
West Karwal Nagar, Delhi-110094
Phone : 011-22963970, Mob. : 9810396373, 8826258746
e-mail.: prashantpublishinghouse@gmail.com

Water Distribution Conflict : India-China and Pakistan

Reserved
First Published 2019

ISBN : 978-93-88526-21-0

PRINTED IN INDIA
Published by Mr. R.K. Jha M/s Prashant Publishing House and Published at H.S. Offset House Press, Delhi.

Preface

The water distribution treaty between India and Pakistan that was brokered by the World Bank in 1960 to use the water available in the Indus system of rivers originating in India, has come in the limelight once again as New Delhi has decided to stop the flow of its share of water from the three eastern rivers - Beas, Ravi, and Sutlej - to Islamabad.

With tensions rising between India and Pakistan in the wake of a deadly terrorist attack earlier this month that killed more than 40 Indian police officers in Kashmir, New Delhi has decided to retaliate in part by cutting off some river water that flows downstream to Pakistan. The decision to build a dam on the Ravi River, whose waters are allocated to India by treaty but a portion of which had been allowed to flow through to Pakistan, adds an extra source of conflict between two nuclear-armed neighbors that have repeatedly clashed over the disputed Kashmir territory.

In 2016, after militants attacked an Indian Army base near the town of Uri, Prime Minister Narendra Modi said "blood and water can't flow together" and his government threatened to do the same thing. Instead, the Indian military staged what it called surgical strikes against targets just across the border in Pakistan. This time around, India seems more serious about using water as punishment. Under the Indus Water Treaty, a World Bank-brokered agreement that goes back decades, India and Pakistan divided the rights to the enormous Indus River and its tributaries that wind across the subcontinent.

Meanwhile, China and Pakistan are employing water as a tool against India. Pakistan's water war strategy is centred on invoking the IWT's conflict-resolution provisions to internationalise any perceived disagreement with India. China's cut-off of hydrological data to India in 2017 — an action that not only breached bilateral accords but also caused preventable flood-related deaths in Assam — helped highlight how Beijing is fashioning unconventional tools of coercive diplomacy. Only by asserting its Indus leverage can India hope to end Pakistan's unconventional war. Modi's new, unified water power ministry aims to rectify a splintered, piecemeal approach that has compounded India's water challenges. But without institutionalised, integrated policymaking, it will not be easy to develop a holistic approach to a critical resource increasingly in short supply or to fashion an effective hydro-diplomacy that advances long-term water interests.

Nearly a year after their standoff on the Doklam Plateau began, India and China are trying to get their relationship back on track. Indian Prime Minister Narendra Modi met with Chinese President Xi Jinping late last month in Wuhan with just that goal in mind, and though their summit was more spectacle than substance, it was nonetheless a necessary step toward resolution. The informal meeting gave the two leaders a prime opportunity to lay aside, however briefly, their countries' long-standing differences and focus on topics of mutual concern, such as climate change, food security and natural disasters. Yet one related issue was missing from the agenda: water. If Beijing and New Delhi fail to address the matter, the repercussions will likely be devastating for the region, its inhabitants and its environment.

This is a reference book. All the matter is just compiled and edited in nature, taken from the various sources which are in public domain.

This is a pioneering study of Asia's murky water politics and the relationships between fresh water, peace, and security. In this unique and highly readable book.

—Editor

Contents

1

Introduction

ASIA'S WORSENING WATER CRISIS

Of all the natural resources on which the modern world depends, water is the most critical. There are replacements for oil, but there is no substitute for water. It is essential to produce virtually all the goods in the marketplace, from food to industrial products, as well as to produce electricity, to refine oil and gas, and to mine coal and uranium.

Put simply, water scarcity and rapid economic advance cannot go hand in hand. Yet water scarcity now affects more than two-fifths of the people on Earth, and by 2025 two-thirds of the global population is likely to be living in water-scarce or water-stressed conditions. Water-scarce nations face very tough choices and serious socioeconomic consequences. And the majority of the world's people living in water-related despair will be in Asia.

Water has emerged as a key issue that will determine if Asia heads toward greater cooperation or greater competition. Asia is the world's driest continent, with availability of freshwater less than half the global annual average of 6,380 m^3 per inhabitant. Asia's rivers, lakes and aquifers give it, per capita, less than one-tenth the water of South America or Australia and New Zealand, less than one-fourth of North America, almost one-third of Europe, and moderately less than Africa.

Yet the world's fastest-growing demand for water is in Asia, which now serves as the locomotive of the world economy. Today, the most dynamic Asian economies, including China, India, Indonesia, South Korea and Vietnam, are all in or close to being in conditions of water stress. The exceptions are few: Bhutan, Brunei, Burma, Cambodia, Laos, Malaysia and Papua New Guinea. Yet Asia continues to draw on tomorrow's water to meet today's needs.

Worse still, Asia has one of the lowest levels of water efficiency and productivity in the world. Against this background, it is no exaggeration to say that the water crisis threatens Asia's economic and political rise and its environmental sustainability. For investors, it carries risks as potentially damaging as non-performing loans, real-estate bubbles, infrastructure overbuilding and political corruption. The water crisis means that the cost of doing business in Asia is set to rise. Water has also emerged as a source of increasing competition and discord within and between nations, spurring new tensions over shared basin resources and local resistance to governmental or corporate decisions to set up water-intensive industries.

WATER CRISIS LOOMS COUNTRYWIDE

Water has become the most commercial products of the century. This may sound bizarre, but true. In fact, what water is to the 21st century, oil was to the 20th century. The stress on the multiple water resources is a result of a multitude of factors. On the one hand, the rapidly rising population and changing lifestyles have increased the need for fresh water. On the other hand, intense competitions among users in agriculture, industry and domestic sector is pushing the ground water table deeper.

To get bucket of drinking water is a struggle for most women in the country. The virtually dry and dead water resources have lead to acute water scarcity, affecting the socio-economic condition of the society. The drought conditions have pushed villagers to move to cities in search of jobs, whereas women and girls have to trudge further. This time lost in fetching water can very well translate into financial gains, leading to a better life for the family. If opportunity costs were taken into account, it would be clear that in most rural areas, households are paying far more for water supply than the often-normal rates charged in urban areas. Also, if this cost of fetching water which is almost equivalent. to 150 million women days each year, is covered into a loss for the national exchequer, it translates into a whopping 10 billion rupees per year.

The government has accorded the highest priority to rural drinking water for ensuring universal access as a part of policy framework to achieve the goal of reaching the unreached. Despite the installation of more than 3.5 million hand pumps and over 116 thousand piped water supply schemes, in many parts of the country, the people face water scarcity almost every year, there by meaning that our water supply systems are failing to sustain despite huge investments.

In India, there are many villages either with scarce water supply or without any source of water. If there is no source of potable water in 2.5

kilometres, then the village becomes no source water village or problem village. In many rural areas, women still have to walk a distance of about 2.5 kms to reach the source of water. She reaches home carrying heavy pots, not to rest but to do other household chores of cooking, washing~ cleaning, caring of children and looking after livestock. Again in the evening she has to fetch water. Thus a rural woman's life is sheer drudgery.

Water is the biggest crisis facing India in terms of spread and severity, affecting one in every three persons.

Even in Chennai, Bangalore, Shimla and Delhi, water is being rationed and India's food security is under threat.

With the lives and livelihood of millions at risk, urban India is screaming for water. For instance, water is rationed twice a week in Bangalore, and for 30 minutes a day in Bhopal; 250 tankers make 2,250 trips to quench Chennai's thirst. Mumbai routinely lives through water cuts from January to June, when some areas get water once in three days in Hyderabad.

Harrowing midnight for a precious bucket of drinking water is a regular feature for many families of Vypuri, an Island off the mainland of Kochi. Women have to queue up in front of the public water taps, being at the lag end of the pipeline system, they get water only after the users ahead in the pipeline finish collecting water. There are nights when water pressure dips so low that some women get it after midnight. They split their day between household chores and collecting water.

Apart from the water scarcity caused by Coca-cola in Plachimada, the other districts in the state are facing a water crisis. For instance, in Kottayam district at some places, the water scarcity is so acute that people hesist to offer a glass of water to the visitor, which hitherto was a common custom.

In the upper Kuttanadu area of the district during summer people collect water from a distance of 3-4 kms. Water supply from public taps is erratic and very often even after standing for an hour in the queue; people are not able to get a bucket of water. Most women and girls in Rajasthan find themselves searching water for much of the year.

They trudge bare foot in the hot sun for hours over wastelands, across thorny fields, or rough terrain in search of water, often life the colour of mud and brackish, but still welcome for the parched throats back home.

On an average, a rural woman walks more than 14000 km a year just to fetch water. Their urban sisters are only slightly better off- they do not walk such distances, but stand in the long winding queues for hours on end to collect water from the roadside taps on the water lorries.

In every household, in the rural areas in Rajasthan, women and girl children bear the responsibilit of collecting, transporting, storing, and managing water. In places, where there is no water for farming, men migrate to urban areas in search of work leaving women behind to fond for the old and the children. Women spend most of their time, collecting water with little time for other productive work. This impacts on the education of the girl child, if the girl is herself not collecting water, she is looking after the home and her siblings when her mother is away.

In brief:

- Water source being open dug well, the quality of water is poor; dirty, saline and has turbidity
- Women have to make at least three trips at 5 am, 11 am and 5 pm
- Sometimes, the number of trips is more
- Total distance traveled is 9-10 km, even higher
- Total Time spent is 6-9 hours
- Total number of pots/buckets is about 3 pots, 30-45 litres (one pot of 10-15 litres per trip)
- Due to long distance, they have to take rest in the middle of the way. Dust storms aggravate their problem
- At some villages water from tubewells is too saline to drink. Even animals particularly cow gets indigestion after drinking this water, so the villagers add water from the dug well. The entire life of women in rural areas like Jaisalmer is spent on water collection and cooking. Even the girls of 8-10 years cannot be spared. They cannot afford the luxury of school. For instance for Pappu a girl of hardly 10 years, water collection has become her main job. In the words of her grandmother "Water fetching is the schooling for Pappu." There are so many Pappus in the villages and dhaanis of Jaisalmer.

In Sriganganagar, the Indira Gandhi canal is the main source for drinking water. However, during the crisis period (either because of no water in the main canal/sub canal or due to the erratic power supply), the rich remain unaffected.

In such crisis women from poorhouse hold draw water from the village diggis, which is totally unfit for any kind of human activity. They use this water not only for washing cloth and bathing but also for drinking. Due to the formation of algae, water becomes greenish and filthy. Women add alum to purify it.

In Orissa drinking water is being privatized. The government first insists on the formation of water associations and conveniently pass the responsibilities on to these association. When this proves inefficient, water distribution rights are given away to private contractors. For example, the Orissa government initially stressed on the formation of Paani Panchayats (water associations). Later using police the government suppressed these panchayats justifying this by claiming that the villages were not being responsible enough. Titlagarh is the hottest town of India, but it has no water, causing great misery to the women. As the highest temperature, is recorded here 52 degrees centigrade which is also the highest temperature in India.

People called "Titlagarh" as "Tatlagarh", in local language Tatla means hot. In Titlagarh water problem is acute. People are buying water throughout the year for drinking and cooking purpose.

In the month of May and June the rate of water increase three times, from Rs 2 per Dabba to Rs.8 per Dabba (container). This is the picture of urban areas, but in rural areas the problem is worse, where the tubewells all are becoming dry but people have no money to buy water. Due to the water problem some villagers are migrating to other places.

In Uttranchal women are suffering a lot in every village where water problem is severe. Natural sources are drying up which adds the kilometres for women everyday to quench the thirst of their family as well as animals.

Women are the major part of the workforce in Garhwal. They work from early morning to late evening to serve the family. They do all household work from cooking to cleaning and washing clothes and soiled utensils as well as look after their children and animals. Women also collect the water required for cooking, cleaning, washing, bathing and drinking both for human beings and animals.

During the survey in Jaunsar area of district Tehri Garhwal, in villages such as Nagthat, Duena, Vishoi, Gadol, Jandoh, Chi tar, Chichrad and Gangoa, it was observed that water in the region is mostly acidic in nature.

The water problem in Chi tar and Gangoa villages is very severe, where men and women carry water on mules from 8-10 Km to the village. Because of the poor water quality, most of the villagers in the regions are suffering from many diseases related to skin and teeth. Natural resources of water in the area are very few and they are also disappearing very fast. During the survey, Smt. Nisha Devi of Chi tar village explained that they are not getting enough water for their animals so they take their animals to the spring about 2-3 kms away.

In Bundelkhand, women have no work but to collect drinking water on their heads from long distance. The grim situation of water may be best illustrated by one Bundelkhandi saying which roughly translated as "let the husband die but the earthen pot of water should not be broken".

The scenario is worst in Patha in Chitrakut district where women have to travel a long distance to collect water for drinking. Half of the time of women is spent to collect water, which affects their health and the well-being of their children. The paucity of time due to water crisis aggravates the domestic problem.

Instead of solving the water crisis, attempts are being made to create a disastrous situation in the region. Banda city entirely depends on the Ken river. If Ken is linked with Betwa, then it will not affect only Banda, but would also jeopardize the survival of farmers who depend on Ken.

Even in Delhi the water scenario is no better, being worst in Delhi slums. For example Sanjay colony slum of New Delhi has population about 15,000-20,000 with about 4500 households in the locality. Majority of the population is self-employed and are engaged in making daris, mats and other clothes for sale. In this area people collect water from different sources depending on the availability such as DJB tanker, MCD pipe water supply and from Sulabh International. DJB tanker comes daily but it has no fixed time for water distribution. The water that comes from MCD pipe water has fixed time for water supply but it only comes for 1-2 hr in the evening (around 4.30 p.m.). At MCD pipe line people made bore and fetch water from it. If the people don't get water from the above sources they are forced to get it from Sulabh International near Kalkaji temple for which they have pay @ Rs. 2 for 20 litre or so.

The Water crisis is same in West Bengal. In all the districts, the water commons have ceased to exist, and have become open-access resources, with hardly anyone responsible to take care of the resources. In North Bengal, some women reported they had opinions regarding the use of the water body, but their importance in management decisions is cipher. The absence of the community from the management of the water resources is indeed a tragedy, because now the resources are at the mercy of either the market or government officials.

Punjab; the name stands for abundance of water, but the present situation of water resources in the state is highly critical. The ground water availability is drastically hampered. The village ponds are drying day by day. Women in the villages desperately need water. Near Talwandi Sabo, for some villages, the source for drinking water is about 8 km away. Near Jajjal due to contaminated water, women are suffering from a number of diseases including cancer. There have been several deaths attributed to polluted water.

For Maharashtra, water is an abiding concern. In many villages women have to walk more than 3 kilometres everyday to fetch two huge vessels of water illegally from a government reservoir. They have to make at least three trips everyday. The state government do not send tankers to the villagers. At some places, women spend Rs 5 for two canes of water. Images of women carrying the pots of water, walking miles and miles for one single pot are common in the state of Maharashtra.

Women in Maharashtra have carried the water burden both as a result of scarcity and abundance. Drought displacement due to dams and irrigation have contributed to increasing water burden of women. Women in Nandurbar district of North Maharashtra share their woes "forget about getting safe drinking water from wells, we spend most of our time locating streams and springs that quench our thrust".

Many Women came as brides, their hair have gone dry, but the search for water has not ended. Karnataka is facing the worst kind of water crisis. In Bangalore, only 35% of the city gets water on daily basis, the rest on alternative days.

In addition to the scarcity, erratic water supply is another problem. In Samadhanagar area, water generally comes in the morning at 11 A.M or in the middle of the night. Both these timings make it very difficult for women to collect water as they leave early in the morning to go to work. In Doddanagar slums in the city, women and children who are also breadwinners of the family spend 3-4 hours filling water, losing their wages. In Hosapalya locality women get severe joint pain in their shoulders, hips and knees due to carrying water pits from water sources outside their colony. In Peenya industrial area, many street fights occur among the women over water. Social conflict and tension is high due to water crisis.

In brief, at an estimate about 150 Million-Woman Days and Rs 10 Billion are lost in fetching water.

CURRENT ISSUES ON INDUS WATER SHARING

Issues External to Pakistan

There are a host of factors external to Pakistan that could also affect the Indus River System. One is the climatic changes leading to reduced flows on the Indus *per se*. Another exogenous factor is the growing demand within India, especially the state of Jammu & Kashmir (J&K) where people feel that the IWT has wrongfully deprived them of water resulting retarding the growth of agriculture, power generation, and irrigation from rivers that originate and flow from their very state. There was also a widespread demand within India for abrogation of the IWT after the attack on the Indian Parliament on December 13, 2001 by terrorists supported directly by the Pakistani state apparatus.

The Tulbul Navigation Lock/Wullar Barrage Issue

The 74 Sq. Km. Wullar Lake (original size 202 Sq. Kms.) is the largest freshwater lake in India and is situated on the Jhelum and supplies 40% of

J&K's fish catch. The stretch of 22 Km between Sopore and Baramulla becomes non-navigable during the lean winter season with a water depth of only 2.5 ft. It is only in spring that rainfall causes the snow to melt at higher elevations on the surrounding mountains and causes floods.

In order to improve navigation, India started constructing in 1985, a barrage 439 feet long and with a lock, at the mouth of the lake to raise the flow of water in winter to 4000 cusecs with a depth of 4 ft with an added storage of 0.3 MAF. Pakistan objected to this project and construction was halted in 1987. Pakistan's objection stems from two issues, one India needs to get concurrence of the design from Pakistan and two, it cannot store waters as per IWT on the Jhelum Main anything in excess of 0.01 MAF as "incidental storage work").

Pakistan 's real objections may be due to its fear that such a barrage may damage its own Triple-Canal project linking Jhelum and Chenab with the Upper Bari Doab Canal. Pakistan also says that such a barrage would be a security risk enabling the Indian Army to make the crossing of the river either easy or difficult through controlled release of water. India 's argument is that such a barrage would not reduce the quantum of water flow and it would also be beneficial to Pakistan by regulating water flow to Mangla Dam by controlling floods and also improve the Pakistani Triple-canal irrigation system.

The water flow would indeed double during the lean winter period from the current 2000 cusecs. Also, the project does not envisage building any new storage capacity as the Wullar lake already existed and the water is only for non-consumptive use (this term includes such usage as navigation, floating of timber, flood protection or control, and fishing with no diminution in volume of water returned to the river/tributaries after use) which is allowed by the IWT. The Wullar barrage is not a storage project but a control project permissible under the treaty. The two countries had indeed reached an agreement in October, 1991 but then Pakistan suddenly introduced an irrelevant element in February, 1992 by linking the termination of Kishenganga Hydroelectric project with further movements in the Tulbul Navigation Lock project and India 's refusal stalled further work.

The 1991 draft agreement stipulated that India would build a 40-feet wide lock but leave ungated 6.2 Metres of the lake at a crest level of 1574.9 Metres and would also forego 0.30MAF storage while Pakistan would allow the lake to fill to its full capacity at 1578 metres.

When the agreement was reached in 1991, the only contention that remained was the timing of the filling up of the lake. The crucial period was between June 21 and August 20 every year. Between October, 1987, and August, 1992, experts from the two countries met eight times to settle the issue. The matter was taken up during the Foreign Secretary-level talks between 1990 and 1994 also. The ninth round was held in July, 2004.

The Salal Hydroelectric Project

This was the first major dispute successfully resolved bilaterally under IWT. On April 14, 1978, the governments of India and Pakistan entered into a treaty on the Salal project. The Salal hydroelectric project on the Chenab in Jammu and Kashmir was negotiated by the Janata Party government in India and the Bhutto administration in Pakistan and has not been disputed by subsequent governments in Pakistan.

The negotiations and discussions took place for a period of four years between 1974 and 1978 between the Indus Commissioners and the foreign offices. The project provides waters to Pakistan in a regulated manner but involves no diversion by India.

However, Pakistan successfully objected to the building of the anti-siltation sluice gates, which were six low-level outlets normally used for controlling sedimentation, resulting in decreased power generation capacity of this project. India also agreed to reduce the heights of the spillway gates from 40 feet to 30 feet.

The Ranbir and Pratap Canals

The Ranbir Canal, built in 1870, was intended to feed the areas of Miran Sahib, Vijaypur and Madhopur. Poor maintenance has ensured that it can now carry just 300 cubic feet per second of water, rather than the 1,000 cusecs it was designed for when originally built. The Pratap Canal, meant to meet the needs of the Akhnoor-Sunderbani belt, has also silted up. These canals off take from Chenab between Salal and Marala headworks. These two canals need urgent repair work to restore their earlier capacities. Under the treaty, India is allowed to take out a fixed quantity of water for these channels. Many restrictions, such as quantum and dates of withdrawal have been imposed on India by the IWT.

The Kishenganga Project

India started the 330 MW Kishenganga hydroelectric projects across River Kishenganga after protracted negotiations between the Central Electricity Authority (CEA), the Defence Ministry, and the environmentalists who fear the loss of the serene Gurez valley. The project involves a 103 metre dam across the river before it crosses the Line of Control (LoC) and a channel and a 27 Km long tunnel through the North Kashmir ranges to bring the water to the Wullar lake where a hydroelectric power station will be built as part of an integrated project. The Kashmir Chief Minister Dr. Farooq Abdullah signed an MoU with the Union Power Minister in July, 2000 for the project. The National Hydroelectric Power Corp. (NHPC) was entrusted with this project on a Build-Own-Operate-Transfer (BOOT) basis. The CEA cleared the project only in June, 2004.

Pakistan objects to the Kishenganga project fearing an adverse impact on its envisaged 969-MW Neelum- Jhelum power plant to be constructed with Chinese assistance. This project was initially planned for 1994-1997 but lies dormant because of lack of funds. The Indian Kishenganga project is expected to lead to a shortfall of 21% loss of water flow in Neelum resulting in a 9% reduction in power for the Pakistani project. The IWT allows India to store waters on Neelum for power generation and so Pakistan wants to start its project first in order to deny waters to India claiming the principle of "prior appropriation", per Paragraph 15(iii), states *"where a Plant is located on a Tributary of The Jhelum on which Pakistan has any Agricultural use or hydroelectric use, the water released below the Plant may be delivered, if necessary, into another Tributary but only to the extent existing Agricultural Use or hydroelectric use by Pakistan on the former Tributary would not be adversely affected"*.

India also claims that the waters will ultimately reach Pakistan through Jhelum though not through Kishenganga (Neelum). In the meanwhile, Pakistan has felt the urgency to take up its USD 1.6 Billion Neelum –Jhelum Hydropower Project by appointing a private company, NESPAK, as consultants and complete the international bidding and evaluation by April 2005.

The Baglihar Project

This project, currently under construction by the Jammu & Kashmir Power Development Corp. on the Chenab in Doda Distt, will generate 450 MW of power when commissioned by end-December, 2005. The contract was extended in 2002 to raise the capacity to 900 MW by Dec., 2007.

Pakistan claims that this dam will result in a loss of 7000-8000 cusecs of water a day during the *rabi* season. India has assured Pakistan that the quantum of water will not be diminished in any way. Pakistan disputes India 's contention that this is a run-of-river project and the site is unsuitable for an ungated spillway.

The works involve the construction of a "Pondage" of 15 Million Cubic Metre (IWT allows for 'Pondage', a term meaning Live Storage, of only sufficient magnitude to meet fluctuations in the discharge of the turbines arising from variations in the daily and the weekly loads of the plant) capacity and an underground power station.

Pakistan claims that the submerged gate spillways of this 429-feet high 1046-feet long dam, allow India to increase the reservoir's storage capacity to 164,000 acre feet and the ability to stop water for about 26 days during December, January and February affecting canals taking off Marala headworks.

The IWT specifies the following with respect to gated spillways, *"If the conditions at the site of a plant make a gated spillway necessary, the bottom level of the gates in normal closed position shall be located at the highest level consistent with sound and economical design and satisfactory construction and operation of the works"*.

This project, Pakistan believes, could also lead to inundation of Bajwat Area above Marala headworks due to sudden synchronized releases from Dulhasti, Baglihar and Salal reservoirs on Chenab. Pakistan also claims that India adopted a stonewalling tactics by not allowing the Permanent Indus Commission members of Pakistan from visiting the dam site for four years after having been officially informed of the project in 1998, little recognizing that the 1999 Kargil conflict and the general mobilization of Indian troops as part of *Op.*

Parakram following the Dec. 13, 2001 Parliament attack, both events of Pakistan's own making, prevented such site visits. In fact, India suspended the site visit on Dec. 24, 2001 following the decision to mobilize troops. Pakistan also contests that it was informed only in 1998 about the Bagilhar project, though the GoI had informed Pakistan as early as 1992.

The Pakistani Commissioner of the Permanent Indus Commission had recommended to his government to appoint a neutral expert in Feb. 2003 and accordingly Pakistan claims to have served two notices to GoI in May and November of the same year. Following the February meeting, India allowed a visit by Pakistani experts to the Baglihar project site in October.

The Pakistani Commissioner is reported to have made the same recommendation to his Government in January 2004 after another round of PIC meeting. On December 15, 2004, India supplied Pakistan with more data on the project as a goodwill gesture and rejected Pakistan 's claims of violation of IWT. However, Pakistan rebuffed India 's explanations, refused India one week time to study and reply, and decided to discontinue the talks-illustrating Pakistani leadership uncompromising attitude and intransigence.

By mid January 2005, Pakistan requested the World Bank to appoint a neutral expert under Article 9(2)(A) of the IWT, claiming one week later that the World Bank chief Mr.Wolfensohn, honored with Pakistan's highest award of Hilal-e-Pakistan during a visit to that country in early February 2005, had assured Gen. Musharraf that there would be no delay in appointing such an expert.

While responding to enquiries from World Bank, India advised the Bank that rather it should allow the suspended bilateral course of action to resume rather than get involved at that stage especially as some convergence of views had appeared in the last round of talks in New Delhi. Meanwhile, Pakistan 's Minister for Education and former head of the ISI, Javed Ashraf Qazi, warned the Pakistani National Senate that the nation might go to war with India over Baglihar "controversy."

Embankment on Ravi

Pakistan claims that India has built a 15-Km long embankment (also known as River Training Works, RTWs) on river Ravi in the Narowal sector in 2002, in front of Kot Naina, a village in Shakargarh Distt.

Pakistan claims that such a construction "so close to the international border" is violative of both the IWT and the Border Ground Rules, 1961 and has caused flooding on its side. By 2002, Pakistan had also decided to build a similar embankment on its side.

Issues Within Pakistan

The Indus River system, which accounts for 65% of water flow within an arid Pakistan, poses several major challenges to Pakistan today. Pakistan faces both political and non-political problems with respect to The Indus River System. On the political front, there have been serious differences among the various provinces about sharing of the waters. In Sind, sea water has intruded as much as 54 miles into the estuary of the Indus river due to low or no flow.

On the basis of a series of meetings among provinces in March 1991, an agreement, Water Agreement Accord (WAA), was reached on the sharing of the river waters. It stipulated the following allocations

Table : Water Allocation among Pakistani Provinces, 1991 (in MAF)

Province	Kharif	Rabi	Total
Punjab	37.07	18.87	55.94
Sindh *	33.94	14.82	48.76
NWFP **	3.48	2.30	5.78
Civil Canals	1.80	1.20	3.00
Balochistan	2.85	1.02	3.87

* - Including requirements of Karachi

** - Ungauged Civil Canals above the rim stations where measurements can be made

It was also decided to set up in 1992, an "Indus River System Authority" (IRSA), as per provisions of the 1991 Accord, with representation from all four provinces. However, actual water allocations have been made on the basis of "historic use" rather than on the 1991 settlement leading to more resentment in Sindh.

The climatic changes due to global warming have led to depleting flow in all Indus River system of rivers, especially the Indus, which depends on glacial runoffs for 90% of its waters. Generally, the Himalayan rivers also carry a very heavy sediment load especially during summer and rainy season, which in turn leads to river shifting and silting of dams and barrages.

The three largest dams in Pakistan, Tarbela, Mangla and Chashma have already lost ~ 25% of their capacity due to silting. This is a serious problem in a country which depends on river irrigation, rather than the monsoon rains, for 74% of its total cultivated land.

It is generally agreed that 40% of all the water drawn through the canals at barrage heads is lost because of seepage due to un-lined and porous beds and banks of the canals. Such problems exacerbate the already poor yield of the crops In addition, there is excessive system-loss of water due to improper and antiquated agricultural techniques and heavy cropping of water-intensive varieties like sugarcane and rice. While reeling under increasing drought for the last six years, it is also predicted that Pakistan will have a certain level of drought conditions for the next 15 years.. Since the dams mostly act as storage reservoirs during *Kharif* season and draw-down reservoirs during *Rabi*, there is an acute need within Pakistan for more storage.

There have been widespread protests against the proposed dams of Kalabagh at Mianwali, and Basha at Chilas, Gilgit area and the raising of the Mangla dam in Mirpur. Out of the four provinces of Pakistan, three viz. Sindh, Balochistan and NWFP are against these dams. Even the illegally occupied PoK and Balawaristan oppose the dam projects of Mangla and Basha. The proposed raising of the height of Mangla Dam in Mirpur, PoK, by another 40 feet, will further submerge that district. It is also possible that if India exercises its rights to store 1.5 MAF on Jhelum, the raised Mangla Dam will not fill up. The crux of the matter is the lack of agreement among provinces on the total water availability within the country.

Meanwhile, the dwindling flows of water and siltation have led to reduced power generation from the hydroelectric plants that are part of the Indus River System.. There is a real possibility of shutting down power generation permanently at Tarbela, leaving it for irrigation purposes only.

The dams, barrages and canals built to satisfy the increasing demands of water upstream have made water scarce in the Indus at the estuaries of the Arabian Sea causing the sea to push in and increase the salinity in 1.2 Million acres of farmlands. The discharge of freshwater from the Indus into the Arabian Sea has declined steadily from 85 MAF in the 1940s to about 10 MAF in the 90s and probably less today. Pakistan also uses the waters of the Indus rivers for another purpose, fortification of its defences along Indian borders. It has built a series of "defence canals" at strategic locations which are flooded at times of wars and tensions to prevent crossing by Indian armour and artillery. In 2002, after India mobilized its forces as part of Operation Parakram, Pakistan diverted waters to these "defence canals" accentuating the then already severe water shortage of 50% to over 70%.

The Indus remains important to both India and Pakistan in another less visible way. The extension of the exclusive economic zone (EEZ) beyond the 200 nautical mile (nm) limit from coastal baseline depends on the ability to prove the sedimentation of the Indus river into the sea and has to be claimed before May, 2009 The United Nations Convention on the Law of the Seas protocol allows the EEZ to be extended under several conditions. In places like the sedimentary basin of the Indus river, the sediment thickness of the rivers beyond the foot of the continental slope can be used to establish the outer limit of the continental shelf of a claimant. This requires baseline and bathymetry survey data. A crucial part of the claim is the delineation of the Territorial Sea Baseline (TSB) which is the set of coordinate points that define the line from which the seaward boundaries are to be measured. The continuing Pakistani wrangle with regards to Sir Creek has delayed the compilation and validation of the TSB thereby delaying the computation of the zone boundaries. This is important for India in view of the potential it has for national security, energy prospecting, mining, laying pipelines etc.

Conclusions

Pakistan faces one of the severest water shortages in the world as seen in its' per capita availability of water per annum fall from 5300 m^3 in 1951 to less than 1100 m^3 today. This figure is alarming given that it is below the internationally recommended level of 1500 m^3 and precariously close to the critical 1000 m^3 level. Compounded with the failure to fill the country's two largest reservoirs to capacity, declining flows in the Indus River System, elusive and contentious the inter-provincial water accord due to mutual suspicions among provinces, and an unsustainable population growth rate of 2% do not bode well for Pakistan's water situation. Disagreements on construction of new reservoirs, declining groundwater potential, and growing number of disputes with India after a relatively uneventful period of 44 years of water sharing will further complicate matters. In summation, the water situation in Pakistan (a country whose landscape is largely arid to semi-arid) is truly disastrous in spite of the Indus, its tributaries, and a treaty with generous concessions that has been implemented faithfully by upper riparian India to date in spite of grave provocations. Pakistani farmers may be forced to change to higher yielding earlier maturating crops, modify their sowing patterns, and employ micro irrigation in coming years to mitigate shortages-all of which will entail higher costs. Its frivolous objections to Indian projects and a general unwillingness to engage India constructively are partly to force India to amend the IWT to accommodate the emerging patterns of water use in Pakistan, such as water sharing during periods of shortage-a situation not envisaged in the treaty.

WORLD BANK INVOLVEMENT

In this same year, David Lilienthal, formerly the chairman of the Tennessee Valley Authority and of the U.S. Atomic Energy Commission, visited the region to write a series of articles for Colliers magazine. Lilienthal had a keen interest in the subcontinent and was welcomed by the highest levels of both Indian and Pakistani governments. Although his visit was sponsored by Colliers, Lilienthal was briefed by state department and executive branch officials, who hoped that Lilienthal could help bridge the gap between India and Pakistan and also gauge hostilities on the subcontinent. During the course of his visit, it became clear to Lilienthal that tensions between India and Pakistan were acute, but also unable to be erased with one sweeping gesture. In his journal he wrote:

"India and Pakistan were on the verge of war over Kashmir. There seemed to be no possibility of negotiating this issue until tensions abated. One way to reduce hostility... would be to concentrate on other important issues where cooperation was possible. Progress in these areas would promote a sense of community between the two nations which might, in time, lead to a Kashmir settlement. Accordingly, I proposed that India and Pakistan work out a program jointly to develop and jointly to operate the Indus Basin river system, upon which both nations were dependent for irrigation water. With new dams and irrigation canals, the Indus and its tributaries could be made to yield the additional water each country needed for increased food production. In the article I had suggested that the World Bank might use its good offices to bring the parties to agreement, and help in the financing of an Indus Development program. "

Lilienthal's idea was well received by officials at the World Bank, and, subsequently, by the Indian and Pakistani governments. Eugene R. Black, then president of the World Bank told Lilienthal that his proposal "makes good sense all round". Black wrote that the Bank was interested in the economic progress of the two countries and had been concerned that the Indus dispute could only be a serious handicap to this development. India's previous objections to third party arbitration were remedied by the Bank's insistence that it would not adjudicate the conflict, but, instead, work as a conduit for agreement.

Black also made a distinction between the "functional" and "political" aspects of the Indus dispute. In his correspondence with Indian and Pakistan leaders, Black asserted that the Indus dispute could most realistically be solved if the functional aspects of disagreement were negotiated apart from political considerations. He envisioned a group that tackled the question of how best to utilize the waters of the Indus Basin - leaving aside questions of historic rights or allocations.

Black proposed a Working Party made up of Indian, Pakistani and World Bank engineers. The World Bank delegation would act as a consultative group, charged with offering suggestions and speeding dialogue. In his opening statement to the Working Party, Black spoke of why he was optimistic about the group's success:

One aspect of Mr. Lilienthal's proposal appealed to me from the first. I mean his insistence that the Indus problem is an engineering problem and should be dealt with by engineers. One of the strengths of the engineering profession is that, all over the world, engineers speak the same language and approach problems with common standards of judgment. Black's hopes for a quick resolution to the Indus dispute were premature. While the Bank had expected that the two sides would come to an agreement on the allocation of waters, neither India nor Pakistan seemed willing to compromise their positions. While Pakistan insisted on its historical right to waters of all the Indus tributaries, and that half of West Punjab was under threat of desertification the Indian side argued that the previous distribution of waters should not set future allocation. Instead, the Indian side set up a new basis of distribution, with the waters of the Western tributaries going to Pakistan and the Eastern tributaries to India. The substantive technical discussions that Black had hoped for were stymied by the political considerations he had expected to avoid.

The World Bank soon became frustrated with this lack of progress. What had originally been envisioned as a technical dispute that would quickly untangle itself became an intractable mess. India and Pakistan were unable to agree on the technical aspects of allocation, let alone the implementation of any agreed upon distribution of waters. Finally, in 1954, after nearly two years of negotiation, the World bank offered its own proposal, stepping beyond the limited role it had apportioned for itself and forcing the two sides to consider concrete plans for the future of the basin. The proposal offered India the three eastern tributaries of the basin and Pakistan the three western tributaries. Canals and storage dams were to be constructed to divert waters from the western rivers and replace the eastern river supply lost by Pakistan.

While the Indian side was amenable to the World Bank proposal, Pakistan found it unacceptable. The World Bank allocated the eastern rivers to India and the western rivers to Pakistan. This new distribution did not account for the historical usage of the Indus basin, or the fact that West Punjab's Eastern districts could turn into desert, and repudiated Pakistan's negotiating position. Where India had stood for a new system of allocation, Pakistan felt that its share of waters should be based on pre-partition distribution. The World Bank proposal was more in line with the Indian plan and this angered the Pakistani delegation. They threatened to withdraw from the Working Party and negotiations verged on collapse.

But neither side could afford the dissolution of talks. The Pakistani press met rumors of an end to negotiation with talk of increased hostilities; the government was ill-prepared to forego talks for a violent conflict with India and was forced to reconsider its position.

India was also eager to settle the Indus issue; large development projects were put on hold by negotiations and Indian leaders were eager to divert water for irrigation.

In December 1954, the two sides returned to the negotiating table. The World Bank proposal was transformed from a basis of settlement to a basis for negotiation and the talks continued, stop and go, for the next six years.

One of the last stumbling blocks to an agreement concerned financing for the construction of canals and storage facilities that would transfer water from the western rivers to Pakistan. This transfer was necessary to make up for the water Pakistan was giving up by ceding its rights to the eastern rivers. The World Bank initially planned for India to pay for these works, but India refused. The Bank responded with a plan for external financing supplied mainly by the United States and the United Kingdom. This solution cleared the remaining stumbling blocks to agreement and the Treaty was signed by the Prime Ministers of both countries in 1960.

TURNING WATER CHALLENGES INTO OPPORTUNITIES

Water is vital in South Asia, where most countries are still largely agrarian. As such, water is inherently political – its socio-ecological flows are implicated in competition by economies, individuals and nations, while its distributional regimes have the capacity to alter lives and livelihoods. Competing water-use for agriculture, industry, and domestic purposes have led water to become an increasingly scarce resource with limited and threatened supply. In 2012, a total of 1023.8 billion cubic meters of water was withdrawn in the eight SAARC nations (including agricultural, industrial, domestic use, as well as desalination plants), out of a total 1982.0 billion cubic metres of renewable internal freshwater sources available (including river flows, rainfall and groundwater). Climate change, volatile rainfall patterns, groundwater depletion and the inefficient usage have precipitated a resource shortage, verging on a crisis in the region. Water disputes amongst the SAARC member nations, then, primarily centre on India's access to rivers and its competition with Nepal, Pakistan and Bangladesh for water 'rights'. Despite the various disputes for river water, there have been efforts at regional cooperation.

The Indus Water Treaty (1960) granted India rights over the eastern rivers (Sutlej, Beas and Ravi) and Pakistan the rights over the western rivers (the Indus, Jhelum and Chenab). Despite the treaty, there have been several disputes: Pakistan objected to the construction of the Kishenganga Dam, terming it a clear violation by India of the Indus Water Treaty, while contesting four more dams proposed by India on the Chenab. A second round of talks in August 2014 yielded no compromise.

Since the Kosi River Agreement between Nepal and India to manage flooding in 1954, talks between the two have stalled. As a result of mismanaged flood control, poor communication, and lack of cooperative maintenance, a dam neglected for decades by both led to the catastrophic flood in 2008, destroying 300,000 homes, 800,000 acres of cropland and displacing over 3 million individuals. More recently Nepal and India have agreed to expedite the 17-year-stalled Pancheshwar project, to generate 6,720 MW of hydropower along with increased irrigation facilities. Nepal has also cleared a GMR Company proposal to build a 900 MW Upper Karnali hydroelectric power plant as part of a scheme aimed at exporting electricity to India.

Despite the 1972 Joint River Commission for Water Management, tensions between India and Bangladesh on sharing resources came to a head in a dispute over the Teesta River. The 1996 comprehensive river pact established a 30-year water-sharing arrangement between the two countries. This was set to change in September 2011 when India's Prime Minister, Manmohan Singh, was to sign a pact with his Bangladesh counterpart for access and use of the Teesta waters. However, the Chief Minister of West Bengal, Mamata Banerjee, refused to approve the treaty, fearing that loss of higher volume of water to the lower riparian would cause problems in her state, especially during drier months. The Tipaimukh hydroelectric project in India is another similar source of contention. While it is expected to control floods in Assam's Barak valley and generate electricity for states in northeast India, farmers in Bangladesh fear it would reduce the water flow to their land, thus damaging rice crops that depend on seasonal flooding of these trans-boundary rivers during every monsoon. However, there has been a decision between the two countries to conduct a joint Environmental Impact Assessment of the project.

While SAARC initiatives have not addressed water management, storage and sharing, they have focused efforts on disaster management – both short-term (in terms of response) and long-term (primarily combating the effects of climate change). The SAARC Disaster Management Centre (SDMC) mandate serves all eight members of SAARC by providing policy advice and facilitating capacity building services. This includes strategic learning, research, training, system development and exchange of information for effective disaster risk reduction and management in South Asia.

The SDMC initiative stressed priorities for action on integrating disaster risk reduction, climate change adaption and a sustainable development agenda; increasing knowledge management (South Asia Disaster Knowledge Network (SADKN)) as an effective tool for networking, information sharing and knowledge transfer; and facilitating regional cooperation for trans-boundary disasters.

A multilateral forum like SAARC gives members the invaluable opportunity to develop bilateral cooperation on protection of water sources from pollution, degradation or denudation; dealing with drainage in the Indus Basin; addressing the issue of arsenic-poisoned aquifers in India and Bangladesh; and flood management, to name a few. Apart from sharing of river water, a major cause for dispute has been the construction of large hydroelectric projects which divert shared river water. The upcoming SAARC summit can encourage joint water management solutions and joint hydroelectric projects. Greater focus on watershed management and storage in Nepal would generate hydro and irrigation benefits there and flood control benefits in Bihar. Water storage in northeast India could provide hydropower, flood control and dry season water augmentation in Bangladesh; similar prospects exist between Afghanistan and Pakistan.

Cross-border management of water resources could help control flooding across countries sharing a basin while simultaneously enhancing the availability of water. Improved inland water transport linkages and trade facilitation could have multiple benefits, particularly to enhance regional trade. All SAARC member need to operationalize the declaration of the 17th Summit in 2013, which emphasized water sanitation, availability and access to drinking water.

COLONIAL CONFLICTS OVER RIVER WATERS

Under colonial influence, water was diverted from its role in the survival economy and nature's economy and was transformed into a source of revenue and taxes, or as an input to commodity production for the generation of profits. The introduction of market forces in the water economy of the country created new conflicts over water resources between the market and survival economies.

The Salt Economy and Water Conflicts

On 5 April 1930 Mahatma Gandhi launched the national noncooperation movement with the campaign for the production and distribution of salt at

Dandi beach in Gujarat, violating the Salt Law of the British that had guaranteed their monopoly in the production and distribution of salt. Salt is a vital resource for the survival of both human and animal life specially in tropical countries like India. It remained a common resource till the British monopolised its production and distribution to transform it into a source of revenue. The growth imperative compelled the expansion of the salt industry, as monopolised by the British, at the cost of diversion of resources from essential economic activities like food production. Further, in order to increase revenue the British government raised the salt tax in 1923 through the Indian Finance Bill of the Viceroy. This triggered off strong protests all over the country since a basic resource like salt was being denied to the people in order to increase revenue. The anguish of Gandhi on this appropriation of a common resource was clear when he said,

They even tax our salt-a necessity of life, only less necessary than air and water. It ought to be free as they are.... Nature bestows it on us and we may not use it. There is salt beside the sea and they forbid us to gather it's

The production of salt in certain pockets like Rajasthan and in the coastal areas as well as its distribution in all parts of the country had been a part of the living history of the Indian civilisation. Salt is one of those commodities which cannot be produced everywhere notwithstanding the self-sufficiency of the village economies. The demand for salt from all parts of the country led to the establishment of salt industries wherever it was possible to extract salt from saline water. All along the coastline except in Bengal, salt was manufactured by digging hollows in the ground and allowing the saline water to evaporate.

The Sambhar Lake in Rajasthan was a major inland source of salt for the whole of Central India. The manufacture and trade of this essential commodity and the possibility of a high margin of profits in case of monopoly in production, led to the East India Company securing the entire lake. In 1870 the British government forced a treaty on the States of Jodhpur and Jaipur through which it acquired the right of not only manufacturing and selling salt but also levying a duty on it. The peculiarity of the Sambhar Lake is that there is no rock salt bed in the geological formation of the area. The salt granules in the great salt marsh of Kutch are carried north-east by the trade winds in the summer and deposited in the catchment of the Sambhar Lake. In the monsoons the salt granules are dissolved and the solution is carried into the lake by a large number of streams. the largest of which is Rupnagar. Through the quick evaporation of water from the lake. millions of tons of salt get deposited in the Sambhar Lake. According to the British estimates of that period. 46 million people in India depended on supplied from this lake. This made the control of this 90 sq miles lake economically valuable for the growth of the salt industry.

Though the British salt industry in India grew by more than 33 per cent in the first twenty years of its existence, it was not content with only monopoly in production and distribution. To enhance the profits and growth of the industry, the British had maximised the inflow of water into the Sambhar Lake by denying the more basic uses of water for irrigation and drinking. Rupnagar, the largest stream feeding the lake, was the main source of water for the State of Kishengarh whose most important economic activity was agriculture which depended solely on the water of Rupnagar for irrigation. Thus the British attempt to increase the inflow of water into the lake came into direct conflict with the survival needs of the people in Kishengarh.

In 1900, a famine year, Kishengarh wanted to store some water by constructing an embankment tank on Rupnagar. The salt authorities strongly opposed this use of water for drinking and irrigation by the people. The Finance and Commerce Department of the then Government of India promptly accorded higher priority to the interest of the salt industry as opposed to the water needs for the survival of the people of Kishengarh. In a note dated 13 July 1901 the Department issued the following statement:

In view of the way in which the manufacture of salt depends on a sufficient supply of water in the lake and the precariousness of the supply, the Govt. of India consider that it is most inadvisable that anything should be done in the shape of constructing new reservoirs, irrigation works, or of extending any existing works on any of the feeder streams of the lake, either in the British territory or in native states which will be likely to diminish supply....

The Government of India desires that in future the Salt Commissioner may be consulted before any of the existing works' in British territory or the native states are enlarged, strengthened or improved.

In 1906 the villages of Kishengarh faced a severe drought. In sheer desperation to ensure a minimum supply of water for the biological survival of human and animal life, the people built an earthen dam which the British promptly destroyed. In the same year the rulers of Kishengarh pleaded for permission to construct low masonry weirs across Rupnagar and to sink some wells. The Salt Commissioner made sure that these projects could not be undertaken. It is this undisclosed destruction of agricultural ecosystems in the catchment of the Sambhar Lake that made possible and visible the growth of the salt industry there. By 1922 the prosperous and populated Kishengarh was desolate. Large areas of cultivable land became waste and wells could no longer be used. Another desperate attempt by the kingdom of Kishengarh to construct four irrigation tanks was postponed for twenty-four years, thus ensuring the total destruction of the local agricultural economy.

This was the general pattern of destruction of the survival base of the people in all regions of the country where the salt monopoly led to economic growth for British interests. This monopoly forced the people to give up the production of a basic resource like salt, which was being produced by them with simple technologies that required no capital input. The control made people totally dependent on the British supply, to be bought at a price determined by British interests. It was this exploitation by the British through the denial of a basic need as well as the associated destruction of other related resources that led to non-violent violation of the Salt Law as an assertion of the people's right to vital natural resources for survival. As a mode of protest it spread throughout the country with people breaking the Salt Law in large numbers. Its impact, both immediate and long-term was immense. By 5 March 1931 the British government was compelled to retrace its steps and issued a notification that people could produce salt for their own use.

WATER CONFLICTS IN THE KRISHNA BASIN

The east flowing krishna river originates in the mahadev range of the western ghats, north of the hill station of Mahabaleshwar in Maharashtra, and after flowing over a distance of about 1,40(1 km it meets the Bay of Bengal, south of Vijayawada. In between its origin at 1,337 metres above the MSL and its delta, the river fows across the entire width of the Indian peninsula through the states of Maharashtra, Karnataka and Andhra Pradesh.

The Krishna river is joined in its course by a large number of tributaries, big and small, draining a total basin area of about 256,000 sq km of which the share of the three riparian states of Maharashtra, Karnataka and Andhra Pradesh is 26.8 per cent, 43.8 per cent and 29.4 per cent, respectively. The basin drains a length of approximately 700 km of the Western Ghats which is the predominant source of water of the river. As the river flows about 135 km from its origin near Mahabaleshwar Hills, it is joined by the Koyna river flowing from the western side of the same hill. Further along its course. it is joined by tributaries like Varna, Panchaganga and Dodhganga draining about 150 km of the Western Ghats. As the river emerges from the eastern slopes of the Western Ghats, it is joined by Ghataprabha and Malaprabha from the south at a distance of approximately 500 km from the origin.

After traversing the Deccan proper the east flowing Krishna then enters the alluvial lands and at a distance of about 800 km from the source, just before it enters Andhra Pradesh, a major tributary Bhima, draining the Western Ghats, north of Mahabaleshwar joins it from the north. Near Kurnool the river is joined by another major tributary, Tungabhadra from the south, draining a major section of the Western Ghats in Karnataka. Within a short distance from this confluence, the river enters the Naliamali Ranges characterised by peep gorges. At this place the Srisailam Dam and further downstream the Nagarjunasagar Dam have been constructed. At this point the major water sources of the Western Ghats have all been united. Tributaries like Dindi, Musi, Palleru and Muneru draining the dry north-eastern parts of the basin join the river between Srisailam ad Vijayawada but do not add much water. Below Vijayawada, where the Krishna is blocked by the barrage constructed during the British period, the river spreads out into the delta and below the last major village Nagailanka it joins the Bay of Bengal in three branches, thus ending the long eastward journey of the waters of the Western Ghats.

Since water flow creates an interconnectedness within the basin, each intervention in land and water use, depending on its scale, can become the source of conflicts. The mining of iron ore at Kudremukh and Manganese ore in Sandur in the upper catchments of Tungabhadra has seriously affected the stability of the catchment and has led to severe soil erosion and silting of the Tungabhadra reservoir, thus conflicting with irrigation needs. The Krishna river system has a large number of small, medium and major dams starting from Dhom which is located within 5 km of its origin.

This storage and diversion of water from the original river course has destroyed the fishing economy which was dominant on both banks of the river as well as the indigenous irrigation system that existed throughout the course of the river. Further, large dams have also generated conflicts by creating waterlogging in the command areas. The hydroelectric power generation from the river water has come into conflict with irrigation needs both in terms of the spatial and temporal characteristics of water storage and distribution. The maximisation of power generation from Koyna demands that the water of the Krishna basin, draining into Bay of Bengal, be diverted to the Arabian Sea.

Industrial uses of the river system are a major source of conflict. For example, the pulp based industries on Tungabhadra have polluted the river and destroyed the fishing economy 20 km downstream. Moreover, the large-scale cultivation of pulpwood species like Eucalyptus in this part of the basin has impaired the groundwater recharge potential.

In the Krishna basin comprising mostly of arid and semi-arid regions water management had reached a high level of sophistication, both for surface as well as groundwater utilisation. An aerial view of the basin reveals a network of a large number of tanks, some pre-historic, others constructed by the local people or the rulers at different times in history. In general the technology used for all these tanks involved the construction of an earthen embankment at the exit of a natural water collection point that is a result of topography.

These tanks were used for surface irrigation of approximately 500 acres of land as well as for enhancing ground water recharge to support the wells. These tanks formed a network so that water did not drain out easily and was conserved at the site. To some extent indigenous water management techniques also included the diversion of streams to irrigate land by canals. The total number of tanks in the basin may be around 30,000. By arresting the scanty rainfall, these tanks actually provided a cushioning effect against variations in rainfall which is common in the basin. This decentralised water conservation system met both drinking water and agricultural needs. There was no major long distance transfer of water and the local cropping pattern evolved in accordance with the local water endowment.

The needs of the Vijayanagar Empire led to the first major intervention in the natural water flow. In the sixteenth century, specially during the reign of King Krishnadevaraya, there were many attempts to divert the water of Tungabhadra through seven canals in the Bellary district, these are now known as the Vijayanagar Canals.

The canals provided water for irrigation as well as satisfied the needs of the large army stationed in the capital city of Hampi. The interests of the Vijayanagar rulers were not limited to canals. Understanding the crucial role of tanks in food production as well as in providing drinking water supply, the kingdom undertook a systematic programme of tank construction. The Daroji tank and the Vyasayaraya Samudram in Cuddapah district are the result of this programme.

The first large-scale intervention in the natural flow of water in the Krishna river basin was seen in the late nineteenth century. It was motivated both by the irrigation needs of export crops like cotton and groundnut, as well as for transporting these products easily to major ports like Madras.

The Krishna delta canal system based on the Vijayawada barrage was constructed in 1855 The Nira Canal in Maharashtra was constructed in 1835 to irrigate about 150,000 acres and the Kurnool Cuddapah Canal was constructed in 1886 to irrigate 100,000 acres. With the passage of time. an increasing number of government aided large and medium projects came up and today the Krishna river has numerous dams including the Dhom Dam which is at a distance of 5 km from its source. Midstream, we find the Alamatti and Narayanpur Dams of the Upper Krishna Project while further downstream Srisailam and Nagarjunsugar Dams generate electricity and divert water for irrigation. The tributaries have also been used extensively in this respect.

The Koyna Dam is situated 58 km below the origin of the river. The Tunga river is impounded at Gajanur and Bhadra at Lakavalli. The Tunga and Bhadra meet and the Tungabhadra Dam is located 265 km from the origin. In Ghataprabha the reservoir at Hidkal in Karnataka is the major irrigation project while Malaprabha is impounded at the peacock gorge near Manoli. The spread of water-intensive cultivation throughout the basin has dramatically altered the water balance, leading to major conflicts between water for cash crop cultivation and staple food production on the one hand, and between irrigation and drinking water needs on the other. The case of sugarcane cultivation in Maharashtra and grapes in Hyderabad are two instances of over-exploitation of water resources in the basin for cash crop production and a consequent destabilisation of the water cycle, leading to water scarcity in large parts of the basin.

Dams for irrigation and/or power are also a source of conflict between the traditional rights of people to land and water and the rights of the state to displace and uproot them for building river valley projects as in the case of Srisailam Dam. Large dams require massive submergence areas, and hence necessitate the displacement of large numbers of people. Big dams also allow large diversions of water. Major diversions from the river basin as in the case of the Telugu-Ganga Canal taking off from Srisailam Dam, affect the riparian rights of the states and have generated unresolvable inter-state conflicts.

FUNDAMENTAL WATER ISSUES BETWEEN PAKISTAN AND INDIA

There is growing feeling in Pakistan that while India is increasingly building dams on its western rivers, it is simultaneously engaged in activities aimed at stopping Pakistan, the lower riparian, from building storage dams on Pakistani rivers. In the case of its upper riparian neighbour, Nepal, India has even deployed heavy artillery to partially destroy dams which were being constructed by the Nepalese. India's water strategy thus boils down to construction of more and more dams on cross-boundary rivers inside its own territory while obstructing dams in lower- riparian neighbours and destroying those in upper-riparian Nepal.

Honorary vice-president of the International Commission on Large Dams (ICOLD), Asif H. Kazi in his column titled "Misusing the Indus Treaty" argues that: "Pakistan's farmlands have been deprived of the uses of the waters of three eastern rivers, Ravi, Beas and Sutlej. The flows of these rivers were allocated to India under the 1960 Indus Waters Treaty. Authorities on the subject accept that when rivers and canals in Pakistan's demarcated area were classified as Pakistan's assets under the Partition Act, 1947, it meant only one thing: that these rivers and canals were to continue to receive water in the same way as before. Under the treaty, Pakistan was to enjoy the unrestricted use of the Indus, the Jhelum and the Chenab. However, exceptions were inserted as annexure which allowed India to develop and use certain specified quantities of water of the three western rivers as well".

Indian storage limits on the western rivers, which add up to 3.6 MAF (million acre feet). However, India deliberately followed a pattern of filling water behind Baglihar Dam constructed on the Chenab River by impounding flows in the low-flow month of September, a clear breach of the treaty which prescribes the filling period as being from June 21 to Aug 31 (Ibid).

Obviously, the foregoing was not the intent of the Indus Waters Treaty. And it is precisely for this reason that Pakistan has been insisting that India adopt well- known dam design features, especially for the outlets, which can easily ensure that the reservoir operators would not be able to manipulate flows of the western rivers at their own sweet will. India is opposing this using as an excuse the need for the prolongation of the reservoirs' lifespan through sediment flushing (Ibid).

BACKDROP: THE INDUS WATERS TREATY (IWT)

Analysts are of the opinion that, "the highly sensitive and charged water issues between Pakistan and India have emerged out of the way the 1947 partition lines were drawn. A seemingly minor change, but one with far-reaching consequences, was introduced in the partition map, in violation of all principles laid down by the British government. It came about at the very last minute when, upon the insistence of the Indian leaders, the partition award turned over to India three vital districts that were originally allocated to Pakistan, with the sole objective of providing India with access to Kashmir. The three remaining western rivers on which Pakistan now relies upon all originate in or pass through Kashmir before entering Pakistan. In other words, India, after having obtained the waters of the three eastern rivers through Indus Waters Treaty, is now trying to take control of three western rivers as well".

Momin Iftikhar provides further detail: "The Indus Waters Treaty (IWT) signed in Karachi on September 19, 1960, by India's Prime Minister Jawaharlal Nehru, Pakistan's President Muhammad Ayub Khan and Mr W.A.B. Illif of the World Bank has shown a remarkable endurance and resilience in withstanding the jolts of the Indo-Pak turbulent relations. The treaty allocates the water of the three western rivers of the Indus Basin (Indus, Jhelum and Chenab) to Pakistan, while the eastern rivers (Ravi and Sutlej) have been assigned to India for utilisation. The treaty allows India to tap the hydroelectric potential of the Pakistan specific rivers; with the important proviso that generation of power should not interfere with the timings and the quantity of flow of waters into Pakistan".

In his column titled "Tackling the Kishanganga knot" Iftikhar held the view that: "If India and Pakistan had normal and trustful relations, with a credible monitoring mechanism in place, this would not have been too demanding a task to accomplish within the parameters provided by the IWT. However, with emerging water shortages for agriculture in Pakistan, and the sensitivity of timings to the flow of water in the rivers that feed the defense-oriented canals and sustains the capacity for the generation of hydroelectric power, it is easier said than done" (Ibid).

CONSTRUCTION OF KISHANGANGA HYDRO - ELECTRICITY PROJECT (KHEP)

The water sharing environment in South Asia is fast deteriorating. The Pakistani frustration at Indian inflexibility was evident when it referred the matter of Baghliar Dam on River Chenab to the World Bank in January 2005. The verdict by a neutral expert, appointed by the bank ultimately settled the issue in February 2007. The decision accommodated both the parties and each country felt that its respective stance had been addressed and vindicated. The problem did not end there; within four years, the two countries are back for arbitration over the water issue and the bone of contention this time is construction by India of the Kishanganga Storage-cum-Hydroelectric Power Project on River Neelum (Indians call it Kishanganga), which is a major tributary of River Jhelum. Iftikhar (2011) points out that: "The matter is sensitive because not only the dam will curtail the flow of water for agriculture, but Pakistan is also constructing the Neelum-Jhelum Hydroelectric Project on River Neelum, downstream of Kishanganga Project."

Pakistan's fundamental objection to Kishanganga is that it involves diverting the water of Neelum River through a 21km long tunnel towards the Wullar Lake to generate 330MW power. This is manifestly not allowed by the IWT. Iftikhar indicates: "This diversion is against the provisions of the IWT and has not only serious consequence for the 969MW power generation capability of Neelum- Jhelum Hydrolectrical Project, but will also reduce the water supply for agriculture in the areas of Azad Kashmir, which are dependent on the Neelum River flow. It is estimated that the diversion of water towards Wullar Lake will reduce flow into Pakistan by 27 percent (Ibid).

According to the available data, it is estimated that, "the dry spell is likely to extend to eight months per year. The lack of water is going to have an adverse impact on the agriculture in over thousands of acres in Azad Kashmir, which are dependent upon the flow of River Neelum, besides causing damage to the environmental aspects of flora and fauna nurtured by the rivers flow in the Neelum Valley" (Ibid).

Kazi (2011) supports the view that, "the proposed Kishenganga project violates the treaty in a most glaring way. Firstly, the hydroelectric plant is not located on the Kishenganga but way off the channel at the end of a long tunnel that discharges into another tributary. And, secondly, the recipient tributary ultimately outfalls upstream of the Wullar Lake, and this completely changes the patterns of the flows of both Kishenganga and Jhelum Rivers."

The International Court of Arbitration's Decision

In response to Pakistan's appeal for 'interim measures' against the dam which may inhibit the restoration of the river flow to its natural channel, "The International Court of Arbitration (ICA) barred India from any permanent works on the controversial Kishanganga hydro-electricity project (KHEP) on River Neelum at Gurez in occupied Kashmir".

Farhatullah Babar, Spokesman for President Asif Ali Zardari, said that, "The arbitration court took the decision on an appeal filed by Pakistan that India was diverting the flow of the river and violating Indus Water Treaty (IWT) between the two countries" (Ibid).

The court order said: "India shall not proceed with the construction of any permanent works on or above the Kishanganga/Neelum River bed at the Gurez site that may inhibit the restoration of the flow of the river to its natural channel. Pakistan and India shall arrange for periodic joint inspections of the dam site at Gurez in order to monitor the implementation of the court's order" (Ibid).

Irfan Raza reports that, "Islamabad had submitted its version in the World Bank's arbitration court in July (2011). The major contention was that under the law India cannot divert the route of River Neelum. Pakistan fears that the Kishanganga dam would rob it of 15 per cent water share – a violation of the Indus Water Treaty. Islamabad accused Delhi of trying to divert the water of Neelumriver in order to harm Pakistan's Neelum-Jhelum hydro-electricity project (Ibid).

In its request Pakistan had required: "A stop work order; An order that any steps India has taken or may take in respect of the KHEP are taken at its own risk without prejudice to the possibility that the court may order that the works may not be continued, be modified or dismantled, that India be ordered to inform the court and Pakistan of any imminent and actual developments on the Kishanganga Dam that may adversely affect the restoring of the status quo ante or that may jeopardise Pakistan's rights and interests under the treaty; Any further relief the court considered necessary" (Ibid).

Indian Response

Indian experts denied the allegations raised by the Pakistani Government on building Kishanganga Dam. Former Secretary, Water Resources, Ramaswamy R Iyer in his column titled "Pakistan: Water on the Boil Again" writes: " So far as one knows, India has not built any storage, not even the 3.6 MAF permitted by the Treaty, nor does it intend to cause harm to Pakistan by diverting Indus waters. In any case, there is such a thing as the Permanent Indus Commission. How can India store or divert waters to the detriment of Pakistan under the watchful eyes of the Indus Commissioner for Pakistan" ?

On violations of the provisions of the Indus Treaty by India, Iyer elaborates that, "The Treaty envisages and permits Indian projects on the western rivers, and so the projects in themselves cannot be violations of the Treaty. They can be violations of the Treaty if they deviate from certain restrictive provisions, but that will be questioned by the Indus Commissioner for Pakistan. The questions may be resolved within the Commission, or become differences and get referred to a Neutral Expert (as happened in the Baglihar case), or may be in the nature of disputes to be referred to a Court of Arbitration (as has now happened in the Kishenganga case)".

Vibha Sharma in a column titled "India confident of winning Kishanganga dispute" writes: "India today termed as "favourable" the International Court of Arbitration (ICA) order last week which prevents the country from undertaking permanent works above the riverbed level at the Gurez site of the Kishanganga hydropower project.

The final orders are expected either in 2012-end or in early 2013".

Water Resources Minister Pawan Bansal asserting that "the stay was merely an interim legal position and in no way signified any "loss of position" for India, as was being projected by Pakistan. Bansal told The Tribune that "the neighbouring country had raised two issues-stopping the work and dismantling the construction already done -and the court did not agree to either of its two contentions" (Ibid).

"India can go ahead with construction of powerhouses, tunneling works, coffer dams, temporary bypass tunnel and concretisation under the riverbed for the dam. The only thing we cannot do is go above the surface of the river bed, which is not a problem since we would only be able to complete these works by 2012- end and 2013 beginning, by when the court will give its final decision," Bansal said (Ibid).

For now, India is compiling a rejoinder to emphasize its point before the International Court of Justice. "The Hague-based ICA has directed India to submit a report on environmental hazards to the ecosystem due to this project" (Ibid).

Former Secretary, Water Resources, Ramaswamy R Iyer also maintained that "the ruling was neither a win nor a loss for either country. It is just a temporary stay. India can still continue with related works except constructing the dam" he said (Ibid).

However, taking into account political and environmental consequences of the project, Sharma is of the view that "there appears to be some amount of skepticism with an expert saying that investments could go waste if the final award goes against India, which in other words also means that the power problem in Kashmir will continue."India will be taking a risk by carrying out with other works till the final ruling," said the water resources expert, who did not wish to be quoted" (Ibid).

Confidence Building Measures

Daily *The Telegraph* reports that "Ahead of another round of Indo-Pak water talks scheduled in mid-September (2011), the Jammu and Kashmir government quietly abandoned the controversy-ridden plan to construct a concrete barrage where the Jhelum meets the Wullarlake in north Kashmir". Thakur, Sankarshan (2011) believes that: "It's a small move with big implications: a persistent irritant in bilateral ties, the dumping of the barrage could prove a significant confidence-building measure between India and Pakistan". Giving further details Thakur writes that "Work on the venture, christened the Tulbul Navigation Project by New Delhi but better known as the Wullar barrage, was stopped two years after it commenced in 1984 upon strong objections from Pakistan which argued the lock-cum-control barrage would not only deprive it of water but could also be used as a "natural weapon" against it" (Ibid).

The Jammu and Kashmir minister for irrigation and flood control, Taj Mohiuddin, confirmed that "the state government had resorted to alternative measures to prevent flooding in the Jhelum's upper catchments and ensure navigability in the river" (Ibid). "We have given up the barrage project in favour of temporary rubber dams, which can work as effectively," Mohiuddin told The Telegraph. "Why should we want to erect a huge concrete structure when modern technology allows us to solve problems with more flexible methods" (Ibid)?

He did say the barrage had become "an unnecessary source of tension and suspicions" between the neighbours. "We had not been able to move on the project, it was stalled, this new rubber damming technique can probably help us a win-win way out," he said (Ibid). Mohiuddin appeared convinced that "the new initiative would address reservations that Pakistan has had with the erection of a concrete barrage" (Ibid).

Role of Media

Zahra (2011) argues that the "Paucity of direct communication between the two states has increased the role of the media. The two nuclear neighbours are caught in a warp where the status quo in bi-lateral relations vacillates between improvement and deterioration but does not sway beyond a certain point — either way — so as to achieve anything decisive."

This part of the study glimpse at the role of the media on the water issues between Pakistan and India during 2011. Excerpts from the editorials and news reports of two leading newspapers from each country i.e. daily *Dawn* and *The Nation* from Pakistan and *The Tribune* and *The Kashmir Times* from India have been included.

Pakistani Media

An elite Pakistani newspaper daily *Dawn* in its editorial captioned "Controversial Project" expressed concerns on the Kishanganga hydropower project being constructed by India. The paper reads: "A series of disputes on hydropower generation projects initiated by India has given rise to concerns that New Delhi is trying to control the river water and thus `strangulate` Pakistan`s agriculture and economy. Many experts also believe that, given the situation, a future war over water between India and Pakistan cannot be ruled out" ('Controversial Projects', 2011).

Dawn extends its comments by saying that: "Repeated Indian attempts in the past to find loopholes and technical flaws in the 50-year-old water treaty that can be used to New Delhi`s advantage have hardly been helpful in easing tensions over water-sharing between the two neighbours" (Ibid).

In its course of discussion the paper writes, "We will have primarily ourselves to blame in case of such an eventuality. Successive governments in Islamabad have failed to raise and resolve crucial water issues, including this one, that have arisen from time to time with India to the peril of Pakistan's agriculture and economy. While Islamabad must vigorously pursue the case at international forums to protect its economic interests, India should remember that the failure to satisfy Pakistani concerns will only delay the realisation of the dream of a prosperous South Asia whose various parts are at peace with one another" (Ibid).

Another leading English language Pakistani newspaper *The Nation* criticizes Indian policy on water sharing. In its news report *The Nation* reads, "The Treaty has in great detail covered a just distribution of water of rivers flowing from India to Pakistan. Under the Treaty India in no case can hold the water or hamper the flow of water during various seasons to Pakistan" ('Pakistan likely to win', 2011).

The paper further writes, "The Kishanganga project is a part of the India move to build a series of water reservoirs on all the three major rivers including river Chenab to utilize water at the upstream for the purposes of irrigation and power generation depriving a huge agricultural lands of waters which have been irrigating from these sources for centuries" (Ibid).

Commenting on the World Court of Arbitration's decision that stayed India's construction of a dam across the Neelum at Kishenganga, *The Nation* in its editorial "Kishanganga stayed" reads: "This stay order is not a final injunction, though it is the first sign that Pakistan is taking India's constant violations of the Indus Waters Treaty (IWT) with some seriousness.

Earlier this year, in bilateral secretary-level talks, Pakistan had conceded acceptance of a revised Indian design of the Wuller Barrage, something which only encouraged Indian ambitions in this direction, and which furthered its ambitions to turn Pakistan into a barren wasteland, by using its illegal occupation of Kashmir to stop Pakistan's water from getting to it".

The Nation suggests the Pakistani government to follow a two-pronged strategy. "First, to pursue this case with full vigour, and ensure that the stay is confirmed; second, to utilize this breathing space to start building irrigation-cum- generation projects on the Indus, and thus rid itself of this charge which is justified only because certain pro-Indian lobbies have been working against the Kalabagh Dam.

The stay order, when confirmed, will also provide a useful precedent which will help stop Indian depredations on the Indus. However, a permanent solution will involve a settlement of the Kashmir issue. It would mean a general Indo-Pak settlement, ridding us of threat of water projects in Held Kashmir" (Ibid).

Indian Media

Daily *The Tribune* is published from Chandigarh. In news report it provides details about Pakistan's stance in the ICA. The paper writes, "Pakistan has moved the Court of Arbitration asking it to direct India to stop work at the 330-MW Kishenganga hydropower project in Jammu and Kashmir. The project is likely to be completed by 2015. A seven-judge Bench has started arbitration proceedings from January 14 this year in the Hague".

The report further reads, "Incidentally, this is the first case referred for international arbitration under the provisions of the Indus Water Treaty, 1960. Earlier, India and Pakistan had sought the services of a neutral expert appointed by the World Bank to resolve their differences over the Baglihar Dam under construction on the Chenab. The Bench – comprising Justice Stephen M Schwebel (head), Justice Sir Franklin Beman, Prof Howard S Wheater, Justice Bruno Simma, Jan Paulsson, Justice Peter Tomka and Lucius Caflisch – has three neutral umpires, including the head of the Bench, and four arbitrators nominated by India and Pakistan. Noted lawyer and expert on International law Shankar Das and legal luminary Fali s Nariman, both of whom had argued India's case in the Baglihar dam issue, are representing India" (Ibid).

Another newspaper *The Kashmir Times* from Jammu published a news report on the Nimoo-Bazgo hydropower project being built by India on the Indus River. It reads, "Pakistan wants to raise objections to the project, saying it allegedly violates the Indus waters treaty. The decision to approach the ICJ on the Nimoo- Bazgo project was made after Pakistani officials made their first visit to the project site and concluded it was allegedly in "total violation" of the Indus waters treaty of 1960, a senior unnamed member of Pakistan's Indus Waters Commission told the media.

The unnamed official claimed India would be able to complete the Nimoo-Bazgo project by July 2012 and thus "suffocate" the water flow in the Indus. The design of its gated spillways and the depth of the dam allegedly breach the Indus waters treaty. The Pakistani side has raised five objections to the design of the project" (Ibid).

TRANSBOUNDARY PROBLEM

Water contamination until now has been mainly a domestic issue as highlighted by the pollution problems affecting the Yellow River in China and the Ganges in India. But the contamination of the Siang signals that this problem is becoming a transboundary problem, which will increase tensions and discord between neighboring countries.

Sino-India tensions have already increased due to freshwater disputes. Beijing has withheld hydrological data from New Delhi on upstream river flows in 2017 in breach of two bilateral accords. This undermined India's flood early-warning systems during the critical monsoon season. In India's Assam state, which suffered record flooding despite below-normal monsoon rainfall, many deaths were preventable. The data denial was apparently intended to punish India for boycotting China's Belt and Road summit and for the border standoff on the remote Himalayan plateau of Doklam.

Asia's water crisis, meanwhile, has given rise to grand but environmentally problematic projects such as China's South-to-North Water Diversion Project. China has already completed two of the three legs of the world's most ambitious water transfer program, which is now diverting billions of cubic meters of river waters yearly to its parched north. Because this program's highly controversial third leg is to divert waters from rivers flowing to other countries from the Tibetan Plateau, China refuses to divulge any details about it.

More broadly, even as threats to Asia's sustainable water supply are intensifying, geostrategic factors are raising the specter of water wars. Dam building and other diversions are often at the center of tensions and recriminations between states.

Asia illustrates that once shared water becomes a political and diplomatic battleground between countries, it begins to insidiously exact geopolitical costs in ways not dissimilar to the legacy of an armed conflict. The casualty usually is sub-regional stability and cooperation.

Asia also exemplifies another important trend -- that dams and democracy do not go well together. Dam building has run into major grassroots opposition in Asian democracies like Japan, South Korea and India, driving up project costs and acting as a damper on hydropower expansion. In the absence of grassroots empowerment, however, there are few impediments to dam construction in Laos, Myanmar, Pakistan, China and elsewhere.

Indeed, China has become the global leader in dam building, boasting more large dams than the rest of the world combined. What is intensifying concern among downstream nations about China's dam frenzy is the shift in its focus from domestic rivers to ones that cross borders. The Siang River's contamination triggered a political furor and grassroots protests in India's northeast, forcing Beijing to break its long silence and claim that a Nov. 18 earthquake in southeastern Tibet "might have led to the turbidity (clouding)" of the river. But the river waters turned dirty and gray before the quake struck.

The plain fact is that the environmental futures of China and its many neighbors are inextricably linked. Environmental degradation on the world's largest and highest plateau -- Tibet (which is warming at a rate three times the global average) -- carries pan-Asian implications. With its height and other unique features, the Tibetan Plateau influences climatic and rainfall patterns across Asia.

Several other developments are also undermining Asia's hydrological and climatic stability and fostering a cycle of chronic flooding and droughts. In many Asian countries, watersheds, watercourses, coastal ecosystems and the broader environment are being degraded, resulting in shrinking wetlands and forests, increased water pollution and other ecological problems.

These developments spur global warming. Natural water flows, evaporation and condensation help to propel the earth's biogeochemical cycles and regulate its climate. Environmental degradation creates a vicious circle. It affects the hydrological cycle that shapes regional climate. A warming climate, in turn, has a significant impact on water resources.

DEMAND-SIDE OPTIONS

Jakarta illustrates how Asia's mounting threats from climate change are fostered by changes in the hydrological cycle. The Indonesian capital, home to over 10 million people, is sinking faster than any other major city in the world because of accelerated groundwater depletion. Tens of thousands of wells across Jakarta pump out groundwater at such a rate that it is causing large-scale subsidence, with as much as 40% of the city now said to be below sea level. Groundwater depletion is also contributing to the rise of the Java Sea, thus exacerbating Jakarta's troubles. Some of the waters extracted from Jakarta's underground aquifers ultimately end up in the sea.

A surfeit of water but not enough to drink is a scenario likely to confront many coastal Asian cities. One study estimates that groundwater depletion contributes 0.8 millimeters per year to the rise of ocean levels globally, or about a quarter of the total rise. Groundwater depletion, by inviting seawater intrusion into aquifers, is already compounding freshwater shortages in some Asian cities. Meanwhile, the plethora of upstream dams on rivers is causing a perceptible retreat of Asia's heavily populated deltas that are home to megacities like Bangkok, Dhaka, Guangzhou, Kolkata, Shanghai and Tianjin.

Given that Asia is likely to face a hotter, drier future, governments there must initiate action to mitigate the impacts. The freshwater crisis that many Asian countries already confront should be tackled in a way that contributes to combating climate change. The imperative is to move from purely supply-side approaches to demand-side options that emphasize water conservation and quality as much as quantity. Even on the supply side, nontraditional measures, from recycling of water to rainwater capture, must be embraced.

If unsustainable practices and mismanagement of water resources are not addressed, freshwater will become a precious commodity whose control will spark conflicts in Asia. The rise of water nationalism at a time of increasing water stress highlights the linkage between water and peace. Cooperative institutional mechanisms and sustainable resource utilization constitute the building blocks of water peace. Water is a key test of whether Asian leaders have the political will and good sense to think and act long term. What Asia confronts today, other continents are likely to face tomorrow.

CENTRAL ASIAN COUNTRIES INITIATIVE FOR LAND MANAGEMENT

This initiative is a collaborative ten year project facilitated by the Asian Development Bank (ADB) to combat land degradation, desertification and declining agricultural yields that impact over 20 million people in the region. All five governments signed a framework agreement with ADB and Global

Environment Facility and global partners in 2006. CACILM has received commitments on country level and on the international level to raise $1.4 billion for the initiative. This includes support from international development agencies from Canada, Germany and Switzerland, as well as various United Nations agencies and the World Bank.

CACILM has identified eight national projects in the five Central Asian states and two multi-country projects that focus on land degradation, eco-system stabilization, sustainable agriculture, pastoral management and sustainable forestry.

By 2015, the initiative aims to increase private investment and make major improvements in degraded farmland, develop an integrated approach toward land-use planning and train more government workers and citizens in sustainable land management practices. Among the anticipated global environmental benefits of this initiative are a significant reduction in the loss of soils from sand storms, the reduction of soil and pesticide runoff into rivers that run downstream and into transboundary rivers as well as improvements in water availability, which should moderate the harsh climate related to desertification. Other environmental benefits include a reduction in the loss of carbon sinks in soils and forests and a reduction in greenhouse gases created by unsustainable agricultural practices. CACILM is a new initiative and it is too early to evaluate its success or failure, but so far there are good indications of wide participation of all five countries in dealing with the legacy of poor irrigation practices resulting in salinization and water logging which has hurt agricultural yields.

The World Bank

The World Bank (WB) has been heavily involved in Central Asia since each state joined following independence. One type of involvement has been the development of Country Partnership Strategies (CPS) with both Tajikistan and Kyrgyzstan. The CPS identifies key issues affecting the states, such as water and energy, and the best ways to address them by utilizing past experience and knowledge gained from similar projects. Another type of assistance, relevant to this report, is environmental and techno-economical assessments done prior to the commencement of hydropower projects.

The World Bank has also collaborated with potential donors in collecting investments needed for the Central Asian states. One important regional donor is Russia, who recently signed onto two new agreements to expand this role.

The first asks for a $30 million contribution towards improving the region's financial management systems and the other puts $9 billion towards the EURASEC Anti-Crisis Fund, which Tajikistan, Kyrgyzstan and Kazakhstan are part of. Another key regional donor is China, who invested $267.2 million and $58 million towards two electricity lines in Tajikistan.

In recent years, the World Bank launched a new initiative with the five Central Asian governments and regional institutions, such as IFAS, called the Central Asia Energy-Water Development Framework.

This program aims to show each state how to utilize their resources in a socially sustainable and environmentally-friendly manner, with regards to each others' national priorities and regional stability. This initiative has three specific aims: 1) balance energy options while addressing winter energy shortages; 2) strengthen investment in infrastructure to expand energy trade within and outside the region; and 3) work with regional organizations to encourage dialogue among the states and improve water usage for the energy and agricultural sectors. If successful, this program will help the states realize the changes they need to make with regards to these issues, for they are part of the overall problem and have not yet fully been addressed.

As a stakeholder, the World Bank has played a positive role in collecting investments and addressing country specific issues in Central Asia. Also, it is worth mentioning once again the Bank's involvement in building of the Kokaralsk Dam and the Aral Sea Basin Programme 1, as these are just a few of its attempts in addressing the Aral Sea crisis. The Bank may also be able to put one other positive role in the region, depending on the outcome of feasibility study currently being done on the Rogun Dam. The World Bank should be further utilized by the Central Asian states since it seems very interested in helping address the key issues that continue to plague them.

European Union

The European Union (EU) has been engaged with the five countries in Central Asia since they gained their independence, a relationship that has developed significantly over the years and revealed shared economic and security interests. Central Asia's energy resources are of particular interest, as the EU is dependent on external energy sources in order to increase energy security. As a result of this development, in June 2007, the EU adopted the "EU and Central Asia: Strategy for a New Partnership" that marked an upgrade in the relations between the EU and Central Asia.

As part of its Central Asia Strategy, the EU-Central Asia Environmental Dialogue has been established to foster environmental protection and better manage water resources. The EU has increasingly focused on working with the five Central Asian countries to improve the management of lands and forestry resources, and supporting the stabilization of the Aral Sea. To promote and increase capacity building for renewable energy sources and improve energy efficiency, recent activities include trainings and seminars of government officials and financing feasibility studies regarding the installation of small sized hydropower stations and the use of renewable energy sources in the region.

The EU is also trying to alleviate the problems arising from the conflicting needs for water access and use between upstream and downstream countries by actively promoting efficient and economic usage of this resource. Several initiatives have been launched to tackle these issues, for example, better use of resources, better management and rehabilitation of irrigation systems and energy transmission lines. The EU has stated that reducing the demand for these resources is a fundamental component of a possible solution.

The work undertaken under the EU Water Initiative, through its main operational instrument- National Water Policy Dialogues- is the centerpiece of EU efforts to achieve the water-related Millennium Development Goals and targets of the Integrated Water Resource Management (IWRM) network. The overall objectives of National Policy Dialogues are to initiate country-specific activities regarding water supply and sanitation, financing strategies and IWRM to improve regulatory and administrative frameworks, help setting country priorities, identify projects and develop capacity in the region through a dialogue that involves public authorities and representatives of the civil society. National Water Policy Dialogues was launched in Kyrgyzstan in 2008 and Tajikistan and Turkmenistan in 2009.

The EU has in collaboration with UNDP addressed integrated water resource management (IWRM), where the idea is that by looking at national coordination a model for cooperation can be developed. However, it has been pointed out that Uzbekistan has marginalized itself from these multinational projects, making progress difficult, and moreover the EU projects have been largely focused on water quality issues. This does not contribute to resolving the main issue of sharing and allocation of water resources. Although dialogues have been held under the EU Water Initiative, they have mostly been on the national level. In practice, the EU involvement, similarly to efforts by UNDP and the World Bank to some extent, has remained focused on providing technical assistance.

UN Special Programme for the Economies of Central Asia (SPECA)

SPECA was established in 1998 by the presidents of Kazakhstan, Kyrgyzstan, Tajikistan, Turkmenistan and Uzbekistan. Azerbaijan joined in 2002 and Afghanistan in 2005. It is jointly supported and implemented by the UN Economic and Social Commission for Asia and the Pacific (UNESCAP) and UN Economic Commission for Europe (UNECE). What distinguished SPECA from other actors involved in the region, such as the EU and the UNDP is the direct involvement from political leaders and the focus on how important political efforts are in order to solve issues related to the mismanagement of water in the region. At the same time, the program has the "neutral protection" from the UN, which can be beneficial in promoting cooperation. Problems hindering regional cooperation in Central Asia are often political, and SPECA has been able to offer a neutral UN umbrella and a broad range of international legal instruments of which UNECE is the custodian to resolve bilateral and regional disputes.

SPECA states that the "objective of the Programme is to support the Central Asian states in developing their cooperation, creating incentives for economic development and integration into the economies of Europe and Asia." It is working to provide a framework for dialogue and cooperation as well as for broader cooperative initiatives. Its activities include the development of Euro-Asian transport linkages, including the possible extension of railway and road networks into the region as well as the positive development of institutionalized cooperation between the Kazakh and Kyrgyz Governments in the management of water installations on the Chu-Talas Rivers.

2

Water Distribution Conflict in Indus Water Treaty

The India Independence Act enacted in 1947 by British Parliament and the subsequent British withdrawal from India left the subcontinent partitioned between two independent states marred by demarcation problems along their international boundaries, the peculiar circumstances leading to the division, and the accession of a number of princely states especially that of Jammu & Kashmir straddling India and Pakistan as well as the complex riverine systems of Indus, Ganges, and Brahmaputra. Of these three rivers, the Indus presented a complicated set of issues stemming from thousands of kilometres of man-made irrigation canals and headworks that regulated the flow of its waters.

While all the rivers, except Indus and Sutlej, originated within Kashmir, the headworks located mostly in the Eastern Punjab were awarded to India. Aside from the Punjab Boundary Commission suggestion that the canal-headworks system be treated as a joint venture, a proposition rejected by both countries, it had not deliberated water sharing of Indus River Basin due to a hasty partition that was completed in a mere 73 days.

Water sharing issues of Indus River System would later take over a decade to resolve. Further complicating this issue, Pakistan covertly and later overtly sought to grab Jammu & Kashmir for various reasons including the desire to control the waters of these rivers that succeeded in instilling only distrust among Indian minds.

After the Partition, both the nations agreed to a "Standstill Agreement" on Dec. 30, 1947 freezing the existing water turn systems at the two headworks of Madhopur (on the Ravi) and Ferozepur (on the Sutlej) until March, 31, 1948. Any dispute that could not be resolved by the Punjab Partition Committee was to be decided by the Arbitral Tribunal (AT) which had been setup under Section Nine of the Indian Independence Act by the Governor General to sort out difficulties arising over the division of assets. However, on the expiry of the arrangement and after not receiving an encouraging response to a reminder for talks issued by the East Punjab Government on 29th March 1948, and in the absence of a new agreement, the then Indian Punjab Government promptly stopped the water supply through Madhopur on April, 1, 1948. By a coincidence, the Arbitral Tribunal's term also expired on the same day.

In the meanwhile, the AT had accepted India 's claims regarding seigniorage charges for the waters and ordered payment of the same by Pakistan. At the invitation of East Punjab, the Engineers of the two divided-Punjab States met in Simla on Apr. 15, 1948 and signed two Standstill Agreements regarding the Depalpur Canal and Central Bari Doab Canal to be in effect until Oct. 15, 1948. The West Punjab Government agreed to pay: (1) seigniorage charges, (2) proportionate maintenance costs, and (3) interest on a proportionate amount of capital. In its defence, the GoI cited such charges levied by the Punjab on the Bikaner state under the British.

However, the West Punjab Govt. refused to ratify the Agreement and the Prime Minister of Pakistan, then Liaqat Ali Khan, called for a meeting. The Finance Minister of Pakistan, Ghulam Mohammed, along with the Pakistani Punjab ministers, Shaukat Hayat Khan and Mumtaz Daulatana visited Delhi to work out an agreement in the Inter-Dominion Conference held on May, 3-4, 1948.

India agreed to resume release of water from the headworks, but made it clear that Pakistan could not lay claim to these waters as a matter of right and would levy seigniorage charges specified by the Prime Minister of India to be deposited in Reserve Bank of India, establishing Indian sovereignty over these rivers. The Indian side also made assurances that the waters would be diminished slowly giving enough time for West Punjab to develop alternate sources. The West Punjab Government, for its part, also recognized "*the natural anxiety of the East Punjab Government to discharge the obligations to develop areas where water is scarce and which were underdeveloped in relation to parts of West Punjab.*" Soon the Pakistani Government falsely accused that they were coerced into signing this Agreement and made futile appeals to the Governor General Lord Mountbatten. However, due to the hostilities between India and Pakistan on account of Kashmir and in the general environment of distrust and animosity, no further talks took place. Pakistan 's suggestion in June 1949 to take the matter to the International Court of Justice at The Hague and widen the conflict across all rivers, was rejected by India. On November 1, 1949, Pakistan unilaterally invalidated the Delhi Agreement and by July, 1950 stopped seigniorage payments into RBI. However, India continued to abide by the Agreement and supplied waters.

In 1951, David Lilienthal, former chairman of the Tennessee Valley Authority and a former Chairman of Atomic Energy Commission, USA visited the two countries ostensibly to write a series of articles for the Colliers magazine *(since defunct)*. Having had access to both the Governments at the highest level, Lilientahl wrote in one of his articles, *"I proposed that India and Pakistan work out a program jointly to develop and jointly to operate the Indus Basin river system, upon which both nations were dependent for irrigation water. With new dams and irrigation canals, the Indus and its tributaries could be made to yield the additional water each country needed for increased food production. In the article I had suggested that the World Bank might use its good offices to bring the parties to agreement, and help in the financing of an Indus Development program."* Inspired by this idea, Eugene R. Black, then President of the World Bank visited the two countries and proposed a Working Party of Indian, Pakistani and World Bank engineers to tackle the "functional", rather than the "political" aspects of water sharing. The two countries accepted this mediation (which also had the backing of President Truman who wanted to remove the *"kind of unfriendliness"* that existed then between the US and India) offer in March 1952 and sent their technical teams to Washington for further discussions. Subsequent meetings took place in Karachi in Nov., 1952 and New Delhi in Jan. 1953. The World Bank suggested that each side submit its own plans, which they did on Oct. 6, 1953. The two plans, while concurring on the available supply of water, differed widely on allocations. The table below, shows the initial, negotiated and final positions of both the countries.

Table : ***Indus River System Estimates and Allocations***

Plan	India	Pakistan
Initial Estimate	119 MAF	118 MAF5
Initial Indian	29 MAF	90 MAF
Initial Pakistani	15.5 MAF	102.5 MAF
Revised Indian	All of the Eastern rivers + 7% of Western rivers	None of the Eastern rivers plus 93% of the Western rivers
Revised Pakistani	30% of Eastern rivers and none of the Western rivers	70% of the Eastern rivers + all of the Western rivers
World Bank	Entire flow of the Eastern Rivers	Entire flow of the Western Rivers

However, despite all efforts, the wide gaps in the stands of the two countries could not be bridged, mainly due to the intransigence of the Pakistani side as the revised and final allocations show clearly above. The World Bank felt that an ideal approach to joint development of an integrated plan for Indus Basin as proposed by David Lilienthal was now impossible. In order to resolve the dispute, it finally stepped in with its own "settlement" proposals on Feb. 5, 1954 offering the three Eastern rivers to India and the three Western rivers to Pakistan. India accepted the proposal *in toto* on Mar. 25, 1954 while Pakistan gave only a "qualified acceptance" on July 28, 1954. The settlement offered by the World Bank was closer to the Indian position as it repudiated the claims of Pakistan based on "historic usage". An angered Pakistan threatened to withdraw from further negotiations. The World Bank proposal was then transformed from a "settlement" to a "basis for further negotiations" and the talks eventually continued for the next six years. In the meanwhile, the two countries signed an Interim Agreement on June 21, 1955. As no conclusive agreement could be reached, the World Bank announced on Apr. 30, 1956 that the negotiation deadline has been indefinitely extended. As is its wont, Pakistan, through its then Prime Minister H.S.Suhrawardy, issued a direct threat of war with India over waters, escalating tensions.

Under the World Bank plan, Pakistan was asked to construct barrages and canals to divert the Western river waters to compensate the loss of Eastern rivers on the Pakistani side. During the period needed to do this, called the Transition Period, India was required to maintain the "historic withdrawals" to Pakistan The World Bank then suggested a "financial liability" for India as replacement costs by Pakistan for the loss of the three Eastern rivers.

In the 1958 meeting, the replacement works and the financial liability to India were considered. India rejected Pakistan 's proposal, known as the "London Plan", for two large dams on the Jhelum and the Indus and three smaller ones on Ravi and Sutlej and several canals, all in all totaling USD 1.2 Billion.

India 's alternate proposal, known as the "Marhu Tunnel Proposal", was unacceptable to Pakistan as leaving too much leverage on water flows in Indian hands. In May, 1959, the Bank's President visited both countries and suggested a way out which involved India paying a fixed amount of £ 62.060 Million to be paid in ten years in equal installments and the Bank assisting Pakistan with help from donor countries. The international consortium of donors pledged USD 900 Million for Pakistan and the drafting of the IWT began in Aug., 1959. The treaty was signed in Karachi by Pandit Jawaharlal Nehru, Field Marshal Ayub Khan H.P., H.J. and Mr. W.A.B. Illif, President of the World Bank in a five-day summit meet starting Sep. 19, 1960. However, it was deemed effective from Apr. 1, 1960. The two governments ratified the same in January 1961 by exchanging documents in Delhi. Simultaneously an

Indus Basin Development Fund was established with contributions from Australia, Canada, Germany, New Zealand, the UK and the US along with India 's share of the cost.

The Eisenhower Administration contributed roughly half the cost of the Fund, while the World Bank provided US$ 250 Million and the other donor countries together provided a similar amount. The Water and Power Development Authority (WAPDA) of Pakistan was entrusted with the task of completing these tasks. The fund was subsequently extinguished after the completion of the projects as per Article XI of the IWT. The May 4, 1948 accord stood annulled after the signing of IWT. The Indus Basin Project involved construction of two large dams, five barrages to transfer 14 MAF of water from the Western rivers. There are three systems of link canals. Two of the systems, the Rasul-Qadirabad-Balloki-Suleimanki System (R.Q.B.S.) and the Trimmu-Sidhnai-Mailsi-Bahawal System (T.S.M.B) connect the Jhelum River through to the Sutlej and the third system Chashma-Jhelum System (C.J) connects the Indus with the Jhelum.

The IWT also enunciated a mechanism to exchange regularly flow-data of rivers, canals and streams. A Permanent Indus Commission (PIC) was constituted, headed by two Commissioners, one from each country. The PIC is expected to meet at least once a year alternately in India and Pakistan and submit an annual report to their respective Governments before June, 30th every year. So far, the Commission has met 92 times. The IWT also sets out the procedures for settlement of differences and disputes both bilaterally and through International arbitration. Given below is an abridged version of the dispute settlement process that may be of interest in the present context:

A. Any question that might be a breach of IWT shall be first examined by the PIC.

B. A difference is deemed to have arisen if the PIC could not reach an agreement.

C. The difference shall be dealt with by a neutral expert who may opine if it is a dispute or not. If not, he shall resolve it. Such a neutral expert shall be a highly qualified engineer and appointed by the two Governments in consultation, or failing which, by the Bank. The expert's decision is final and binding.

D. In case of a dispute, the Commissioners report to their respective Governments which shall then strive to resolve the dispute.

E. A Court of Arbitration shall be setup to resolve the dispute, if no decision is reached by the above process.

F. Such a Court will consist of seven members, two from each party and three including a Chairman from a panel to be chosen by the two

Governments. If no consensus on names can be arrived at, the IWT has given a list of persons from whom to choose such as the Secretary General of the U.N. or International Bank for Reconstruction and Development (IBRD) for the Chairmanship and the President of M.I.T., Cambridge, the Rector of Imperial College, London, the Chief Justice of the USA, or the Lord Chief Justice of England for panel membership.

Many Pakistanis feel that Pakistan surrendered to India the waters of the three Eastern rivers in 1960. Their argument is along the following lines.

On the basis of over fifty years' record the mean flow in Indus River System (IRS) totalled 175 MAF on the eve of Partition of Punjab in 1947. This comprised of 93 MAF including 27 of Kabul for Indus, 23 for Jhelum, 26 for Chenab, 6 for Ravi, 13 for Beas and 14 for Sutlej annually.

Out of this 175 MAF, 167 flowed into Pakistan at the time the boundaries of partitioned Punjab were fixed according to the Radcliffe Award. This means that the Indian East Punjab drew only 8 MAF of a total of 33 MAF of water that annually flowed in three eastern rivers Ravi, Beas and Sutlej. Under the Internationally agreed rights of lower riparian states and also Indian Independence Act 1947, the balance 25 MAF waters of three eastern rivers were to be shared between India and Pakistan. The Pakistanis feel that those who negotiated the IWT on their behalf did not sufficiently press for the sharing of this quantum of water.

However, there are several fallacies in these arguments. First, leaving the claim on the quantum of waters aside, the arrangement entered into at Partition time was interim in nature until a final agreement could be reached and the provisions of such an interim arrangement were in no way binding on the parties concerned. Secondly, the Indus Agreement was reached eventually in 1960 during that time the utilization of the waters of these rivers had grown enormously in the states of East Punjab, Rajasthan, and Jammu & Kashmir. To claim the waters on the basis of the flow thirteen years before, when agriculture and economy had been dictated by different circumstances of a united India is patently unfair. In fact, the IWT itself treats water flows and usage based on the situation existing as on Apr. 1, 1960, the effective date of the Treaty. Thirdly, as a lower riparian state, all the unused river waters would naturally flow to Pakistan. This, by itself, cannot bestow any rights on that country and again, a quantum of 80 MAF of water was reaching the Arabian Sea unutilized out of the total flow of the Indus River systems. All these are summarized by the following statement of N.D.Gulhati, the principal negotiator from the Indian side to the IWT, *"After ten years of hard and devoted work, we had secured almost a world-wide recognition of our claim to use in India all the waters of the Eastern Rivers, including the 12 MAF which was actually being let down for use in Pakistan as at the time of partition... In India, we had already allocated all these waters, including the 12 MAF referred to above, between Punjab (including the present Haryana), Rajasthan and Jammu and Kashmir. The scope of the Bhakra-Nangal project had been considerably increased, the Madhopur-Beas Link and the Sirhind Feeder had been completed and opened for operation, several new channels had been built on the Upper Bari Doab Canal and the Rajasthan Canal was under construction."*

INDIA RE-THINKING INDUS WATER TREATY

"Many of the wars of the 20th century were about oil, but wars of the 21st century will be over water", said Dr Isamil Serageldin, former Vice President of the World Bank. Water is surpassing oil as the world's scarcest critical resource as water has no substitute. There's an increasing feeling in the world that everyone has a basic right to a minimum 13 gallons of water a day for basic human health. Today, the world stands divided between water haves and have-nots and Pakistan is facing critical water issues. Water management and distribution has always been an important but cumbersome process in Pakistan being a semi-arid country and its economy based mainly on agriculture and related industry.

The positive thing is that Pakistan has the largest contiguous supply-based canal irrigation system in the world. In Pakistan, the muddy plains of the Indus basin cover approximately 25 percent of the land area of Pakistan. Whereas in India, the basin includes only 9.8 percent of the total geographical area of the country. On negative side, the aqua environment of Pakistan has been shrinking since last two decades as the World Bank had put the country in the category of "water-stressed" in 2000. The availability of water in Pakistan has been declining over the past few decades from 5000 cubic meters per capita 60 years ago to 1200 cubic meters per capita in 2010.

Unfortunately, Pakistan's water problem is not new, as soon after independence, the country faced water problems due to blockage of its water in canals by India. Political boundary between Pakistan and India was drawn right across the Indus Basin making the country the lower riparian to India. The headwaters went to Indian side leaving Pakistan vulnerable as India got the physical capacity to cut-off vital irrigation water. Adding insult to injury, India started demanding proprietary rights on the water of Punjab Rivers, denying Pakistan its due share as a lower riparian.

INDUS WATER TREATY (IWT) 1960

Negotiations commenced between Pakistan and India in 1951 under the World Bank and resultantly the famous Indus Waters Treaty (IWT) was signed on September 19, 1960. It was the partition of waters like land in 1947. Pakistan got the rights of the waters of the three western rivers, i.e., Indus, Jhelum, and Chenab, while the three eastern rivers, i.e., Beas, Sutluj, and Ravi went in total jurisdiction of India. India was not allowed to build storages on the western rivers except to a very limited extent and also restrictions were imposed on the extension of irrigation development in India. The permanent Indus Commission was appointed for both states. International financial assistance was given to Pakistan for the development of irrigation works utilizing the waters of western rivers.

Strain & Stress on IWT and Violations by India: There is no denying the fact that the IWT survived in the midst of wars and border clashes between the two states but the Indian projects on Pakistani rivers created stress and strain as India could either reduce water flows to Pakistan or cause floods by releasing the stored-waters. There are numerous water disputes between the two, e.g., Wular Barrage, Kishanganga Project, Baglihar Dam, etc. Salal Dam was started by India without informing Pakistan, in violation of the IWT. Though an agreement was reached between the two countries, yet there is no guarantee that India would not do the same in future. Now India has got the leverage to hold water for 25-26 days which can cause acute shortage of water for winter crops in Pakistan. This, besides causing electricity shortage, can greatly affect wheat crop in the Punjab. According to Dr John Briscoe, Professor of the Environmental Engineering and Environmental Health at Harvard University and former Senior Water Advisor to the World Bank on the Baglihar case, "in case of Baghliar, Pakistan's vulnerability was driven home when India chose to fill Baglihar exactly at the time when it would impose maximum harm on farmers in downstream Pakistan. Following Baglihar is a veritable caravan of Indian projects, i.e., Kishanganga, Sawalkot, Pakuldul, Bursar, Dal Huste, Gyspa…The cumulative live storage will be large, giving India an unquestioned capacity to have major impact on the timing of flows."

Implications for Pakistan: Water flows in river Chenab declined to about 6000 cusecs from a 10 year average of 10000 cusecs, mainly because of construction of over a dozen Hydro-electric Projects (HEPs) upstream by India. To fill Baglihar Dam, India had consistently obstructed River Chenab's flow. Resultantly, Pakistan received lesser water when it should have been receiving a minimum of 55,000 cusecs per day. In order to achieve the required growth targets in agriculture, Pakistan needs an estimated 277 MAF in 2025. Otherwise, the shortage of surface water will result in drought and more dependency on ground water for irrigation; hence water table will go down causing water constraints to the population. Indian water regulation capability has increased as with the completion of Salal Dam, India has enhanced its water regulation capability over river Chenab by 6-7 times. After completion of Baglihar Dam, India will be able to stop the flow of water in the river for 30-40 days as compared to previous capability of only 8-10 days. Kishanganga HEP will also enhance Indian storage capability over river Jhelum with a stoppage capability of 14 days. Also, Wullar Barrage will further enhance Indian storage capability in river Jhelum for additional 30 days. So, depending upon the degree of water regulation capability, India can create three types of effects:

- Drying up of rivers-related canal
- Flooding of rivers
- Fluctuate discharge of rivers

Possible Impacts on Global Security: Since water security has become a principal concern for sustainable development, so availability of freshwater is one of the greatest challenges that the world is going to face in the near future. As water shortages are growing, the result could be a series of disasters and confrontations leading to regional crises. Nowhere else on earth are the prospect of water wars more serious than in South Asia, where two of the world's greatest river systems crisscross the international boundaries of the world's largest and most densely-populated countries being:

- Indus River System (IRS)
- Ganges-Brahmaputra-Meghna (GBM)

Water issues are likely to continue as a major source of conflict between India and Pakistan in coming decades as forecasted by many analysts. As populations rise, levels of economic development increase and the adverse effects of climate change become more extreme, the South Asian region will struggle to meet its growing demand while managing dwindling water supplies and the trans-boundary rivers, especially those in the IRS and GBM basins. These disputes could prove to be dangerous for world security since war over water between two nuclear armed states, i.e., Pakistan and India, would be dangerous. The possibility of such a war can not be ruled out since water poses a survival issue there is no substitute of this commodity.

INDIA RE-THINKING IWT

Indians consider IWT generous to Pakistan and Pakistan thinks it discriminatory right from its inception. At official levels, there is no such demand by the Govt. of India/Indus Water Commission India and so is the case with Pakistan as there is no such demand from the Govt. of Pakistan/ Indus Water Commission Pakistan. But at non-governmental level, intellectuals/ academia in India have started asking for re-visiting/re-thinking the IWT and probably they are making a case for the future. Brahma Chellaney, a Professor of Strategic Studies at the New Delhi-based Centre for Policy Research, said that "Pakistan's reopening of the water-sharing agreement could backfire, as it might prompt India to rethink a treaty that was extremely generous to Pakistan. There was no treaty in the world which had been so generous on the part of the upper riparian to the lower riparian state. India was starving its own northern regions and reserving four-fifths of the water for Pakistan. If Pakistan played this dangerous game, they would make India review its generosity."

IDSA Report: Institute for Defence Studies and Analyses (IDSA) had published its book/task force report in 2010 titled "*Water Security for India—The External Dynamics*" in which they have given reasons and plans for re-visiting the IWT. According to the report, "...with Pakistan, given some stringent provisions in the IWT that thwart India's plans of developing projects on the western rivers, a 'modification' of the provisions of the treaty should be called for. Whether it is done through re-negotiations or through establishing an Indus-II Treaty, modifications of the provisions are crucial in case of the western rivers.

Under the draft provisions of the International Law Commission 'Responsibility of States for Internationally Wrongful Acts, 2001', India can consider the abrogation of the treaty...Pakistan aids and abets terrorist actions from its soil. India should quantify the damage it has sustained over the decades because of Pakistani support to terrorism and seek as a first step suitable compensation. If Pakistan does not comply, India can possibly threaten to walk out of various bilateral agreements including the IWT." Pakistan is using water propaganda to get international attention on Kashmir so India should "talk" to Pakistan but not "negotiate". The talks should be about "water needs" and not "water rights".

Five Constituencies/Point of Views in India on Re-thinking the IWT: According to the same IDSA report, there are five constituencies that ask for revision or a re-think. "The first constituency seeks to evolve an Indus-II under the provisions of Article VII and Article XII of the IWT for an integrated or joint development of the Indus water basin. Indus-II should be fed into the current peace process as a means both for defusing current political strains over Indus-I and managing adverse impact of climate change."

"The second constituency while understanding the merits of a new hydrologic relationship on the Indus does not see any viability of Indus-II and contends that a totally new treaty has to be negotiated. The IWT was a partitioning treaty, like the partitioning of the land. How can cooperation be built on that basis?"

"The third constituency is the domestic pressure group in [Indian occupied] Jammu & Kashmir which feels that the IWT has restricted the state's overall development by not allowing it the usage of "its" rivers, i.e., Jhelum, Chenab and Indus. It has been calling for a complete review of the treaty. The [Indian occupied] Jammu & Kashmir government has been contending that in spite of having an untapped hydro-electric potential of 15,000 MW, the state continues to suffer from acute power shortage and related agro-economic underdevelopment."

"The fourth constituency springs into action when the political climate between India and Pakistan becomes acrimonious. While war over water is not an option, this group suggests strong-arm tactics in dealing with Pakistan and using water as a coercive tool and a bargaining instrument in the larger politico-strategic objectives of India."

"There is a fifth constituency that argues that any attempt to review the treaty, can be done only after India exploits the potential already permissible under the treaty. Only a crying child, it is argued, gets the mother's milk. This constituency argues that first India should fully exploit the existing potential and then cry for more. Any attempt otherwise to review the treaty may not be seen as logical. The IWT is a product of its time and could be fruitfully modified and renegotiated to bring it more in line with contemporary international watercourse law, the Helsinki rules, and emerging concerns with water quality, environmental sustainability, climate change, and principles of equitable sharing."

Pakistan's serious projected shortages, India's trend of damming and diverting waters and global warming's expected depletion of water in the IRS are a source of increasing tensions between Pakistan and India. Based on supply and demand projections, India faces its own water scarcity, which would provide India an excuse to store or divert river water that would otherwise reach Pakistan. Water shortages would pressure the Pakistani government to increase its share of water drawn from the Indus system under the treaty as Pakistan is heavily reliant on the Indus and has few alternative water supply sources unlike India. In this environment, renegotiation of the IWT may become an important diplomatic issue between India and Pakistan. With India, water issue will be far more political and strategic than just water. India has also started propagating that Tibet's water is for humanity, not for China alone. But they (Indians) forget that the Indus-Ganges basins are also for humanity, not for India alone.

THE WAY FORWARD

As for as the existing treaty is concerned and keeping pros and cons in mind, there is no need to revisit/review/rethink the IWT. Due to India's continuous hegemonic attitude, Pakistan would not be in a better position to have any revision in its favour. Instead, Pakistan should continue lobbying that India has been violating the IWT and India should be compelled to abide by the IWT in its true letter and spirit. Also, Pakistan should engage with India within the context of the IWT in a comprehensive way. International lobbying should be intensified on the point, i.e., water being the "lifeline" issue for Pakistan and this could trigger war.

Pakistan should be calling for a sophisticated forecasting system, accurately estimating how much water flows into the IRS, as almost 90% of the water in the Upper Indus River Basin comes from remote glaciers of Himalaya and Karakorum mountain ranges, which border Pakistan, China and India. This region is so remote that the authorities in Pakistan do not know the exact weather conditions there. This system will also help in alleviating droughts in the country. The water forecasting system could ultimately help Pakistan in optimizing water allocation at national level by working out how much water is used for irrigation, industry, and domestic purposes.

Internally, water management in Pakistan has been poor. So, keeping in view the dwindling water resources, water must be made part of new "security agenda."

PAKISTAN AND WATER: NEW PRESSURES ON GLOBAL SECURITY AND HUMAN HEALTH

PRESSURES ON THE WATER OF the Indus River, the major water source for the more than 180 million persons living in Pakistan, are increasing, with serious implications for the health of the population. Rural Pakistanis (more than half the population) use irrigation water from the river for domestic purposes, even though it is unfit for drinking and a major cause of stunting and diarrhea. Diarrhea causes 21.6% of infant mortality in rural Pakistan. In Karachi, a megacity of approximately 18 million people, it is estimated that more than 30 000 people, 20 000 of whom are children, die every year because of unsafe water. Control of river flow is still a major challenge for the country, which was tragically demonstrated during recent flooding that affected 20 million people and was described by the secretary general of the United Nations as the worst disaster he had ever seen.

Beyond the direct effect on human health, disputes over the flow of the Indus may erupt into a military conflict between India and Pakistan, endangering the lives and security of millions. The future of water flow in the Indus is also threatened by regional environmental changes. Public health professionals must be fully engaged in the development of this crucial resource for the country and the health of its population.

PAKISTAN AND THE INDUS RIVER

Pakistan was created in 1947 with the partitioning of British India, becoming the first Islamic republic. With one of the fastest growing populations in the world, Pakistan had a population of 180.8 million in 2009 and is projected to reach 208 million by 2020. Approximately 20% of the population lives below the international poverty line of US $1.25 a day. Health and social indicators have lagged behind those of other South Asian countries whose economic conditions are poorer than Pakistan's.

The strategic importance of Pakistan has gone through important shifts, first with the Pakistan–India conflict that began after the 1947 partition, then with the Cold War's denouement, and now with the war on terror. The geopolitical importance of Pakistan, which shares borders with Iran, India, China, and Afghanistan, also intensified when it became a nuclear power in 1998.

The majority of the people in Pakistan live near the Indus River, the longest river in the country, and the 21st largest river in the world in annual flow. The snows and glaciers of Tibet, India, and Pakistan feed the river. Beginning in the Himalayas, the Indus courses the entire length of Pakistan—a total of 1976 miles—and empties into the Arabian Sea near Pakistan's major port, Karachi. As much as 65% of agricultural land in Pakistan is irrigated by water from the Indus, which accounts for approximately 90% of the country's food and fiber production.

THE INDUS WATERS TREATY

During the early years after partition, disagreements over the flow of the Indus River led to the danger of military conflict; by 1951, the two sides were no longer meeting, and the situation seemed intractable. India's control of the headwaters of the Indus gave it the power to turn fertile Pakistan into a desert. With the conflict over Kashmir and the trauma of partition still in vivid memory, the threat of a "water" war became imminent.

David Lilienthal, a former chairman of the Tennessee Valley Authority and the US Atomic Energy Commission, visited the region in 1951 to write a series of articles for *Collier's*magazine. Working behind the scenes with the US Department of State and the World Bank, he engaged the governments of Indian and Pakistan in negotiations that lasted nine years. Those negotiations led to the Indus Waters Treaty, signed in 1960. This agreement has been faithfully implemented and upheld by both India and Pakistan and has been the longest-running accord ever between the two countries. The treaty gives India exclusive use of all of the waters of the Eastern Rivers and their tributaries before the points where the rivers enter Pakistan. Similarly, Pakistan has exclusive use of the Western Rivers. Pakistan also received a one-time financial compensation for the loss of water from the Eastern Rivers.

Continuing tensions between India and Pakistan, however, have begun to erode confidence in the treaty. India has greater bargaining power over Pakistan because the upper stream is in its territory, and Pakistan's water rights under the treaty are hard to enforce. Critics of the treaty suggest that benefits have gone to major players and not to those most in need. For Kashmir, where only 40% of cultivated land is irrigated, the result has been limited economic development. One quarter of the people of Kashmir lack electricity, and 55% lack safe drinking water. Kashmir also remains at the heart of the political tensions between India and Pakistan.

India's plan to build a dam on a tributary of the Indus within its borders has created new tensions. The construction of the dam would give India even more control over the flow of the river. The collapse of a dam could cause a disaster in the Northern Areas of Pakistan, and India's history with dam failure is considerable. Ongoing political confrontation between India and Pakistan makes the future of the Indus Waters Treaty uncertain. Even worse, war—globally the worst threat to public health—appears increasingly likely to break out over Indian–Pakistani water issues. Rapidly changing issues related to water quality and access to water for basic human needs have given a new direction to global security discussions. UN Deputy Secretary General Asha-Rose Migiro said,

Projections are that by the year 2050, water accessibility for human consumption will have dropped by 40 percent. Probably the next major conflict will be about water.

NEW PRESSURES ON THE RIVER

Intensification of water use in Pakistan threatens the quality of water in the Indus. Rapid population growth over the past half century has intensified the pressure on agriculture and the need for irrigation water. The management of the flow has historically been inefficient because of poor water storage capacity, seepage, and inadequate maintenance of reservoirs. Heavy irrigation and seepage have overwhelmed the drainage of irrigated land, leading to accumulation of salts on the surface of the soil and rendering large tracts of land unfit for agricultural production. These inefficiencies have prevented Pakistan from attaining food self-sufficiency.

Environmental degradation of the Indus River and other wetlands in Pakistan has created additional health risks for the population. Water pollution in the Indus comes from a number of sources, including return flow from agriculture, which adds sodium nitrates, phosphates, and pesticides to the river. Additionally, untreated or incompletely treated sewage from cities along the Indus is discharged into the river. The river also receives a wide range of industrial waste: organic matter and ions such as sodium, potassium, calcium, magnesium, carbonates, bicarbonates, and chloride as well as inorganic wastes such as fluoride, silica, and cyanide. Finally, thermal power plants along the Indus cause sudden increases in surface water temperature that harm marine life.

Little research has been carried out to date on the effect of river pollution on human health in Pakistan, but the problem should not be underestimated. Much of the population along the Indus depends on the river for drinking water, and boiling does not remove polluting chemicals. Water pollution in the Indus River has reduced the species diversity of fish and decreased the supply of subsistence food for many who live near the river. In parts of the lower Indus delta, mangroves that were once abundant with marine life and an important source of food for coastal populations have almost disappear because of the toxic effect of polluted water that flow into this ecosystem.

Cities near the river are major water users. Karachi needs enormous quantities of water for both human and industrial use. The Indus River to the east and the Hub River to the west are the main water sources for Karachi. Water management in the city is a serious problem; one quarter of the population has no piped water, and as much as a quarter of the city water is wasted in faulty pipes.

Sewage management has been chaotic in Karachi for many years. The sewage system established by the British during colonial days has been overwhelmed and is in a poor state of repair. Open sewers, raw sewage overflowing into streets, and contamination of water lines with sewage are all common in Karachi. The city has annual outbreaks of cholera. Newspaper reports document thousands of hospitalizations attributable to sewage lines breaking and merging into water lines. Half of middle-class children in Karachi have intestinal parasites.

Also dependent on the Indus are Lahore (population six million) and Faisalabad (population five million). The groundwater table in Lahore is falling at a rate of 30 centimeters per year in the central part of the city because of heavy water use by the growing urban population.

Regional climate change also threatens the future of the Indus water flow and the millions of people who depend on it. The recent fast pace of glacier melt and warmer temperatures may lead to a serious diminution of river flow. One of the suspected reasons for the rapid melting of these glaciers is settling of aerosolized soot and particles on the icy surface. This "Asian brown cloud," caused by the burning of fossil fuels and biomass by the more than one billion people who live on the subcontinent, can be seen from outer space. As the cloud settles on the white glacial ice, light and heat are absorbed rather than reflected, melting the ice. Even a small decrease in the flow in the rivers fed by these glaciers (the Indus and Ganges) would have huge consequences for agricultural production and human life.

NEW DIRECTIONS FOR HEALTH DIPLOMACY

Health has emerged as a global security issue, and the water needs of human populations have become part of that issue. After the partitioning of British India, Pakistan and India began sharing the Indus River, but the contentious relations between the countries have already sparked two wars and water issues could cause further conflict. New pressures on water in Pakistan include intensification of use to meet the rapidly growing needs of agriculture and industry, environmental degradation of the river, and increasing use by cities.

These new problems will have serious public health consequences for people living in the region and must be added to the agenda of health diplomacy. Improved management of the Indus River could improve the health of the people of Pakistan. Public health has an important role in achieving this goal and in global diplomacy to safeguard water supplies and human health.

BREACH OF INDUS WATER TREATY

India and Pakistan used to share the River Indus and its five contributories Jhelum, Chenab, Ravi, Beas and Sutlej under British rule. The Pakistani areas had no dam to store water, therefore 80% of the water from six rivers would eventually fall into the Arabian Sea. When water conflicts started intensifying after the division of British India in 1948, the World Bank's President Eugene Black acted in an arbitration procedure between Pakistan and India which resulted in 1960 in the Indus Water Treaty. Under this agreement three eastern rivers Ravi, Beas and Sutlej were given to India and three western rivers the Indus, Chenab and Jhelum were given to Pakistan. It was "water division" rather than 'water sharing". Pakistan also agreed to allow India to use some of western rivers' waters for local agriculture around rivers in India and produce run-of-river style hydroelectricity provided tyhe water flow did not fall below 55,000 cusecs at Marala and other interface barrages that went below 20,000 in 2009.

The Indus Water Treaty worked well up to the 1980s before the Indian Government decided to build dams in Shiwaliks (Himalchal, Punjab, Jammu & Kashmir) on the western rivers. Geotechnical studies were carried out in

Ballowal, Takarla and Karoan areas from 1984 to 1995. Generally pre-monsoon, monsoon and post-monsoon rain fall in Kashmir valley (Handwara) used to be 305, 161.8 and 89mm from 1903 to 1982 which increased to 1117 to 1249mm in 1990s that prompted India to go for multiple dams on western rivers without seeking permission of lower river riparian.

Building dams on active faults in Zone-V was in violation of the Indus Water Treaty.

The Indian Government conducted several more studies on geotechnical and hydrological parameters for the design of small earth filled dams in the 1990s.

Initially, the small dams construction experience using local expertise led to micro-earthquakes around Thien Dam in Himalayas in 1980s which forced them to seek international assistance on dams. Feasibility studies on 400 MW Hasti Dul (400 MW) and other dams were carried out in Kashmir valley and the adjacent provinces of Himachal and Punjab in the 1990s.

Uri-I (240 MW) dam on river Jhelum and Nathpa (1650 MW) dam on river Sutlej were carried out to test geological and geotechnical responses which hardly complied. If the Indian dams were to fail for technical reasons or as a result of earthquakes the people who would suffer would be Kashmiri or Pakistanis.

Building tens of dams without consulting lower riparian renders the Indus Water Treaty virtually defunct. Under the Indus Treaty of 1960, India is supposed to inform at least six months before launching any hydropower project. India did not comply in this regard.

India has several dam projects including water diversion tunnels and canals. India had allocated RS.33 billion for the 330 MW Krishanganga project and Rs. 18 billion for the 240 MW Uri-II hydropower dam on River Jhelum, Rs.51 billion for 1000 MW Pak Dul and 1200 MW Sawalkot dams projects on Chenab. The Sawalkot dam is 646-feet height which is more than the 485-feet height Tarbela and 453 feet height Mangla in Pakistan. These dams are 160 km away from Kangra where a 8.0 Richter scale earthquake occurred in 1905 on record.

India has already built 60 MW Madekheda dam on Indus river and is constructing 130 MW Chuttak, 600 MW Monpreet n Randeep, 44 MW Dumkhar and 60 MW Nimo Bazgo dams on river Indus. After completion of 330 MW Wular barrage and 240 MW Uri-I dam India is further constructing 330 MW Krishanganga and 240 MW Uri-II dams on the river Jhelum.

India completed 450 MW Baglihar, 345 MW Salal-I and 345 MW Salal-II on river Chenab on which Pakistan objected seriously. India has diverted Jhelum river water to Chenab through a 80km long tunnel which is clear breach of Indus Water Treaty. India is constructing another 1200 MW Bursar dam on this tunnel. Instead of respecting Indus Water Treaty India has started construction of 400 MW Hasti Dul, 460 MW Rattle, 400 MW Gyspa, 100 MW Pakdul, 800 MW Karthai, 180 MW Raoli, 725 MW Seli, 1200 MW Sawalkot, 90 MW Tangat, 50 MW Pattan, 50 MW Teling, 100 MW Tandi, 180 MW Sach Khas, 300 MW Dueli/Dugli, 100 MW Rashal, 100 MW Myar, 190 MW Gondhala, 240 MW Dogar, 100 MW Shatru, 110 MW Dang, 20 MW Thai Rot and Chenai dams. After completion of so many dams all the western rivers will become dry. Bhutan has a hydropower potential of 23,000 MW out of which 4,484 MW is expected to be harnessed by constructing six dams by 2024. Pakistan has 50,000 MW hydro potential which is under threat due to 39,000 MW power Indian dams on western rivers. Pakistan is generating 71.9% thermal, 25.2% hydel and 2.9% nuclear power. Our energy mix consists of 43.5% oil, 41.5% gas, 0.3% LPG, 4.5% coal, 9.2% hydropower and 1.1% nuclear electricity. Pakistan has over 40,000 MW wind, 30,000 MW solar and 800 MW geothermal potential.

India has already contributed to the drying up of the eastern rivers Ravi, Sulej and Beas. Water only flows in these rivers when India has significant dam overflows. India is digging a Sulej-Ganges Link canal to divert waters to the southern Indian states on which Indian riparian have taken stay from the Indian court.

India has built 390 MW Pong, 360 MW Pandoh and 126 MW Larji dams on river Beas, 1000 MW Bhakra, 1650 MW Nathpa and 800 MW Kol, 1000 MW Karcham Wang and 77 MW Nangal dams on river Sutlej, 1200 MW Baira Siul, 540 MW Chamera and 600 MW Ranjeet Agar, 120 MW Sewa-II and 70 MW Budhil dams on river Ravi. Indian dam mania is causing drought to both eastern and western riparian farmers.

Pakistan has only two dams which usually stay partially filled throughout the year except monsoon months Wikipedia, 2010). Unfortunately, 95% Indian dams in Himachal, Jammu and Kashmir regions are located on dangerous earthquake faults zones.

Recently India has launched another dams construction drive in Himachal Pardesh to build 300 MW Baspa, 231 MW Holi, 70 MW Dhamwar, 2050 MW Parbati, 192 MW Allian, 162 MW Swara, 370 MW Sham Not, 560 MW Rattle, 430 MW Kiru, 320 MW Kawar and 35 MW Bichlari dams. United Nations water experts must formulate global water legislation to avoid water wars especially between India and Pakistan which may engulf many others.

When Pakistan came to know of water shortages in rivers India had completed 70% of 48 dams. Indus river system is spread over 944,473 km2 out of which 553,416 km^2 lies in Pakistan. Pakistan declared failure of Indus

Commission in 2005 referring the case to neutral expert. India has 34 large dams out of which 10 are in Kashmir. Indian links between Neelum, Jhelum, Chenab through Tavi river uplift canal, Ravi, Beas, Sutlej and Yamana transfer western rivers water to Indian highlands.

There is no dam on Chenab, Ravi, Beas and Sutlej rivers on the Pakistani side. However, India is building over three dozens dams on Western rivers which are viewed as a matter of grave concern by Pakistan.

Science news and global warming observations conclude that the Himalaya region will be affected in the near future. Dams worth 150,000 MW have been proposed in India, Nepal, Bhutan and Pakistan. International Rivers point it out that these projects are environmentally determinental (ie from a global warming perspective). Melting glaciers, like Dig Tsho Glof in Nepal in 1985, may lead to glacial lake bursts causing flash floods. Bhutan noted 25 dangerous glacial lakes in 2009.

Over one billion people rely on Himalaya waters. Upstream countries should not store waters in dams to starve lower riparian. India must focus on other sources of energy instead of blocking the flow of water to Pakistan.

United Nations and Indian scientists and engineers must advise the Indian Government to curtail dam construction in fault zones on western rivers under 1960 Indus Treaty to discourage water war for long term regional security. We have long history of using waters amicably but energy crisis is driving the conflicts. Global irrigation potentials exists 68% in Asia, 17% in Americas, 9% in Europe and 1% in Oceania. Indus Basin western rivers contribute to 15-20% of Asian food cycle. Transboundary rivers are not local rather global assets which need due attention on merits. Indus water treaty went well for last 50 years but recent Indian dam drive is worsening the scenario.

Salaman's claim the lower riparian (Pakistan) can harm upper riparian (India) is not a valid argument as Pakistan and India have divided rivers instead of sharing them. Eastern rivers Sutlej, Beas and Ravi were chosen by India and Western rivers Indus, Jhelum and Chenab were left for Pakistan due to geographical locations. Eastern rivers had annual water capacity of 41 billion cubic meters (33 MAF) whereas western rivers had capacity of 188 billion cubic meters (135 MAF). Uri dams have storage capacity of 3.07 MAF in 1999 which increased to 6.37 MAF in 2002. Sutlej-Yamana (SYL) can transfer 3.5MAF water. India is transferring this water from western rivers into eastern rivers through Tavi-Ravi 31 meter high uplift link canal. India stopped Neelum River to divert water to Wular Barrage through 27 km long tunnel which is further diverted from Jhelum to Chenab through 77 km long tunnel. Asia Times called it race to death over Kashmir waters.

RECENT WATER CONFLICTS

Not surprisingly, this situation has already led to numerous small-scale local conflicts, began in the late 1980s when the central authorities weakened their grip on Central Asia. In 1990, the outbreak of conflict in the Kyrgyz town of Osh, on the border with Uzbekistan, claimed over 300 lives and was provoked by fierce competition for water together with high population density, limited arable land and ethnic dimension (large population of Uzbeks living in the area).

Since summer 1993, there have been serious water tensions between Kyrgyzstan and Uzbekistan. Kyrgyzstan was blamed by the Uzbek authorities for releasing too much water from the Toktogul reservoir. Extra water did not reach the Aral Sea but was dumped instead into the Aydarkul depression, the large 'sinus' which has developed as a result of years of negligence (Kltzli, 1994). In 1997, Uzbekistan has deployed 130,000 troops on the Kyrgyz border to guard the reservoirs straddling the two countries (Hogan, 2000b; Grozin, 2001). In June 2001, the Kyrgyz parliament adopted a law classifying water as a commodity, and the government followed up by announcing that the downstream countries would be charged for the water they use. Uzbekistan's response was to cut off all deliveries of gas to Kyrgyzstan and accuse Kyrgyzstan of failing to honour the barter agreement to provide Uzbekistan with water in return for oil and gas. Although weaker in political and military terms Kyrgyzstan acknowledged this failure, Uzbekistan would be emboldened to behave in a more aggressive manner towards its neighbours. The two were on the verge of violent conflict for several times (Khamidov, 2001).

Current Water Disputes

Central Asia's two major rivers, as well as their tributaries, have become a focus for growing competition among their riparians, with the Syr Darya being a particular point of tensions. The Amu Darya is rapidly becoming a locus of disputes as the governments of Turkmenistan and Uzbekistan become more hostile towards each other competing also for water, and Afghanistan is about to demand its share. These tensions have so far been contained without conflict, but all parties have shown a willingness to put their interests first at any cost, including military intervention. Due to their reliance on agriculture, Uzbekistan and Turkmenistan view irrigation as a key security issue (ICG, 2002b).

The Syr Darya Basin

The Syr Darya is shared by four states and, in case of Uzbekistan, is shared twice as after flowing from Kyrgyzstan and crossing the Uzbek part of the Ferghana valley the river flows into the Tajik territory in the western

Ferghana Valley and then pours again into Uzbekistan. After crossing the Hunger Steppe, the Syr Darya runs into Kazakhstan.

Kyrgyzstan and Uzbekistan have had particularly discordant history over the use of water from the Syr Darya. Since independence, Kyrgyzstan faces serious economic problems, mainly because of a shortage of energy supply from Russia, Kazakhstan and Uzbekistan. The primacy of energy production over the irrigation needs downstream has already created a major discord between Uzbekistan and Kyrgyzstan (Klötzli, 1994). The 1998 Syr-Darya Framework Agreement between the two has been broken by both sides. The implementation of such barter agreement runs across one major problem – all barter agreements are delayed until the late spring when the downstream countries urgently need water for irrigation. As this might be the case, Kyrgyzstan would have had an incentive to produce less electricity. However, due to Kyrgyzstan's uncertainty whether enough gas would be provided, it produces electricity to protect itself giving rise to a vicious circle (IGC, 2002).

Uzbekistan intensified the tension more than once by acting in a unilateral manner. In July 1997, it cut off 70 percent of downstream flow, which caused a riot among the Kazakh farmers whose 100,000 hectares were threatened (O'Hara, 1998; Hogan, 2000b). History of altering water flow by upstream riparians is no more soothing. In summer 1999, Tajikistan released 700 million cubic meters of water from its Kairakum reservoir without warning its downstream neighbours. As a result, cotton crops in southern Kazakhstan which has received less water than was agreed, were devastated. The situation was seriously aggravated by Kyrgyzstan's concurrent move to reduce the flow to southern Kazakhstan in retaliation for Kazakhstan's failure to supply coal under the barter agreements. After months of talks, the incident was finally settled (Hogan, 2000a).

At issue is also the Naryn-Syr Darya cascade of dams in Kyrgyzstan. Every year Uzbekistan insists on releasing water from it to improve downstream agriculture. Several times, the conflict was on the verge of war. In 1997, Uzbekistan deployed 130,000 troops on the Kyrgyz-Uzbek border, near the Toktogul reservoir, to conduct military exercises aimed at seizure of a 'well guarded object', using the armour and helicopters. Meanwhile, Kyrgyzstan, through media leak, hinted that in case the reservoir would be blown up, the resulting flood would sweep away Uzbekistan's Ferghana and Zeravshan Valleys (Grozin, 2001).

Kyrgyzstan has tried to persuade Uzbekistan and Kazakhstan to share the maintenance and operating costs of the Toktogul reservoir but these attempts were turned down by the downstream countries. Kazakhstan claimed that it would not be able to pay the costs – between US$ 15 and 27 million per annum. Thus, the opportunity for the downstream riparians to settle the dispute was missed. However, by adopting *Law on the Interstate Use of Water Objects, Water Resources and Water Management Installations* on 29 June 2001, the Kyrgyz parliament left the door open to push the downstream countries into negotiations regarding the maintenance costs of the Toktogul reservoir as later Kyrgyzstan stated that in fact it demanded to pay only for the water passing through Kyrgyz reservoirs, i.e. share maintenance costs. This was welcomed by Kazakhstan who agreed to pay for the maintenance of the Kyrgyz water installations, but initially opposed by Uzbeks. However, in March 2002 Uzbekistan reached the agreement with Kyrgyzstan that it would share some costs in return for the guarantee that it would receive water for irrigation. Had more attention have been paid to the barter agreements working properly, the main step to resolving the Syr Darya dispute between Kyrgyzstan and Uzbekistan would be taken (ICG, 2002b).

Shared water storage facilities, like the Andijan reservoir located in the Uzbek part of the Ferghana Valley but supposed to re-channel some water back to Kyrgyzstan, also represent an inter-state problem (Chait, 1998).

The Amu Darya Basin

The Amu Darya is shared by four countries – Tajikistan as the upstream riparian, Afghanistan, Uzbekistan and Turkmenistan – and forms the border in some stretches between Tajikistan, Uzbekistan and Afghanistan, and between Turkmenistan and Uzbekistan.

The Amu Darya is much less regulated and has fewer dams and reservoirs to cause potential problems. However, there are serious tensions along the flow of the river not only between the upstream and downstream riparians, as, for example, between Tajikistan and Uzbekistan, but also between the middle and lower riparians, for example, Uzbekistan and Turkmenistan.

According to the 1992 water quota agreement, Tajikistan is entitled to 9 m^3 of about 75 m^3 of annual flow of the Amu Darya, or 12 percent. This is considered low by Tajikistan who needs to expand its agricultural output to supply the growing population with food. Tajikistan's agriculture is underdeveloped since the Soviet times, and the irrigation system is derelict and in need of urgent repairs. Tajikistan sees the only way out as using more water either by increasing its water quota from the Amu Darya or by diverting the Zeravhsan river. As 95 percent of the latter are used by Uzbekistan, this would cause serious tensions with Tajikistan's much powerful neighbour.

In contrast, increasing the Amu Darya quota seems to be quite easy, since Tajikistan has an upper hand in distributing water resources of the Amu Darya. In principle, nobody could prevent Tajikistan from taking more water than was allocated by the water quota agreement. It is very hard to monitor Tajikistan's performance, as most equipment needed has been destroyed during the civil war in 1992-1997. But even Tajikistan were to increase its water quota moderately, this would have an immediate impact downstream.

The same water/energy complex as with Kyrgyzstan has developed between Tajikistan and Uzbekistan. Tajikistan's central and southern parts are well provided by electricity from the Nurek hydro plant, and northern Tajikistan having no grid lines with the rest of the country relies on Uzbekistan's intermittent supplies of electricity and gas in winter. In return, Tajikistan provides power to southern Uzbek provinces and often requests that Uzbekistan switched off electricity to northern Tajikistan to keep imports within the agreed limit not to pay higher price. This causes serious discontent as Tajikistan is forced to have electricity rationed in many provinces due to poor state of Tajikistan's grid lines. The country desires to develop its hydropower resources to break dependence on Uzbekistan. But increasing hydro consumption would seriously affect the downstream access to seasonal water supplies and to create further discord along the Amu Darya course.

The most dramatic conflict over the Amu Darya water resources is between downstream nations of Uzbekistan and Turkmenistan. Both equally depend on their cotton production and irrigation agriculture and both claim that each of them exceed their water quotas. Due to the very poor state of Turkmenistan's water infrastructure, most water received by Turkmenistan is wasted. The country does not want to spend huge funds for the expensive rehabilitation of crippling Turkmen canals and draws off more water from the Amu Darya instead. The relations between two countries dramatically worsened in the late 2002 when the Uzbek ambassador has been declared persona non grata in Turkmenistan on accusation of participating in the conspiracy to oust and kill President Niyazov. Uzbek-Turkmen relations over water can grow even worse, given Turkmenistan's ambitious plan to complete a huge reservoir in the Karakum desert, called the Golden Century Lake. Another point of contention is the Tyuyamuyun reservoir in the delta of the Amu Darya divided between Uzbekistan and Turkmenistan. Both sides feel displeased with the wasteful use of water, and this led to an outbreak of violence in 1992 over the re-direction of drainage waters and raids by both sides to cut off pipes and irrigation canals (Smith, 1995). Today, the Tyuyamuyun remains one of the several disputed areas in continuing water dispute with Uzbekistan.

Throughout the independence period, rumours have circulated of a small-scale secret war between the two states over the river resources, Uzbekistan troops taking control of water installations on the Turkmen bank of the Amu Darya, and even of a massacre of a large number of Uzbekistan troops in

Turkmenistan in 2001. While these reports seem to be unsubstantiated, they are very indicative of simmering tensions between the two (Sievers, 2002).

THE INDUS WATERS KISHENGANGA ARBITRATION (PAKISTAN V. INDIA)

A Partial Award was rendered in the *Indus Waters Kishenganga Arbitration* between Pakistan and India on February 18, 2013. The inter-State dispute under the 1960 Indus Waters Treaty (IWT) arises from India's proposal to build a 330 megawatt hydroelectric project on the Kishenganga River" a tributary of the Jhelum River in the India-administered part of Jammu and Kashmir. Upon crossing the Line of Control between India and Pakistan, the Kishenganga is rechristened the Neelum River in Pakistan-administered Kashmir, before finally joining the Jhelum. India's Kishenganga Hydro-Electric Project (KHEP) involves the diversion of water from the Kishenganga/Neelum River (the River), at a point in the Gurez Valley, through a network of tunnels to the powerhouse at a distance of 23 kilometers from the River, before emptying the water into another tributary of the Jhelum at a lower elevation.

Downstream, Pakistan has also sought to harvest the hydroelectric potential of the River by constructing the 969 megawatt Neelum-Jhelum hydroelectric project (NJHEP). The Jhelum is an important river within the over-burdened Indus river system, which irrigates large areas of India and Pakistan. Concerned by the impact of the KHEP on its water supply, Pakistan filed a Request for Arbitration under the IWT in May 2010.

THE INDUS WATERS TREATY

The 1960 IWT an outcome of decade-long negotiations between India and Pakistan facilitated by the World Bank sets out the rights and obligations of the Parties for the utilization of the Indus river system's water resources. In a rather unusual approach, the Treaty allocates entire streams, instead of water volumes. India is permitted unrestricted use of the Eastern Rivers (the Sutlej, the Beas and the Ravi), while the Western rivers are allocated to Pakistan (the Indus, the Jhelum and the Chenab), subject to certain exceptions contained in the Treaty. By focusing on the Parties' rights to use the streams, the Treaty avoids addressing the controversial question of sovereignty over the disputed parts of Jammu and Kashmir through which the rivers flow.

The Treaty also establishes the Permanent Indus Commission, comprising a commissioner from each State, for its implementation. Article IX provides for a multi-tiered dispute resolution process based upon a hierarchy of disputes. A "question" between the Parties relating to the interpretation or application of the IWT or the existence of certain facts, if unresolved by the Commission, gives rise to a "difference." If, however, a difference does not relate to the listed technical matters, or if the Neutral Expert considers appropriate, then a "dispute" arises. Such a dispute may be settled by formal negotiations, failing which, or if the Parties agree, it is to be resolved by a seven-member arbitral tribunal called the "Court of Arbitration."

THE DISPUTE AND PROCEEDINGS

This is the first time a dispute under the IWT has been referred to a Court of Arbitration. In its Request for Arbitration, Pakistan identified two questions: first, whether India's proposed inter-tributary transfer as part of the KHEP breached its obligations under the IWT, as interpreted and applied under international law (First Dispute); and, second, whether the IWT allowed India to deplete the reservoir level of a run-of-river plant below the "Dead Storage Level" in circumstances other than unforeseen emergencies.

To answer these, a Court of Arbitration was constituted on December 17, 2010. In June 2011, Pakistan submitted an application for provisional measures, leading to an Order on Interim Measures by the Court on September 23, 2011. Subsequently, the Court undertook two site visits and oral hearings on the merits were held at the Permanent Court of Arbitration in.

The Hague from August 20-31, 2012. The Partial Award of February 18, 2013 allowed India to proceed with the construction and operation of the KHEP, subject to certain operational constraints to be determined in the Final Award. While both Parties agreed that the awards should be published, Pakistan opposed the publication of the pleadings.

The Award

The First Dispute concerned the permissibility of India's KHEP and the inter-tributary transfer under the IWT. The IWT obliges India to "let flow" the waters of the Western Rivers, except for limited, enumerated uses. In the Court's view, these exceptions give India the right to utilize the Western Rivers in some ways, subject to its obligations under the IWT.

The Court began by considering India's general obligations under Articles III and IV(6) of the IWT. Pakistan argued that, since the power generated by the KHEP would be supplied to the whole of India's northern electricity grid, the Project did not conform with Article III(2), restricting India's use of the Western Rivers to "the drainage basin thereof." The Court disagreed: though Article III(2) imposed a geographical restriction on India's use of the Western River waters, such a restriction did not extend to the products (such as electricity) generated from the use of these waters. Pakistan also argued that, by failing to adequately assess the environmental impact of the inter-tributary transfer, India breached its general obligation to "use its best endeavours to maintain the natural channels of the Rivers" under Article IV(6). Although noting that Article IV(6) was obligatory, the Court considered it of no direct relevance as it only required the preservation of the natural, unobstructed paths of the rivers, and not the volume or timing of the flow.

Next, the Court turned to Pakistan's arguments of the IWT prescribing requirements for the design and operation of run-of-river plants. Pakistan contended that, first, permit the permanent diversion of a tributary; second, even if such diversion was permitted, the KHEP did not qualify as a "Plant" under Paragraph 15(iii); and, finally, even if the KHEP was a "Plant," it failed the test of necessity contained in Paragraph 15(iii).

The Court rejected all three arguments. It found that the plain text of Paragraph 15(iii) allowed inter-tributary transfers, provided that the diverting works complied with three conditions. First, the work must be a run-of-river plant. The Court noted that the KHEP was designed and notified to Pakistan as a run-of-river plant. Second, the plant must be "located on" a tributary of the Jhelum. Pakistan pointed out that the actual electricity generation was to take place at a distance of 23 kilometers from the Kishenganga. The Court however saw no reason for "disaggregating the elements" comprising the KHEP, designed to operate as an "integrated whole," and concluded that the condition was satisfied since the works that trapped the water were "located on" the Kishenganga" a tributary of the Jhelum.

Finally, the Court noted that Paragraph 15(iii) required the diversion of water into another tributary to be "necessary" for generating hydroelectricity. On the threshold for necessity, the Court considered "inapposite" the concepts of necessity developed in other branches of international law, such as international trade law, investment law and the law of State responsibility, adopting instead the plain meaning of "necessary" to describe action that was "required, needed or essential." Against this threshold, it found that the diversion was necessary for India to utilize the difference in elevation between the two tributaries in order to generate significant power.

The Court next turned to the "essence" of the First Dispute: the requirement under Paragraph 15(iii) that any Indian inter-tributary run-of-river plant operate "only to the extent that the *then existing* Agricultural Use or hydro-electric use by Pakistan on the former Tributary would not be adversely affected." Pakistan argued for an "ambulatory" interpretation of "then existing use" in Paragraph 15(iii), calling for a "dynamic assessment by India of the agricultural and hydro-electric uses of Pakistan whenever water is released by the KHEP." By contrast, India argued for a "static" approach, focusing on a "critical date," when India communicated to Pakistan its "firm intention" to proceed with a project, such that Pakistan's agricultural and hydroelectric uses must be "frozen" at the stage when design was finalized. In answering whether the NJHEP constituted "then existing use" by Pakistan, which restricted India's right under Paragraph 15(iii), the Court did not accept either interpretation in entirety. With respect to Pakistan's approach, it noted that the "overall structure" of that "the general permissibility of any new Plant's design is determined prior to the commencements of its construction." It ultimately rejected Pakistan's interpretation because it would subject the viability of India's works to the "unilateral will and action of another party."

With respect to India's approach, the Court considered that, in practice, it could be "very difficult to pinpoint" the exact moment at which a firm intention to proceed with a project crystallizes, keeping in mind the "continuum of design, financing, government approval, construction, completion and operation" associated with large infrastructure projects such as the KHEP. Instead, the Court proposed a "'critical period,' wherein a cumulation of facts â€" tender, financing secured, government approvals in place and construction underway â€" has achieved a level of certitude indicating that a project will proceed 'firmly' as proposed." Applying this "critical period" approach to India's KHEP and Pakistan's NJHEP, it found that the KHEP preceded the NJHEP such that the NJHEP did not constitute a "then existing use" by Pakistan. India was therefore permitted to effectuate an inter-tributary transfer under Paragraph 15(iii).

However, the Court accommodated elements of the dynamic approach by subjecting India's right to operate the KHEP to certain operational constraints. In doing so, it recognized that India's rights to divert water for the operation of the KHEP are "tempered" by Pakistan's right to a minimum flow of water for hydroelectric and agricultural uses. The Court observed that Paragraph 15 "delineates a number of operational constraints" for new works and seems to be "operational in character," such that the Treaty imposed a duty on India to ensure that a minimum flow of water reaches Pakistan at all times.

The Court also found support for such a duty in "contemporary customary international law," which requires States to take "environmental protection into consideration when planning and developing Projects that may cause injury to a bordering State." Acknowledging that the IWT must be interpreted and applied in light of the "customary international principles for the protection of the environment in force today," the Court noted that general international law imposes a duty on States "to prevent, or at least mitigate" significant harm to the environment when pursuing large-scale construction activities. Crucially, it recalled the International Court of Justice's observations that the "duties of due diligence, vigilance and prevention" imposed by the principle of sustainable development continue "once operations have started and throughout the life of the project." It acknowledged that India recognized this continuous duty by committing to ensure a minimum downstream flow of water. However, the information presently at its disposal did not allow the Court to objectively fix the exact rate of the minimum downstream flow, and it requested the Parties to provide the relevant information to fix this rate in its Final Award.

Second Dispute

Although Pakistan framed the Second Dispute as relating to the permissibility of reservoir depletion in the abstract, the Court noted that Pakistan in essence took issue with the use of a sediment management technique called "drawdown flushing" by India at the KHEP and other future projects. It clarified that while its findings could not reverse the Neutral Expert's 2007 Determination (permitting this technique for India's *Baglihar* project), or retrospectively affect any plant already in operation or under construction, they would apply to the KHEP and any future Indian run-of-river plants on the Western Rivers.

India put forth two objections to the admissibility of the Second Dispute. First, it argued that except when the two Permanent Indus Commissioners were in agreement to pursue an alternative, the IWT required a Neutral Expert to initially determine whether a matter was a technical "difference" or a "dispute" to be referred to arbitration. With respect to Pakistan's claim, no such initial determination was made. Second, in India's view, the subject matter of the Second Dispute was objectively among the questions consigned to a Neutral Expert. The Court dismissed both objections. In its view, the text of Article IX(2)(a), as confirmed by its object and purpose, did not impose "an additional procedural hurdle" to access the arbitral process, and it was not open to India to assert at this late stage that the Second Dispute was a "difference" and not a "dispute."

Looking at the treaty context, the Court noted that several provisions strongly suggested that some limitation on India's use and depletion of dead storage" a consequence of drawdown flushing technique" was intended. Specifically, it identified a "decisive prohibition" in the Treaty against the depletion of dead storage, except in unforeseen emergencies. Noting that both Parties agreed that sediment accumulation did not constitute an unforeseen emergency, the Court concluded that the text of the Treaty prohibited the depletion of dead storage for drawdown flushing. Next, the Court juxtaposed its understanding of the limitations on the use of dead storage with another object of the Treaty: to allow India to harness the hydroelectric potential of the Western Rivers. Agreeing that "anything you build needs to work," it considered whether drawdown flushing was indispensable to the sustainable generation of hydroelectricity on the Western Rivers. Based on the evidence, it concluded that India's right to utilize the Western Rivers could be "meaningfully exercised without drawdown flushing." In particular, the Court suggested the use of another technique called "sluicing" for sediment management.

WATER SUPPLY AND SANITATION IN INDIA

Water supply and sanitation in India continue to be inadequate, despite longstanding efforts by the various levels of government and communities at improving coverage. The level of investment in water and sanitation, albeit low by international standards, has increased during the 2000s. Access has also increased significantly. For example, in 1980 rural sanitation coverage was estimated at 1% and reached 21% in 2008. Also, the share of Indians with access to improved sources of water has increased significantly from 72% in 1990 to 88% in 2008. At the same time, local government institutions in charge of operating and maintaining the infrastructure are seen as weak and lack the financial resources to carry out their functions. In addition, no major city in India is known to have a continuous water supply and an estimated 72% of Indians still lack access to improved sanitation facilities.

A number of innovative approaches to improve water supply and sanitation have been tested in India, in particular in the early 2000s. These include demand-driven approaches in rural water supply since 1999, community-led total sanitation, a public-private partnerships to improve the continuity of urban water supply in Karnataka, and the use of micro-credit to women in order to improve access to water.

Access

In 2008, 88% of the population in India had access to an improved water source, but only 31% had access to improved sanitation. In rural areas, where 72% of India's population lives, the respective shares are 84% for water and only 21% for sanitation. In urban areas, 96% had access to an improved water source and 54% to improved sanitation. Access has improved substantially since 1990 when it was estimated to stand at 72% for water and 18% for sanitation.

As of 2010, the UN estimated based on Indian statistics that 626 people practice open defecation. In June 2012 Minister of Rural Development Jairam Ramesh stated India is the worlds largest "open air toilet". He also remarked that Pakistan, Bangladesh and Afghanistan have better sanitation records.

According to Indian norms, access to improved water supply exists if at least 40 litres/capita/day of safe drinking water are provided within a distance of 1.6 km or 100 meter of elevation difference, to be relaxed as per field conditions. There should be at least one pump per 250 persons.

Service Quality

Water and sanitation service quality in India is generally poor, although there has been some limited progress concerning continuity of supply in urban areas and access to sanitation in rural areas.

Water Supply

Challenges. None of the 35 Indian cities with a population of more than one million distribute water for more than a few hours per day, despite generally sufficient infrastructure. Owing to inadequate pressure people struggle to collect water even when it is available. According to the World Bank, none have performance indicators that compare with average international standards. A 2007 study by the Asian Development Bank showed that in 20 cities the average duration of supply was only 4.3 hours per day. No city had continuous supply. The longest duration of supply was 12 hours per day in Chandigarh, and the lowest was 0.3 hours per day in Rajkot. In Delhi residents receive water only a few hours per day because of inadequate management of the distribution system. This results in contaminated water and forces households to complement a deficient public water service at prohibitive 'coping' costs; the poor suffer most from this situation. For example, according to a 1996 survey households in Delhi spent an average of 2,182 (US$39.5) per year in time and money to cope with poor service levels. This is more than three times as much as the 2001 water bill of about US$18 per year of a Delhi household that uses 20 cubic meters per month.

Achievements. Jamshedpur, a city in Jharkhand with 573,000 inhabitants, provided 25% of its residents with continuous water supply in 2009. Navi Mumbai, a planned city with more than 1m inhabitants, has achieved continuous supply for about half its population as of January 2009. Badlapur, another city in the Mumbai Conurbation with a population of 140,000, has achieved continuous supply in 3 out of 10 operating zones, covering 30% of its population. Thiruvananthapuram, the capital of Kerala state with a population of 745,000 in 2001, is probably the largest Indian city that enjoys continuous water supply.

Sanitation

Most Indians depend on on-site sanitation facilities. Recently, access to on-site sanitation have increased in both rural and urban areas. In rural areas, total sanitation has been successful. In urban areas, a good practice is the Slum Sanitation Program in Mumbai that has provided access to sanitation for a quarter million slum dwellers. Sewerage, where available, is often in a bad state. In Delhi the sewerage network has lacked maintenance over the years and overflow of raw sewage in open drains is common, due to blockage, settlements and inadequate pumping capacities. The capacity of the 17 existing wastewater treatment plants in Delhi is adequate to cater a daily production of waste water of less than 50% of the drinking water produced. Of the 2.5 Billion people in the world that defecate openly, some 665 million live in India. This is of greater concern as 88% of deaths from diarrhoea occur because of unsafe water, inadequate sanitation and poor hygiene.

Environment

As of 2003, it was estimated that only 27% of India's wastewater was being treated, with the remainder flowing into rivers, canals, groundwater or the sea., For example, the sacred Ganges river is infested with diseases and in some places "the Ganges becomes black and septic. Corpses, of semi-cremated adults or enshrouded babies, drift slowly by.". News Week describes Delhi's sacred Yamuna River as "a putrid ribbon of black sludge" where fecal bacteria is 10,000 over safety limits despite a 15-year program to address the problem. Cholera epidemics are not unknown.

Health Impact

The lack of adequate sanitation and safe water has significant negative health impacts including diarrhoea, referred to by travellers as the "Delhi Belly", and experienced by about 10 million visitors annually. While most visitors to India recover quickly and otherwise receive proper care, the World Health Organisation estimated that around 700,000 Indians die each year from diarrhoea. The dismal working conditions of sewer workers are another concern. A survey of the working conditions of sewage workers in Delhi showed that most of them suffer from chronic diseases, respiratory problems, skin disorders, allergies, headaches and eye infections.

Water Supply and Water Resources

Depleting ground water table and deteriorating ground water quality are threatening the sustainability of both urban and rural water supply in many parts of India. The supply of cities that depend on surface water is threatened by pollution, increasing water scarcity and conflicts among users. For example, Bangalore depends to a large extent on water pumped since 1974 from the Kaveri river, whose waters are disputed between the states of Karnataka and Tamil Nadu. As in other Indian cities, the response to water scarcity is to transfer more water over large distances at high costs. In the case of Bangalore, the 3,384 crore (US$612.5 million) Kaveri Stage IV project, Phase II, includes the supply of 500,000 cubic meter of water per day over a distance of 100 km, thus increasing the city's supply by two thirds.

Responsibility for Water Supply and Sanitation

Water supply and sanitation is a State responsibility under the Indian Constitution. States may give the responsibility to the Panchayati Raj Institutions (PRI) in rural areas or municipalities in urban areas, called Urban Local Bodies (ULB). At present, states generally plan, design and execute water supply schemes (and often operate them) through their State Departments (of Public Health Engineering or Rural Development Engineering) or State Water Boards.

Highly centralised decision-making and approvals at the state level, which are characteristic of the Indian civil service, affect the management of water supply and sanitation services. For example, according to the World Bank in the state of Punjab the process of approving designs is centralised with even minor technical approvals reaching the office of chief engineers. A majority of decisions are made in a very centralised manner at the headquarters. In 1993 the Indian constitution and relevant state legislations were amended in order to decentralise certain responsibilities, including water supply and sanitation, to municipalities. Since the assignment of responsibilities to municipalities is a state responsibility, different states have followed different approaches. According to a Planning Commission report of 2003 there is a trend to decentralise capital investment to engineering departments at the district level and operation and maintenance to district and gram panchayat levels.

Policy and Regulation

The responsibility for water supply and sanitation at the central and state level is shared by various Ministries. At the central level, The Ministry of Rural Development is responsible for rural water supply through its Department of Drinking Water Supply (DDWS) and theMinistry of Housing and Urban Poverty Alleviation is responsible for urban water supply. However, except for the National Capital Territory of Delhi and other Union Territories, the central Ministries only have an advisory capacity and a very limited role in funding. Sector policy thus is a prerogative of state governments.

Service Provision

Urban areas. Institutional arrangements for water supply and sanitation in Indian cities vary greatly. Typically, a state-level agency is in charge of planning and investment, while the local government (Urban Local Bodies) is in charge of operation and maintenance. Some of the largest cities have created municipal water and sanitation utilities that are legally and financially separated from the local government. However, these utilities remain weak in terms of financial capacity. In spite of decentralisation, ULBs remain dependent on capital subsidies from state governments. Tariffs are also set by state governments, which often even subsidise operating costs.

Furthermore, when no separate utility exists there is no separation of accounts for different activities within a municipality. Some states and cities have non-typical institutional arrangements. For example, in Rajasthan the sector is more centralised and the state government is also in charge of operation and maintenance, while in Mumbai the sector is more decentralised and local government is also in charge of planning and investment.

Private sector participation. The private sector plays a limited, albeit recently increasing role in operating and maintaining urban water systems on behalf of ULBs. For example, the Jamshedpur Utilities & Services Company (Jusco), a subsidiary of Tata Steel, has a lease contract for Jamshedpur (Jharkhand), a management contract in Haldia, another contract in Mysore (Karnataka) and since 2007 a contract for the reduction of non-revenue water in parts of Bhopal (Madhya Pradesh). The French water company Veolia won a management contract in three cities in Karnataka in 2005.

In 2002 a consortium including Thames Water won a pilot contract covering 40,000 households to reduce non-revenue water in parts of Bangalore, funded by the Japan Bank for International Cooperation.

The contract was scaled up in 2004. The Cypriot company Hydro-Comp, together with two Indian companies, won a 10-year concession contract for the city of Latur City (Maharashtra) in 2007 and an operator-consultant contract in Madurai (Tamil Nadu).

Furthermore, the private Indian infrastructure development company SPML is engaged in Build-Operate-Transfer (BOT) projects, such as a bulk water supply project for Bhiwandi (Maharashtra).

Rural areas. There are about a 100,000 rural water supply systems in India. At least in some states responsibility for service provision is in the process of being partially transferred from State Water Boards and district governments to Panchayati Raj Institutions (PRI) at the block or village level (there were about 604 districts and 256,000 villages in India in 2002, according to Subdivisions of India.

Blocks are an intermediate level between districts and villages). Where this transfer has been initiated, it seems to be more advanced for single-village water schemes than for more complex multi-village water schemes. Despite their professed role Panchayati Raj Institutions, play only a limited role in provision of rural water supply and sanitation as of 2006. There has been limited success in implementing decentralisation, partly due to low priority by some state governments. Rural sanitation is typically provided by households themselves in the form of latrines.

Innovative Approaches

A number of innovative approaches to improve water supply and sanitation have been tested in India, in particular in the early 2000s. These include community-led total sanitation, demand-driven approaches in rural water supply, a public-private partnerships to improve the continuity of urban water supply in Karnataka, and the use of micro-credit to women in order to improve access to water.

Community-led Total Sanitation

In 1999 a demand-driven and people-centered sanitation program was initiated under the name Total Sanitation Campaign (TSC) or Community-led total sanitation. It evolved from the limited achievements of the first structured programme for rural sanitation in India, the Central Rural Sanitation Programme, which had minimal community participation. The main goal of Total Sanitation Campaign is to eradicate the practice of open defecation by 2017. Community-led total sanitation is not focused on building infrastructure, but on preventing open defecation through peer pressure and shame. In Maharashtra where the program started more than 2000 Gram Panchayats have achieved "open defecation free" status. Villages that achieve this status receive monetary rewards and high publicity under a program called Nirmal Gram Puraskar.

Demand-driven Approaches in Rural Water Supply

Most rural water supply schemes in India use a centralised, supply-driven approach, i.e. a government institution designs a project and has it built with little community consultation and no capacity building for the community, often requiring no water fees to be paid for its subsequent operation. Since 2002 the Government of India has rolled out at the national level a program to change the way in which water and sanitation services are supported in rural areas. The program, called *Swajaldhara,* decentralises service delivery responsibility to rural local governments and user groups. Under the new approach communities are being consulted and trained, and users agree up-front to pay a tariff that is set at a level sufficiently high to cover operation and maintenance costs. It also includes measures to promote sanitation and to improve hygiene behaviour. The national program follows a pilot program launched in 1999.

According to a 2008 World Bank study in 10 Indian states, *Swajaldhara* results in lower capital costs, lower administrative costs and better service quality compared to the supply-driven approach. In particular, the study found that the average full cost of supply-driven schemes is Rs 38 (US$0.7) per cubic meter, while it is only Rs 26 (US$0.5) per cubic meter for demand-driven schemes. These costs include capital, operation and maintenance costs, administrative costs and coping costs incurred by users of malfunctioning systems.

Coping costs include travelling long distances to obtain water, standing in long queues, storing water and repairing failed systems. Among the surveyed systems that were built using supply-driven approach system breakdowns were common, the quantity and quality of water supply were less than foreseen in designs, and 30% of households did not get daily supply in summer. The poor functioning of one system sometimes leads to the construction of another system, so that about 30% of households surveyed were served by several systems.

As of 2008 only about 10% of rural water schemes built in India used a demand-driven approach. Since water users have to pay lower or no tariffs under the supply-driven approach, this discourages them to opt for a demand-driven approach, even if the likelihood of the systems operating on a sustainable basis is higher under a demand-driven approach.

Achieving Continuous Water Supply with the Help of a Private Operator in Karnataka

In the cities of Hubli, Belgaum and Gulbarga in the state of Karnataka, the private operator Veolia increased water supply from once every 2–15 days for 1–2 hours, to 24 hours per day for 180,000 people (12% of the population of the 3 cities) within 2 years (2006–2008). This was achieved by carefully selecting and ring-fencing demonstration zones (one in each city), renovating the distribution network, installing meters, introducing a well-functioning commercial system, and effective grass-roots social intermediation by an NGO, all without increasing the amount of bulk water supplied.

The project, known by its acronym as KUWASIP (Karnataka Urban Water Sector Improvement Project), was supported by a US$39.5 million loan from the World Bank. It constitutes a milestone for India, where no large city so far has achieved continuous water supply. The project is expected to be scaled-up to cover the entire area of the three cities.

Micro-credit for Water connections in Tamil Nadu

In Tiruchirapalli in Tamil Nadu, the NGO Gramalaya, established in 1987, and women self-help groups promote access to water supply and sanitation by the poor through micro-credit. Among the benefits are that women can spend more time with their children, earn additional income, and sell surplus water to neighbours. This money contributes to her repayment of the WaterCredit loan. The initiative is supported by the US-based non-profit Water Partners International.

The Jamshedpur Utilities and Services Company

The Jamshedpur Utilities and Services Company (JUSCO) provides water and sanitation services in Jamshedpur, a major industrial centre in East India that is home to Tata Steel. Until 2004 a division of Tata Steel provided water to the city's residents. However, service quality was poor with intermittent supply, high water losses and no metering. To improve this situation and to establish good practices that could be replicated in other Indian cities, JUSCO was set up as a wholly owned subsidiary of Tata Steel in 2004.

Efficiency and service quality improved substantially over the following years. The level on non-revenue water decreased from an estimated 36% in 2005 to 10% in 2009; one quarter of residents received continuous water supply (although the average supply remained at only 7 hours per day) in 2009; the share of metered connections increased from 2% in 2007 to 26% in 2009; the number of customers increased; and the company recovered its operating costs plus a portion of capital costs. Identifying and legalising illegal connections was an important element in the reduction of non-revenue water. The utility prides itself today of the good drinking water quality provided and encourages its customers to drink from the tap. The utility also operates a wastewater treatment plant that meets discharge standards. The private utility pays salaries that are higher than civil service salaries and conducts extensive training programs for its staff. It has also installed a modern system to track and resolve customer complaints. Furthermore, it conducts independent annual customer satisfaction surveys. JUSCO's vision is to be the preferred provider of water supply and other urban services throughout India. Together with Ranhill Malaysia it won a 25-year concession contract for providing the water supply in Haldia City, West Bengal.

Efficiency

There are only limited data on the operating efficiency of utilities in India, and even fewer data on the efficiency of investments.

Concerning operating efficiency, a study of 20 cities by the Jawaharlal Nehru National Urban Renewal Mission with the support of the Asian Development Bank showed an average level of non-revenue water (NRW) of 32%. However, 5 out of the 20 cities did not provide any data. For those that provided data there probably is a large margin of error, since only 25% of connections are metered, which makes it very difficult to estimate non-revenue water. Also, three utilities show NRW levels of less than 20%, two of which have practically no metering, which indicates that the numbers are not reliable and actual values are likely to be higher. In Delhi, which was not included in the ADB study, non-revenue water stood at 53% and there were about 20 employees per 1000 connections. Furthermore, only 70% of revenue billed was actually collected. Concerning labour productivity, the 20 utilities in the sample had on average 7.4 employees per 1,000 connections, which is much higher than the estimated level for an efficient utility. A survey of a larger sample of Indian utilities showed an average ratio of 10.9 employees per 1,000 connections.

Tariffs, Cost Recovery and Subsidies

Water and sewer tariffs in India are low in both urban and rural areas. In urban areas they were set at the equivalent of about US$0.10 per cubic meter in 2007 and recovered about 60% of operating and maintenance costs, with large differences between cities. Some cities such as Kolkata do not bill residential users at all. In rural areas the level of cost recovery often is even lower than in urban areas and was estimated at only 20% in rural Punjab. Subsidies were estimated at US$1.1 billion per year in the mid-1990s, accounting to 4% of all government subsidies in India. 70% of those benefiting from the subsidies are not poor.

Urban Areas

Metering. Water metering is the precondition for billing water users on the basis of volume consumed. According to a 1999 survey of 300 cities about 62% of urban water customers in metropolitan areas and 50% in smaller cities are metered (average 55%). However, meters often do not work so that many "metered" customers are charged flat rates. Bangalore and Pune are among the few Indian cities that meter all their customers. Many other cities have no metering at all or meter only commercial customers. Users of standposts receive water free of charge. A 2007 study of 20 cities by the Jawaharlal Nehru National Urban Renewal Mission with the support of the Asian Development Bank (ADB) showed that only 25% of customers of these utilities were metered. Most other customers paid a flat tariff independent of consumption. Some utilities, such as the one serving Kolkata, actually do not bill residential users at all.

Tariff levels. According to the same ADB study the average tariff for all customers – including industrial, commercial and public customers – is Rs. 4.9 (US$0.1) per cubic meter. According to a 2007 global water tariff survey by the OECD the residential water tariff for a consumption of 15 m^3 was equivalent to US$0.15 per m^3 in Bangalore, US$0.12 per m^3 in Calcutta, US$0.11 per m3 in New Delhi and US$0.09 per m^3 in Mumbai. Only Bangalore had a sewer tariff of US$0.02 per m^3. The other three cities did not charge for sewerage, although the better-off tend to be the ones with access to sewers.

Tariff structure. The tariff for customers that are effectively metered is typically a uniform linear tariff, although some cities apply increasing-block tariffs. Affordability. Urban water tariffs were highly affordable according to data from the year 2000.

A family of five living on the poverty line which uses 20 cubic meter of water per month would spend less than 1.2% of its budget on its water bill if it had a water meter. If it did not have a water meter and was charged a flat rate, it would pay 2.0% of its budget. This percentage lies below the often used affordability threshold of 5%. However, at that time the average metered tariff was estimated at only US$0.03 per m^3, or less than three times what it was estimated to be in 2007. Apparently no more up-to-date estimates on the share of the average water bill in the budget of the poor are available.

Cost recovery. According to a 2007 study of 20 cities the average rate of cost recovery for operating and maintenance costs of utilities in these cities was 60%. Seven of the 20 utilities generated a cash surplus to partially finance investments. Chennai generated the highest relative surplus. The lowest cost recovery ratio was found in Indore in Madhya Pradesh, which recovered less than 20% of its operating and maintenance costs.

Delhi example. In Delhi revenues were just sufficient to cover about 60% of operating costs of the city's utility in 2004; maintenance has, as a result, been minimal. In the past, the Delhi utility has relied heavily on government financial support for recurrent and capital expenditures in the magnitude of Rs. 3 billion (US$54.3 million) per year and Rs. 7 billion (US$126.7 million) respectively.

As financial support for both capital and recurrent expenditures has been passed on as loans by the Government of the National Capital Territory of Delhi, the utility's balance sheet is loaded with a huge debt totalling about Rs. 50 billion (US$905 million) that it is unlikely to be able to service. Accounts receivable represent more than 12 months of billing, part of it being non recoverable. The average tariff was estimated atUS$0.074/$m^3$ in 2001, compared to production costs of US$0.085/$m^3$, the latter probably being a very conservative estimate that does not take into account capital costs. Challenges faced in attempting to increase tariffs. Even if users are willing to pay more for better services, political interests often prevent tariffs from being increased even to a small extent. An example is the city of Jabalpur where the central government and the state government financed a Rs. 130 million (US$2.4 million) water supply project from 2000–2004 to be operated by the Jabalpur Municipal Corporation, an entity that collected only less than half of its operational costs in revenues even before this major investment.

Even so the municipal corporation initially refused to increase tariffs. Only following pressure from the state government it reluctantly agreed to increase commercial tariffs, but not residential tariffs.

Rural Areas

Cost recovery in rural areas is low and a majority of the rural water systems are defunct for lack of maintenance. Some state governments subsidise rural water systems, but funds are scarce and insufficient. In rural areas in Punjab, operation and maintenance cost recovery is only about 20%. On one hand, expenditures are high due to high salary levels, high power tariff and a high number of operating staff. On the other hand, revenue is paid only by the 10% of the households who have private connections. Those drawing water from public stand posts do not pay any water charges at all, although the official tariff for public stand post users is Rs. 15 (US$0.3) per month per household.

Subsidies and Targeting of Subsidies

There are no accurate recent estimates of the level of subsidies for water and sanitation in India. It has been estimated that transfers to the water sector in India amounted to Rs. 5,470.8 crore (US$990.2 million) per year in the mid-1990s, accounting for 4% of all government subsidies in India. About 98% of this subsidy is said to come from State rather than Central budgets. This figure may only cover recurrent cost subsidies and not investment subsidies, which are even higher. There is little targeting of subsidies. According to the World Bank, 70% of those benefiting from subsidies for public water supply are not poor, while 40% of the poor are excluded because they do not have access to public water services.

Investment and Financing

Investment in urban water supply and sanitation has increased during the first decade of the 21st century, not least thanks to increased central government grants made available under Jawaharlal Nehru National Urban Renewal Mission alongside with loans from the Housing and Urban Development Corporation.

Investment

The Eleventh Five-Year Plan (2007–2012) foresees investments of Rs. 127,025 crore (US$23 billion) for urban water supply and sanitation, including urban (stormwater) drainage and solid waste management.

Financing

55% of the investments foreseen under the 11th Plan are to be financed by the central government, 28% by state governments, 8% by "institutional financing" such as HUDCO, 8% by external agencies and 1.5% by the private sector. Local governments are not expected to contribute to the investments. The volume of investments is expected to double to reach 0.7% of GDP. Also, it implies a shift in financing from state governments to the central government. During the 9th Plan only 24% of investments were financed by the central government and 76% by state governments. Central government financing was heavily focused on water supply in rural areas.

Institutions

State Financing Corporations (SFC) play an important role in making recommendations regarding the allocation of state tax revenues between states and municipalities, criteria for grants, and measures to improve the financial position of municipalities. According to the Planning Commission, SFCs are in some cases not sufficiently transparent and/or competent, have high transactions costs, and their recommendations are sometimes not being implemented. An important source of financing are loans from Housing and Urban Development Corporation Ltd (HUDCO), a Central government financial undertaking. HUDCO loans to municipal corporations need to be guaranteed by state governments. HUDCO also on-lends loans from foreign aid, including Japanese aid, to states. The Jawaharlal Nehru National Urban Renewal Mission initiated in 2005 also plays an increasingly important role in financing urban water supply and sanitation through central government grants.

The current system of financing water supply and sanitation is fragmented through a number of different national and state programs. This results in simultaneous implementation with different and conflicting rules in neighbouring areas. In rural areas different programs undermine each other, adversely affecting demand driven approaches requiring cost sharing by users.

External Cooperation

In absolute terms India receives almost twice as much development assistance for water, sanitation and water resources management as any other country, according to data from the Organisation for Economic Co-operation and Development. India accounts for 13 per cent of commitments in global water aid for 2006–07, receiving an annual average of about US$830 million (€620 million), more than double the amount provided to China. India's biggest water and sanitation donor is Japan, which provided US$635 million, followed by the World Bank with US$130 million. The annual average for 2004–06, however, was about half as much at US$448 million, of which Japan provided US$293 million and the World Bank US$87 million. The Asian Development Bank and Germany are other important external partners in water supply and sanitation. In 2003 the Indian government decided it would only accept bilateral aid from five countries (the United Kingdom, the United

States, Russia, Germany and Japan). A further 22 bilateral donors were asked to channel aid through nongovernmental organisations, United Nations agencies or multilateral institutions such as the European Union, the Asian Development Bank or the World Bank.

Asian Development Bank

India has increased its loans from the Asian Development Bank (ADB) since 2005 after the introduction of new financing modalities, such as the multitranche financing facility (MFF) which features a framework agreement with the national government under which financing is provided in flexible tranches for subprojects that meet established selection criteria.

In 2008 four MFFs for urban development investment programs were under way in North Karnataka (US$862 million), Jammu and Kashmir (US$1,260 million),Rajasthan (US$450 million), and Uttarakhand (US$1,589 million). Included in these MFFs are major investments for the development of urban water supply and sanitation services.

Germany

Germany supports access to water and sanitation in India through financial cooperation by KfW development bank and technical cooperation by GTZ.

Since the early 1990s both institutions have supported watershed management in rural Maharashtra, using a participatory approach first piloted by the Social Centre in Ahmednagar and that constituted a fundamental break with the previous top-down, technical approach to watershed management that had yielded little results. The involvement of women in decision-making is an essential part of the project. While the benefits are mostly in terms of increased agricultural production, the project also increases availability of water resources for rural water supply. In addition, GTZ actively supports the introduction of ecological sanitationconcepts in India, including community toilets and decentralised wastewater systems for schools as well as small and medium enterprises. Many of these systems produce biogas from wastewater, provide fertiliser and irrigation water.

Japan

As India's largest donor in the sector the Japan International Cooperation Agency (JICA) finances a multitude of projects with a focus on capital-intensive urban water supply and sanitation projects, often involving follow-up projects in the same locations.

Current projects. Projects approved between 2006 and 2009 include the Guwahati Water Supply Project in Assam, the Kerala Water Supply Project (Phased II and III), the Hogenakkal Water Supply and Fluorosis Mitigation

Project (Phases I and II) in Tamil Nadu, the Goa Water Supply and Sewerage Project, the Agra Water Supply Project, the Amritsar Sewerage Project in Punjab, the Orissa Integrated Sanitation Improvement Project, and the Bangalore Water Supply and Sewerage Project.

Evaluation of past projects. An ex-post evaluation of one large program, the Urban Water Supply and Sanitation Improvement Program, showed that "some 60%–70% of the goals were achieved" and that "results were moderate". The program was implemented by the Housing and Urban Development Corporation, Ltd. (HUDCO) from 1996 to 2003 in 26 cities. The evaluation says that "state government plans were not based on sufficient demand research, including the research for residents' willingness to pay for services", so that demand for connections was overestimated. Also fees (water tariffs) were rarely increased despite recommendations to increase them. The evaluation concludes that "HUDCO was not able to make significant contributions to the effectiveness, sustainability, or overall quality of individual projects. One of the reasons that not much attention was given to this problem is probably that there was little risk of default on the loans thanks to state government guarantees."

World Bank

Current projects. The World Bank finances a number of projects in urban and rural areas that are fully or partly dedicated to water supply and sanitation. In urban areas the World Bank supports the Andhra Pradesh Municipal Development Project (approved in 2009, US$300 million loan), the Karnataka Municipal Reform Project (approved in 2006, US$216 million loan), the Third Tamil Nadu Urban Development Project (approved in 2005, US$300 million loan) and the Karnataka Urban Water Sector Improvement Project (approved in 2004, US$39.5 million loan). In rural areas it supports the Andhra Pradesh Rural Water Supply and Sanitation (US$150 million loan, approved in 2009), the Second Karnataka Rural Water Supply and Sanitation Project (approved in 2001,US$151.6 million loan), the Uttaranchal Rural Water Supply and Sanitation Project (approved in 2006, US$120 million loan) and the Punjab Rural Water Supply and Sanitation Project (approved in 2006, US$154 million loan).

Evaluation of past projects. A study by the World Bank's independent evaluation department evaluated the impact of the World Bank-supported interventions in the provision of urban water supply and wastewater services in Mumbai between 1973 and 1990. It concluded that water supply and sewerage planning, construction and operations in Bombay posed daunting challenges to those who planned and implemented the investment program. At the outset, there was a huge backlog of unmet demand because of under investment. Population and economic growth accelerated in the following decades and the proportion of the poor increased as did the slums which they occupied. The intended impacts of the program have not been realised. Shortcomings include that "water is not safe to drink; water service, especially to the poor, is difficult to access and is provided at inconvenient hours of the day; industrial water needs are not fully met; sanitary facilities are too few in number and often unusable; and urban drains, creeks and coastal waters are polluted with sanitary and industrial wastes."

INDUS RIVER SYSTEM AND ITS IMPORTANCE FOR INDIA AND PAKISTAN

Indus river basin drains the highland of four riparian countries, Pakistan, India, Afghanistan and China. The rough terrains surrounding the river in China and Afghanistan has so far minimized these states ability to develop the river within their border but China and Afghanistan are asserting their rights to a reasonable and equitable share of the Indus tributaries flowing through their territory. Afghanistan has started to build a dam on Kabul River for hydropower generation but mainly India and Pakistan are dependent on the Indus river system. Out of about 193 million total populations, 72% of Pakistan and 23% of Indian live in Indus basin system.

For Pakistan, Indus River is the main source for domestic, industrial and agricultural water. Agriculture is vital for Pakistan's welfare and its role is like a backbone in national economy. This sector employed 43% of Pakistan's labour force and contributed about 25% of Pakistan GDP. In spite of the fact, Pakistan agriculture is mostly dependent on irrigation network because of little rainfall, low quality ground water etc. Of the total irrigated area of Indus River, 74 % is located in Pakistan that provides over 60% of the water utilized for irrigation purposes through the world best and largest irrigational network. The irrigational network comprises of 3 reservoirs (Tarbela, Chashma on Indus River and Mangla on Jhelum River), 19 large river barrage and 45 independent irrigational canal commands, some 1.6 million km water courses and 144 large dams. The irrigational network almost spread out more than one third part of country. About 78% of Pakistan's cultivated area is under irrigation and it ranks second in the world after Egypt.

Background

The canals and barrages built under the British rule to serve Indo-Pak continent were under partition in 1947. As a result of partition, these canals network is divided into East Punjab that is in India and West Punjab in Pakistan. For India, the real problem arose when out of 26 million acres of land annually irrigated by Indus and its tributaries, 21 million acres became part of Pakistan. But, the headworks of the entire network remained in India. During the division of Punjab into East and West regions, Punjab partition committee was established to settle down the dispute related to division of assets between East and West Punjab provinces. In 1947 both east and west Punjab were agree that water shall be divided equally.

Pakistan and India disputes over Indus water erupted soon after eight months of independence, when India cut off the water coming across the border into Pakistan in 1948. East Punjab cut off the supplies of every single canal that crossed the border and declared its decision not to restore the flow of these canals, unless west Punjab recognized that it had no rights to the water and resumed the flows only after Pakistan made a payment to India. This situation was extremely stressful for west Punjab farmers dependent upon them.

In May1948, Simla agreement was signed but, Pakistan rejected it in early 1950s arguing that it has been forced upon them. From the early 1950s the situation had reached to a deadlock and there was no communication over water between both countries for a long period of time.

INDUS RIVER BASIN

The Indus river basin is one of the largest basins in Asia covering an area of 1,165,000 km2. The river flows through four countries in south Asia including, China in north- east, India in east, Afghanistan in north-west and Khyber Pakhtunkhwa and majority of plains of the Punjab and Sindh in Pakistan. The Indus river basin comprise of Indus river, its two western tributaries the Kabul and Kurram rivers and five eastern tributaries the Jhelum, Ravi, Beas, Sutlej and Chenab rivers. Indus and Sutlej originate from Lake Manasarovarin in Tibet. Chenab River originates from Himachal Pradesh in India and flows through Kashmir valley and into Pakistan. Ravi also originates from Himachal Pradesh but directly flows into Punjab and then Pakistan. Beas originates and flows entirely in India. Jhelum originates in the Kashmir valley of India and flows to Pakistan. Kabul River rises in Afghanistan and flows through the Peshawar valley to join the Indus at Attock. These five main left bank tributaries have an aggregate length of more than 2,800 miles and Kabul River and Kurram River together cover more than 700 miles.

The basin is the home to three world's mightiest mountain ranges (Karakoram, Himalayan and Hindukush). The basin originates at 17,000 feet above sea level in Tibetan plateau. The river pass through Indian occupied Jammu and Kashmir, enters into north area of Pakistan and finally merge into an Arabian sea. Most of its flows around 69% originate from India, compared to 12% for Tibet and Afghanistan and 19% for Pakistan.. The drainage area which extends into india is 45,000 square miles and contribute to an average annual inflow (including all rivers) of 175 million acre feet.. The snow melting in the Himalayan- Hindukush regions and precipitations in mountains are the major components of the annual flow of these rivers. Climate is not uniform over Indus basin region. It varies from arid to semi arid to temperate sub-humid in the plains of Sindh and Punjab provinces. Annual precipitations ranges maximum 2000 mm on mountain slopes and between 100 to 500 mm in the lowlands. Abundant flow is during the monsoon season (July-September), which contributes 51% of annual flow.

INDUS WATER TREATY (IWT)

The president of International Bank of Reconstruction and Development, Mr. Eugene Black offered his good office to settle the water dispute. After close to eight years of negotiation the IWT came into existence. The IWT was concluded by India and Pakistan with the World Bank's mediation on 19th of September 1960. IWT based on the allocation of Indus and its tributaries. According to IWT the three Eastern Rivers (Ravi, Beas and Sutlej) allocated to India and three Western Rivers (Indus, Jhelum and Chenab) allocated to Pakistan. India has unrestricted use of the Eastern Rivers and Pakistan has a right for the exclusive use of Western Rivers. India can use the water of Western Rivers for hydropower generations, to meet the domestic, Industrial and irrigation requirements of Jammu-Kashmir and also develop these tributaries for flood protection, floating of timbers and fishing. It clearly mentioned in IWT that, Pakistan has to construct infrastructure to meet the Eastern Rivers needs from the Western Rivers and India has to pay fixed amount of money to Pakistan to build infrastructures. Both parties have to regularly exchange flow data.

A permanent Indus commission (PIC) established to supervise implementation of the IWT. Implementation of IWT with the involvement of PIC is one of the successful agreements for resolving trans-boundary water issues. PIC worked very well for maintaining the soul of treaty. The commissioners are obliged to meet once a year, altering their meetings places between the two countries. During their meetings, they plan and organize their tours, exchange data and information regarding the current and future developments. If either of the countries have questions, regarding the projects and maintenance work, the problems can be referred to PIC. If PIC is unable to resolve the issues, then the question becomes a difference and could be referred to a Neutral expert, either appointed by two members of commission or by a third party. If the neutral expert failed to solve the difference then it should be treated as disputes and then International Court of Arbitration (ICA) could be establish to resolve the disputes..

WATER CRISIS IN THE INDUS BASIN

Pakistan is one of the world's most arid countries with an average rainfall of less than 240 mm. Indus water is the only source of water for domestic agriculture and industrial needs. Agriculture importance is like the backbone in Pakistan's economy. Indus flow plays a major contribution in maintaining and developing Pakistan's economy as it provides over 60% of the water utilized for irrigation purposes. Continuation in population growth with high demand of food, water and energy increasing strains on limited water resources. Now a day Pakistan faces a very severe water crisis. One third of the country population is living under water stress condition. An estimated report of November 2008 shows that out of 165 million population of Pakistan, 25% are below poverty level, 98 million rely on agriculture, 50 million do not have access to safe drinking water and 74 million have no sanitation. The gap between demand and supply is widening. In 2004, water shortfall was 11 MAF which is expected to ascend to 31 MAF in 2013. Water availability has been declining at an alarming rate from 5000 cubic meter per capita in 1951 to about 1100 cubic meter currently and it has been projected to less than 700 cubic meter by 2025. Pakistan's total water demand in 2025 is projected to 338 bcm suggesting a gap of 100 bcm.

Compared to Pakistan, India is a semi arid country. Over 70% of Indian's live in rural areas and agriculture is the primary source of their livelihood. About 200 million people are directly employed by agriculture (Government of India Ministry of Agriculture 2005). Population is growing rapidly after China, India is the second largest country having population of 1,241 million (2011 world population datasheet).

Rising population with high demand of water put more pressure on limited resources. India's per capita water availability has declined from 5000 cubic meters in 1950 to 1800 cubic meters in 2005 and it has been assumed that per capita water availability will fall below 1000 cubic meters by 2050. Growing demand of food and energy pushed India to concentrate for water conservation and power generation projects.

Many analysts argue that GDP growth of 7% per year requires a 10 % increase in annual supply. India booming economy needs energy to grow particularly in Jammu and Kashmir that has many potential hydroelectric sites despite the fact that, Jammu and Kashmir faces energy crisis. Despite the potential of 30,000MW of power, 25% of our population has no access to electricity and 75% is getting episodic electricity.

High demands of water to meet the challenges of rapid increase in population, increased urbanization and industrialization creating a competing environment for a limiting water resource. Limited water availability with high demand also creates some sort of intrastate tensions in Pakistan and India. Both countries desperately need water for booming their economy and trying hard to get access as much as they can. Although, the Indus water treaty has been successful in managing the war between Pakistan and India two and half times and worked very well for more than 50 years. But, there are series of disagreement going on between both these riparian countries.

Baglihar Hydroelectric Dam

Baglihar Dam was one of the most controversial issues. India planned to build Baglihar dam on the Chenab River 60 miles up streams from the Pakistani border. Under the IWT India has a right to build upstream non storage facilities but it must not alter or influence the flow of the river. Pakistan had a number of objections over the construction of this dam. Pakistan claimed that dam design did not following the criteria (a), (c), (e) and (f) of paragraph 8 to the treaty.

- Criteria (a) states that the work shall not be capable of raising the water level artificially above the full pondage level specified in design. Pakistan claimed that dam design is excessive and provided ability to India for raising artificial water level above the full pondage level.
- Criteria (c) requires that the maximum pondage in the operating pool not to exceed twice the pondage required for firm power and Pakistan claimed that the pondage in operating tool mentioned by India is excessive. So it should be reduced.
- Criteria (e) state that if the conditions for gated spillway is necessary, the bottom level of gates in normal closed position shall be located at the highest level consistent with sound and economical design. Bone of contention on this point, Pakistan claimed that design was not based on reality and correct estimates of flood discharge. Pakistan claimed that spillway was not necessary. Either un-gated or surface gated spillway could be provided with the bottom of the gates with the highest level.
- Criteria (f) require that intake for the turbine shall be located at the highest level coherent with sufficient and economical construction and operation of the plant as run off river plant. Pakistan had an objection that the location of intake power is not at the highest level as mandated in IWT.

Although, both countries tried hard to settle the issue by themselves but bilateral negotiation did not bear any productive result. So, first time in the history of IWT, on January 15, 2005, Pakistan asked for World Bank to appoint a neutral expert to resolve the differences over Baghliar dam. After five months of the original request, Raymond Lafitte, professor of Swiss Institute of Technology in Lausanne was appointed as a neutral expert to address the differences regarding Baglihar project.

In February, 2007, Lafitte delivered his final decision to both parties and also one copy of decision to World Bank. In his report he partly addressed some objections of Pakistan like, reduced the pondage capacity, increased 3m height of power intake and acknowledged India's right to construct gated spillway. Both countries agreed to follow the final descision of the neutral expert.

But, the dispute again activated when, India filled the dam during the dry season in 2008, that seriously disturbed the livelihood and agriculture production of Pakistan. Pakistani media and local people blamed that India stole water having rights of Pakistan. The filing of Baglihar dam above Marala reduced the flow as low as 20000 cusec, whereas India obliged to maintain the minimum inflow at the level of 55,000 cusec.

Pakistan lost about 2 MAF of water from August, 25, 2008 to September, 4, 2008 and it adversely affected Pakistan's wheat crop. President of Pakistan even raised the issue in his speech to the UN General Assembly.

Pakistan strongly protested and claimed that India is violating the IWT. But this time, Pakistan decided to solve the issue by negotiation. Indian commission admitted that reduction was because of unavailability of any mechanism to pass the flow at the low level. He explained that this happened because we were expecting heavy rainfall during these days. Pakistan's Indus commissioner in an interview told that although "Pakistan felt that parameter and procedure mentioned in IWT were not followed during the initial filling of the dam. We have resolved the differences on the initial filling of the dam in a spirit of cooperation and good will and India gave us the insurance that it will be careful in future".

Wullar Barrage/ Tulbul Navigation Project

Wullar barrage or tulbul navigation project being constructed by India on Jhelum River just below Wullar lake located 25 kilometers north of Srinagar at 5180 feet above sea level. The project has been started by government of Indian state of Jammu and Kashmir. The dispute emerged in 1985 when Pakistan learnt through the notification of tender notice in newspaper. Pakistan calls it a Wullar barrage constructed by India for storage purposes and India refer it as a Tulbul Navigation project for transportation of fruits and timbers.

Pakistan strongly opposed the construction of this project. Pakistan claimed that construction of such a project on that site had a potential to unfavorably affect the triple canal project in Pakistan namely, Upper Chenab Canal, Upper Jhelum Canal and lower Bari Doab Canal. Pakistan believed that construction of this barrage would provide India with the means to control over River Jhelum that could facilitate India to stop water flow during winter. The Mangla Dam on Jhelum River, which is a main source of irrigation and electricity for Punjab, would be adversely affected. Moreover, Pakistan has an apprehension that India could close the gate of barrage during war so, enhancing the ability of Indian troops to come in Pakistan. Pakistan remembered in the connection of 1965 war, when Indian army had failed to cross the Bambanwali Ravi Bedian Link Canal because of its full flow.

Indian government argues that, the purpose of Tulbul project is only to improve the navigations in Jhelum River during lean month in order to connect Srinagar with Baramula. Indian claimed that 90 percent of this project would be beneficial to Pakistan, as it would increase the power generation capacity of Mangla. The project would regulate the supply of Mangla dam as well as increase the efficiency of irrigation network in Pakistan Punjab. India argues that the Tulbul Project would be effective in reducing the flow of water during the flood seasons and suggest that Pakistan should bear the share of construction. Pakistan assert that the Wullar barrage capacity is more than 300,000 acre feet and according to IWT, the India is only allowed to construct storage work on western tributaries, if it does not exceed 100000 acre feet and the design has been approved by Pakistan. Pakistan referred this issue to the Indus commission in 1986, but commission failed to resolve it. Pakistan then decided to take the case to a International court of arbitration (ICA), but India postponed the construction. About ten rounds of talk have already been done but only with little progress. Pakistan gave an option to stop the construction of Kishanganga project on Neelum River, which would affect the Neelum-Jhelum Project constructed by Pakistan.

Kishanganga Hydroelectric Project (KHEP)

Now the current controversy is related to Kishanganga hydroelectric project (KHEP) that entangled two countries in conflict. This is the 330 MW Hydropower project in India about 160 km upstreasm of Muzaffarabad. The KHEP involves the 100 km diversion of Kishanganga River (called the Neelum Riverin Pakistan) to a tributary named Bunar Madumati Nullah of Jhelum near Bunkot, through a 22 km tunnel. The water will rejoin the Jhelum through Wullar Lake near the town of Bandipur in Baramula district. Neelum is the greatest tributary of Jhelum River and runs about 150 km in Pakistan controlled Kashmir before it joins the Jhelum River near Muzafarabad. Because of this diversion, instead of Muzafarabad it will rejoin Jhelum in Indian controlled Kashmir. This diversion will change the direction of river about 204 km before it joins the Jhelum River near Muzafarabad, the site where Pakistan Neelum-Jhelum hydel Project is situated.

PAKISTAN'S APPREHENSIONS

Pakistan first received a report about the Indian's plan of this project in 1988, while India officially confirmed it in 1994. Pakistan claims that India is violating the IWT by diverting the water and water drawn from a given tributary must be return to the same river. According to IWT, upstream must release as much water as downstream have the capacity to store it and the diversion will also affect the ecosystems, it submerged the Pakistan controlled Kashmir and entire Neelum valley. It will affect 133, 000 hectors of irrigation in the Neelum valley. Pakistan also claims that 11 percent of water flow in summer and 27 percent flow in winter would reduce due to Kishanganga project. The Hydropower generation capacity of 969 MW Neelum-Jhelum Project which Pakistan is constructing on Jhelum River would reduce by 11 percent. The Kishanganga dam could reduce Pakistan's total water availability from an estimated 154 MAF per year and may affect a significant portion of the Mangla dam storage capacity besides declining the pressure required to generate electricity in Neelum-Jhelum Power Project. Pakistan also claims that the feasibility study of Neelum-Jhelum project has acquired right in favor of Pakistan..

INDIA'S APPREHENSIONS

India argues that the diversion will not affect the flow of water because the quantum of water will be the same as it before. The diversion of river is not matter instead of meeting in Pakistan controlled Kashmir it would meet in Indian controlled Kashmir. India also rejected Pakistan's objection of favoring feasibility study by quoted the Indus water treaty according to that the project authorized first would give top priority.

In May 2004, India promised to freeze all its work on the site and hold a meeting with Pakistan to remove its objections. Pakistan raised six objections of which one related to the power generation scheme, two to the diversion of water and three related to the design of dam. The issue was discussed in five meetings from November 2004 to November 2005 but it did not bear any prolific results. In 2006, India submitted the revised plan of the project, brought down the storage capacity by reducing the height of dam from 75.48m to 35.48 m. Pakistan rejected the revised plan having objection over the diversion of the water. Because, it will adversely affect the Neelum-Jhelum Project capacity, that Pakistan has a plan to complete in 2015 one year before the completion of KHEP.

According to the press report Pakistan Indus water commission Sayed Jamat Ali Shah said that New Dahli is not cooperating with us. Indian Government is not providing any project information before according to

Indus water treaty the states have to share information on any new project before six month of starting.

"India never stole or blocked Pakistan's share of waters and has assured Pakistan that New Delhi would implement Indus Water Treaty in letter and spirit". Indus Water Commissioner of India G. Auranganathan.

Chairman Indus Water Treaty Council Hafiz Zahoor-ul-Hassan Dahr has stated that like the 131 round talk between Pakistan and India under Indus water treaty not bore any fruit and the latest series of dialogue would meet the same result. India is still willing and in favor of bilateral talk but Pakistan decided to take this issue to World Bank. So, Pakistan sent a legal notice to India on 20 May 2010 on Kishanganag hydropower project.

Because of the technical and legal objections, first time in the history of IWT, Pakistan took this issue to ICA. Pakistan nominated Jan Paulsson, head of Norwegian international law firm, and Bruno Simma, of the International Court of Justice, as its arbitrators in the Court of Arbitration. India nominated Peter Tomka, Vice-President of the International Court of Justice at Geneva and Lucius Caflisch, a Swiss international law expert who is a professor at the Graduate Institute of International Studies to represent it in the dispute. Although the two countries have rejected each other's nominees for the Court of Arbitration, they decided to set up a panel comprising a chairman, a legal member and an engineer to select the umpires, by drawing lots. In response to the Pakistan appeal, ICA on 25th September, 2011 has barred India from going ahead to work on controversial KHEP on Neelum River.

Limitations in IWT

Agreements on water have the prime importance in water allocation. It brings the national and international community to the same table for the joint management of their common resource. Signing agreements over water sharing might be easy but the real problem is to keep alive the agreements in letter and spirit. Agreements over share water resource not only motivate the riparian states to work together but also can be a source to promote peace and cooperation among states on other mutual issues. But the validity of agreements depends on the mutual interest of all the stakeholders, strength of their relationship, level of interdependency and cooperation. States with a good political relationship and mutual interest tend to co-operate more affectively then adversarial states. Agreements with good characteristics need to be workable for a long period of time. Only then they can positively contribute in peace and cooperation within a basin by addressing the future water needs of the riparian countries.

The 1960, Indus water agreement (IWT) signed for water allocation of Indus River between Pakistan and India. IWT worked very well for more than forty five years. During this time period both states have a difference on many issues but they settle the dispute by themselves. PIC tried hard to work in letter and spirit for the implementation of IWT. But one of the main drawbacks is the amputation surgery of the Indus basin into two. According to IWRM the whole basin should be treated as a single unit so that states can cooperate in more effective way for the sustainable management of river and land resources. But, this division reduced the level of cooperation among states. Although both state are highly interdependent on each other for the construction of infrastructure and pollution control etc. But in this agreement the level of joint basin management seems to be missing.

Another drawback is missing the perception of all stakeholders, their needs and future demands. Jammu and Kashmir is a disputed territory of which major part is under the control of India. At the time of treaty the population of Jammu and Kashmir was 3.5 million which now has increase three times. Increase population demanding more water and energy for boosting their economy. While, according to IWT Jammu and Kashmir can use only 10% of hydroelectric potential and 40% of cultivable land. Due to this restrictive use, people in Jammu and Kashmir facing high energy crisis.IWT signed in 1960, with the simple division of Indus basin without considering the future need. According to IWT, annually 135 MAF water were allocated to Pakistan. Compare to that time Pakistan population now has grown three times. Population growth result in declining per capita water availability. Now, Pakistan is under water scarce situation and the situation become worst in future if the current circumstances go as such.

Lack of Trust and Cooperation

Effective transboundary cooperation over shared water resources is closely related to the establishment of institutional organizations. Sufficient institutional capacities within an enabling environment are necessary for promoting good cooperation in order to manage the international river basins. Cooperation over shared water resource maintains regional stability by promoting peace and improving economic efficiency. Cooperation will enable better management of ecosystem, providing benefits to the river and underpinning all other benefits that can be derived. Cooperation over shared water resource can ease tension and provide gains in the form of savings that can be achieved.

Sustainable international rivers development depends on the cooperative management strategies. The IWRM concept of building cooperation at political, institutional and technical level within an enabling environment is the complimentary element for sustainable river basin management. Transboundary cooperation depends on the political, geographic and cultural circumstances. The countries having a bad history of political relations are less cooperative than others. Even in the presence of bilateral agreements, such countries are more reserve to cooperate unconditionally because of trust deficits. The establishment of an internationally acceptable legal principle to share the common rivers may itself not bring a solution. Complex water disputes can only be solved by co-operations and compromises.

IWT 1960 agreement is a successful bilateral agreement that obliged both states to cooperate on water management issues under the supervision of PIC. The commission is trying hard to monitor and implement of the IWT. As both states are striving to utilize limited resources with full potential by constructing hydropower projects and storage reservoirs. Pakistan claimed that India is not providing fair information on time as obliged in IWT to share information on any project before six month to start. Pakistan as a lower riparian has a fear of flood and drought by the construction of Indian's projects on western rivers and have a perception that India would be able to harm Pakistan during war time. These unilateral actions performed by upstream bear a fear of water scarcity to lower riparian.

Although, India is denying Pakistan's objections but this distrust environment is a result of lack of joint river basin management institutions, poor political relations and lack of cooperation. Due to poor historical political relations and lack of information exchange, a trust deficit environment has been developed between both states, that's became a major obstacle to achieve potential cooperation. This lack of trust and cooperation has led to several negative social, environmental and economic impacts, creating regional instabilities by affecting the livelihood of local people in Pakistan.

High politics

International rivers are more prone to conflict because of the involvement of more than one state interest. Poor state relations and lack of trust makes the water issue more politicize. States focused on other issues like nation security instead of considering the overall cooperative management of shared water resources. The involvement of political bodies in policy making and implementation put the water in less priority.

Indus river system also has the same effect. Because of the hostile relationship between Pakistan and India the element of effective joint cooperation seems to be missing. Kashmir issue and Pressure of fundamentalist group of people from both sides is the major obstacles in resolving water related issues jointly. Moreover, as Indus seems to be a more political case; lack of accountability and transparency is highly observable in Indus water issue. Water governing authorities from India fear to give relevant information before time. All these Situations are the hindrance in joint management of Indus River Basin.

Revision of treaty

Many analysts from Pakistan claim that IWT is not in favor of Pakistan and experts from Kashmir have opinion that IWT is limiting their right to use water. The 1960 agreement of IWT does not fulfill the requirement of IWRM. IWRM is holistic and participatory approach; focus on the integration of all the sectors in decision making and implementation by considering the perspective of all stakeholders for sustainable management. This element of all stakeholder participation seems to be missing in 1960 agreement. The other major limitation of IWT is missing the considerations of future water demands. Treaty was signed when water was abundance and now due to high population growth and climate change both countries are facing water scarcity. Some experts also argue that IWT is not supporting the concept of IWRM because of the partition of Indus into two parts. According to IWRM, the whole basin should be taken as a single unit and it is essential to consider its social, economic and environmental interest for sustainable management. The partition of Indus basin into two has divided the interest of the users and also affected the environment and ecosystem of Indus basin.

IWT worked very well for more than forty five years, till now both countries are striving to implement the treaty with soul and spirit. The current circumstances reveal that IWT does not seem to work efficiently in future. Both countries have high water need for boosting their economy and to meet the future demands. To prevent the future disasters of acute water shortage, there is a dire need to revise the treaty according to the present and future demand of all the states while keeping in mind the environmental sustainability and equity.

Although, IWT obliged both countries to be interdependent before taking any action on Indus river but the level of cooperation is very low. The unilateral actions of India like construction of dams for hydropower generation and navigation projects extremely affecting the livelihood of Pakistan. As Indus is the life blood for Pakistan, is facing a high water scarcity situation and the conditions will become worst in near future. Now, there is a need for both countries to come forward and reconsider the IWT in a comprehensive way by involving the participation of all major stakeholders and considering their interests, needs and future demands.

Sustainable river basin management needs an effective role of river basin organizations. Organizations for managing share water resources could work efficiently, if they are independent to make decisions and willing to cooperate fairly. Under the revised treaty, a joint river basin organization should be established for sustainable and efficient utilization of Indus water resource. The organization should be independent and free to make decisions without any political pressure. There should not be any political interference in decision making and management of river resources. Working efficiency of joint river basin organization become strong by the participation and joint work of technical staff from riparian countries in analyzing the situation and decision making process.

As, in case of Columbia River, the 1964, Colombia river treaty between USA and Canada has provided significant benefits through the coordinated river basin management to both countries. To analyze the future flood and power situation both countries are cooperating on joint river basin management. There is no interference from political sides, only technical staffs are responsible to analyze the future needs and management requirements. After analyzing the whole situation the member of technical staff is free to take decision that is beneficial for both countries (U.S Army Corps of Engineers, 2009). There is a need to organize such type of joint Indus river basin organization for the sustainable management of limited Indus water resource. Establishment of joint river basin organization could be a catalyst to build trust among these two hostile riparian and will also enhance the benefit sharing. Sharing the benefits of cooperative water management is an integral part of the successful treaty design and implementation. In revised treaty, whole basin should be considered as a single unit and all states should oblige to cooperate fairly.

Cooperation at political, institutional and technical level is vital to manage share water resources effectively. Effective cooperation between states on shared resource not only improves the better management, it also enhances the regional stability by reducing the tensions at international levels. Establishment of joint river basin organization will be helpful in promoting cooperation by improving the level of transparency and accountability.

3

Distribution of Water Wars in China

China is often thought of as a country that suppresses internal conflicts, usually to great effect. But there are a number of notable exceptions and, of these, conflicts over water are perhaps the most intriguing. While China is by some definitions water-scarce, its domestic and international water conflicts are driven not by scarcity per se but by the impact of China's rampant economic growth.

Total water availability in China stands at about 2000 cubic meters per person per year — around one-third of the global average. According to one estimate, China faces a shortfall of some 200 billion cubic meters of water annually, due mostly to increasing industrial and urban water demand. But these figures mask considerable regional differences. Most of the provinces where water demand exceeds its supply sit astride the rapidly growing eastern seaboard.

Even more serious is the issue of water pollution, which affects some 85 per cent of major urban waterways and about 80 per cent of tested groundwater in China. Large-scale urbanisation is also seriously damaging China's aquatic ecosystems like lakes and wetlands, and is dramatically increasing flood risk.

These changes are setting the stage for a growing number of water conflicts between China's sub-national jurisdictions, and may portend more difficult relations with its neighbours as well. China's domestic water conflicts typically take the form of disputes between sub-national units like provinces and prefectures. These conflicts arise over a number of issues like dam and hydropower development, but they most commonly pertain to some form of inter-jurisdictional water pollution.

Domestic water conflicts can provoke civil unrest. In a landmark incident in 2001, residents of the city of Jiaxing in Zhejiang province who were fed up with pollution flowing downstream from neighbouring Jiangsu province sunk a number of old boats in the two provinces' shared waterway to form a makeshift dam, which backed up the polluted water across the border.

China's internal water wars have the potential to pose significant problems for China's political system, which is set up to ensure local officials pursue centrally formulated priorities rather than their own. There are relatively few mechanisms to encourage cooperation between neighbouring jurisdictions on issues of shared concern.

Beijing has recently undertaken a number of wide-ranging reforms intended to address the problem of inter-jurisdictional water disputes. A number of regulations have been issued over the past decade to clarify how such disputes are handled, and several provinces have set up 'dialogue mechanisms' to try to prevent and resolve such disputes.

But the overwhelming preference of China's leaders is for a more hierarchical solution, such as the recently established 'river and lake chief' system (hezhang). Under this system, China's local officials are vested with specific responsibilities for ensuring adherence to water quality and other water-related policy measures within their jurisdictions.

The problem with this approach is that issues like pollution and flooding require broad cooperation between officials and residents of neighbouring regions that cannot easily be encouraged by fiat. Decades of research and examples from across the globe show that durable, effective cooperation over shared resources like water requires inclusive institutions that bring interested parties together — the exact opposite of the vertical hierarchy that currently shapes the governance of water and almost everything else in China.

The importance of building good institutions is even greater at the international level, where outside actors can play an important role in fostering cooperation between countries that otherwise might not see eye-to-eye over contentious issues like water. Mistrust over shared rivers remains high between China and its neighbours, especially India and Vietnam, which for different reasons fear the downstream impacts of dam-building and water diversions being planned or undertaken by China.

Outside observers have noted these projects with alarm for some time, especially with respect to China's transboundary rivers. Indian strategist Brahma Chellaney attracted widespread attention for his contention in 2014 that these rivers are destined to become 'Asia's new battleground'.

It is true that China has often been dismissive of its neighbours' concerns that construction of large dams may negatively impact downstream fisheries, flood risk and other matters. But in some cases China has been a constructive neighbour, for instance in helping to establish the Lancang-Mekong Cooperation Mechanism as an alternative to the ineffectual Mekong River Commission.

If China's reputation as a 'hydro-hegemon' that seeks to control Asia's water resources by exploiting its dominion over the headwaters of many of the continent's major rivers is indeed a misrepresentation of its intentions, China's internal divisions over water are at least partly to blame for this perception.

China's peculiar blend of political centralisation and fiscal decentralisation gives sub-national officials an incentive to pursue grand infrastructure projects, regardless of their implications for China's neighbours. The dam-building projects in particular — which are the source of many international transboundary water conflicts between China and its neighbours — appear to largely reflect the economic self-interest of individual jurisdictions rather than grand geopolitical objectives.

According to one analysis, jurisdictions that build dams experience a 16 per cent increase in revenue. Fieldwork evidence has also concluded that local officials are often motivated to support dam construction projects because of their contribution to local economic growth.

While there's no question that China isn't always the ideal riparian neighbour, parochial rather than hegemonic interests appear to better explain China's behaviour on Asia's transboundary waterways.

CHINA'S WATER WOES AND THE PUSH TO THE SOUTHWEST

Water has always been a problem in China, and effective control of it has been associated with both personal heroism and legitimate sovereignty for as far back as our records go – or perhaps even further, since the mythological sage ruler Yu proved his right to rule by controlling floods. But water scarcity has probably been an even greater problem than excesses, especially in the modern period. Surface and near-surface water per capita in China today is roughly ¼ of the global average, and worse yet, it is distributed very unevenly. The North and Northwest, with about 380 million people (almost 30% of the national population) and over half the country's arable land, have about 7% of its surface water, so that its per capita resources are roughly 20-25% of the average for China as a whole, or 5-6% of the global average; a more narrowly defined North China plain may have only 10-15% of the per capita supply for the country as a whole, or less than 4% of the global average. Northern waters also carry far heavier sediment loads than southern ones – most readings on Southern rivers fall within EU maxima for drinking water, while some readings on the middle and lower Yellow River, and the Wei and Yongding Rivers are 25 -50% of that level; water shortages are such that Northern rivers also carry far more industrial pollutants per cubic meter, even though the South has far more industry. Northern China also has unusually violent seasonal fluctuations in water supply; both rainfall and river levels change much more over the course of the year than in either Europe or the Americas. North China's year to year rainfall fluctuations are also well above average (though not as severe as those in North and Northwest India). While the most famous of China's roughly 90,000 large (over 15 meters high) and medium-sized dams are associated with hydro-power — about which more below — a great many exist mostly to store water during the peak flow of rivers for use at other times.

The People's Republic has made enormous efforts to address these problems – and achieved impressive short-term successes that are now extremely vulnerable. Irrigated acreage has more than tripled since 1950 (mostly during the Maoist period), with the vast majority of those gains coming in the North and Northwest. It was this, more than anything else, that turned the notorious "land of famine" of the 1850-1950 period into a crucial grain surplus area, and contributed mightily to improving per capita food supplies for a national population that has more than doubled since 1949. Plentiful water supplies made it possible for much of northern China to grow two crops a year for the first time in history (often by adding winter wheat, which needs a lot of water); and plentiful, reliable supplies of water were necessary to allow the use of new seed varieties and plenty of chemical fertilizer (which can otherwise burn the soil). And, of course, irrigation greatly reduced the problem of rain coming at the wrong time of year, or not coming at all some years. During the previous two centuries farming in northern China had become steadily more precarious in part because population growth had lowered the water table – early 20th century maps show much smaller lakes than 150 years earlier, and there are many reports of wells needing to be re-drilled at great expense – and in part because the safety net the Qing had once provided fell apart. But beginning in the 1950s, and especially in the 1960s (after the setbacks of the Great Leap Forward) things turned around very impressively.

Much of that turnaround, however, relied on very widespread use of deep wells, using gasoline or electrical power to bring up underground water from unprecedented depths. Large-scale exploitation of North China groundwater began in the 1960s, peaked in the 1970s at roughly 10 times the annual extraction rates that prevailed during 1949 -1961, and has remained level since about 1980 at roughly 4 times the 1949-1961 level. But this amount of water withdrawal is unsustainable. The North China water table has been dropping by roughly 4-6 feet per year for quite some time now, and by over 10 feet per year in many places; some people estimate that if this rate of extraction is maintained, the aquifers beneath the plain will be completely gone in 30-40 years. This is by no means a unique situation; in the United States, for instance, the Ogallala Aquifer — which lies beneath portions of western South Dakota, Nebraska, Kansas, Oklahoma, and Texas, and eastern Wyoming, Colorado, and New Mexico — is being depleted at roughly the same rate. (Serious excess withdrawals began there in the 1950s, and as in China, turned areas previously marginal for farming — the land of the 1930s Dust Bowl – into a breadbasket.) But consider the following: while the 175,000 square miles served by the Ogallala Aquifer are home to less than 2 million people, the 125,000 square miles of the North China plain were home to 214,000,000 people in 2000 (80% of them rural). The 2008 North China drought – the worst since the late 1950s drought that exacerbated the Great Leap famines – focused global attention on the problem for a brief moment, but chronic water shortages – both in cities and in the countryside – have been a fact of life for years, and conflicts over scarce and/or polluted water have become common events. So what is to be done?

One hears periodically about various ways water is used inefficiently by urbanites; the Chinese steel industry, for instance, uses about twice as much water per ton produced as steel-makers in the most technologically advanced countries (though the Indian steel industry, for instance, is considerably worse than China's on this score). Leaky pipes and other fairly straightforward infrastructure problems create considerable waste. But relatively speaking, industrial and urban residential losses are small potatoes; agriculture still uses at least 65% of all water in China (though less, even in absolute terms, than 20 years ago) and has by far the lowest efficiency rates. Moreover, urbanites are sufficiently prosperous that price increases – unless they are very large – are unlikely to cause them to cut back on use very much. Certainly this is not where the most water waste is in commercial terms. According to some estimates, a marginal gallon of water sent from the countryside to Tianjin produces as much as 60 times as much income in its new urban locale as it did in the countryside. The best hope in terms of moderating China's overall water demand pressure is probably to keep per capita urban use from growing very much while water use efficiency and living standards there continue improving, and urban population grows sharply. Any significant *reductions* will have to come from the countryside. That process has begun, but it is unclear how far it can go without devastating social consequences.

A great deal of water is wasted in agriculture, in part because costs to farmers are kept artificially low; and since many rural communities have no way to transfer water to those who would pay more for it, anyway, "waste" has very little short-run opportunity cost for them. But it is worth noting here that "waste" has different meanings depending on what time frame one adopts. Irrigation water that never reaches the plants' roots and seeps back into the soil is wasted in the short term – it can't be used for anything else that year. But in the long term, it can help recharge the local aquifer. On the other hand, polluted water that could be re-used if treated properly but instead flows out to sea untreated is wasted in both senses, and thus represents a bigger problem. Chinese agriculture is not necessarily more wasteful in this regard than agriculture in many other places – and the deviations from market prices are no worse than in much of the supposedly market-driven United States – but its limited supplies make waste a much more pressing problem.

Various technologies that would reduce water waste exist, but many are sufficiently costly that farmers are unlikely to adopt them unless they are donated. Center-pivot irrigation systems, for instance, can save a lot of water, but at roughly $35,000 each – almost 60 years' worth of an average North China farmer's income — they make sense only for China's largest farms; they are also poorly suited to the geometry of existing fields, and to the particular requirements of rice and some other crops. Drip-irrigation (sometimes called micro-irrigation) is another technological fix, which has been greeted enthusiastically by many analysts despite being relatively expensive. The idea is that water is moved through small plastic tubes directly to the roots of the plants so that much less of it is wasted; it has been a huge success in Israel (where it was first developed) and in various other water-scarce environments. More recently, however, doubts have been raised about its benefits, in large part because of precisely the ambiguity in defining "waste" mentioned above. Since drip irrigation makes sure that a higher percentage of the water used gets to the roots of the plants, it will enable a fixed, visible water source – for instance, an above-ground tank that catches winter rains for use in the spring – to irrigate more crops than if the water was distributed through traditional ditches or less-precisely targeted (and timed) sprinklers. Alternatively, one could irrigate the same amount of crops, and have some water to sell to other users. But if the water source is an underground aquifer, which can be depleted (in contrast to a system of stored rainfall, where you can't over-withdraw in the same way, because next year's rain isn't yet available), the benefits become less clear. In that situation, much of the water that seeps away through the bottom of ditches and so forth helps recharge the aquifer, so that it isn't necessarily "wasted" from a long-run perspective. On the other hand, precisely because drip irrigation means that almost every gallon of water a farmer buys helps that farmer's crops in the current year, that water is a better buy for the farmer than water run through a less "efficient" system; the farmer is thus tempted to buy more of it. Thus, drip irrigation may be good for maximizing *current*food output while actually exacerbating longer-run water shortages in situations like those in northern China (or, as we shall see, much of northern India and Pakistan) where over-use of ground-water is a big problem. This possibility is not merely a theoretical one; a recent study of drip irrigation in the Upper Rio Grande Valley (on both sides of the US-Mexican border) came to the conclusion that water use increased in precisely this way. In short, selectively implemented high-tech solutions may help in some ways, but they cannot provide a total answer — even if, miraculously, all the funding for them could be found.

Ironically, low-tech solutions may actually have greater potential. It is almost impossible to get a clear sense of how much could be saved by technologically simple measures that can be implemented on either a large or a small scale – re-lining and/or covering irrigation ditches, fixing leaky pipes, and so on. The amounts are probably very big, given the low quality of much of the water infrastructure in China (and elsewhere). But these measures also cost money, and many farmers, or even whole rural communities, are unlikely to invest in them without subsidies and/or greater incentives. More effective pollution control – some, though not all, of which is perfectly possible with fairly simple and relatively inexpensive technologies — could also help enormously, but here, too, there are serious incentive problems. Local officials generally have more to gain by protecting local factories and jobs than by conserving water (especially, of course, the water of people downstream).

More commercially realistic pricing of irrigation water would help provide such incentives – but here there are serious social and political constraints. More expensive water would almost certainly mean decreased agricultural output – and though China certainly has enough foreign exchange to buy more food abroad, the government is quite reluctant to become much more dependent on imports. More expensive water might be particularly bad for the many farmers who have been switching from grain production to fruits and vegetables – crops that it otherwise makes sense for China to produce more of, since they demand much more labor per acre than grain, and can produce relatively high incomes for people with small plots. And even if China – and the world – were content to see Chinese demand for imported food rise significantly, there is the question of what would become of the farmers themselves in such a scenario. With farmers' incomes already lagging far behind those of other Chinese, any significant rise in water prices would probably drive millions of marginal farmers to the wall, and greatly accelerate the already rapid rush of people to the cities. Consequently, further water savings in agriculture, though vital, potentially huge, and far less environmentally risky than large water-moving projects, are likely to come slowly and painfully.

Under the circumstances, many officials see no alternative to technologically ambitious mega-projects: above all, the South-North water diversion scheme. The idea behind this $65 billion plan – which had been tossed around for decades, and was officially green-lighted in 2001 – is simple: to take water from the Yangzi and its tributaries and move it to North China, where water is much more scarce. But implementing the scheme is extraordinarily difficult, and the consequences of any one of several possible failures could be enormous.

If completed, the Diversion will be the largest construction project in history. It would carry almost 45 billion cubic meters of water per year – roughly the average annual flow of the Yellow River. It has three parts:

1) an Eastern route, which would take water from the Lower Yangzi in Jiangsu province up to Tianjin (roughly following the route of the Ming-Qing Grand Canal) and, via a branch line, to the Shandong peninsula. This is the technologically simplest part of the project – though it still raises plenty of questions. Parts of it began operation in 2008; it is scheduled to be complete in 2010.
2) a Central route, running from near the Three Gorges Dam in Sichuan to Beijing. Work on this route was recently suspended – in response to environmental problems that have proved to be more complicated than was originally foreseen, and to problems with the relocation of people in the path of the project. (There were large protests in March near Danjiangkou in Hubei, where over 300,000 people are supposed to be moved.) Still, the official projection is that water will be reaching Beijing through this route by 2014.
3) a Western route that is really two routes, taking water from the Yarlong-Tsangpo, Dadu, Tongtian and Jinsha Rivers (all of which flow into the Yangzi) across mountains and the Tibet-Qinghai plateau, directing it into the Yellow River, which would then carry it across North China. This is by far the most complex part of the project; work is currently scheduled to begin in 2010, but it would not be completed until 2050.

The project carries uncertainties commensurate with its size and cost. Among other things, there is considerable uncertainty about how dirty southern waters will be by the time they arrive in the north; diversions on this scale change flow speeds, sedimentation rates, and other important rates in unpredictable ways, and the original plans have already been modified to add more treatment facilities than were originally thought necessary. (Changes in water volume will also affect the ability of other rivers to scour their own beds – effects on the Han River, one of the Yangzi's largest tributaries, are a particular concern.) Conveyance canals passing through poorly drained areas may also raise the water table and add excess salts to the soil – already a common problem in irrigated areas of North China – and salt water intrusion rates in the Yangzi Delta. For better or worse, we will begin learning about the effects of the Eastern line soon, and probably about the Central line in just a few years.

But despite its long time horizon, it is the Western line – along with other projects in China's far west — which is the big story. First of all, it offers the most dramatic potential rewards. The idea is that it will tap the enormous water resources of China's far Southwest – Tibet alone has over 30% of China's fresh water supply, most of it coming from the annual snow melt and the annual partial melting around the edges of some Himalayan glaciers. These water resources are an aspect of the Tibet question one rarely hears about, but the many engineers in China's leadership, including Hu Jintao and Wen Jiabao, are very much aware of it. (And ordinary Chinese are increasingly aware of it too – advertisements for bottled Tibetan water now adorn the backs of passenger train seats and other common locations, offering an icon of primitive purity of a type long familiar to Western consumers.) And hydro projects in this very mountainous region offer enormous potential rewards in electricity as well as in water supply. How much electricity water can generate is directly proportional to how far it falls into the turbines: the Yangzi completes 90% of its drop to the sea before it even leaves Tibet to enter China proper, and the Yellow River 80% of its decline before it leaves Inner Mongolia. On April 21, the Chinese government announced plans for 20 additional hydro projects on the upper Yangzi and its tributaries; if they are all completed, they would theoretically add 66% to the already existing hydropower capacity on the river (which includes Three Gorges).

But secondly, the western route also poses by far the biggest complications. It is here that the engineering challenges are most complex and the solutions most untested. It is here (and in nearby Yunnan) that the needs of agrarian and industrial China collide most directly with the lives of Tibetans, Yi, Miao, and other minority groups. It is here that the environmental risks of dam building become major *international* issues, with enormous implications for the Mekong, Salween, Brahmaputra and other rivers relied on by hundreds of millions of South and Southeast Asians. And it is here that major water projects – which always include many uncertainties – collide with what has always been an extraordinarily fragile environment, and one which now faces far more than the average amount of extra uncertainty from climate change: Tibet, home to by far the largest glaciers outside the two polar regions, is expected to warm at twice the average global rate during the 21st century.

STATE-BUILDING AND DAM-BUILDING IN THE HIMALAYAS

From the 1950s to the mid-1980s, China built plenty of dams, but relatively few of them were in the far west. This may seem surprising, given the concentration of hydro potential in that region, but makes perfect sense in other terms. The need to maximize energy production was less urgently felt before the boom of the 1990s, and there was much less concern about relying on coal (which still provides 80% of China's electricity). Many of the dams that were built were constructed by mobilizing large amounts of labor (especially off-season peasant labor) in place of scarce capital, and it was a lot easier to use that labor close to home than to send it far away. The supporting infrastructure (e.g. roads) and technology for dam building in remote mountain locations was not available; the far reaches of the upper Yangzi were not even surveyed until the late 1970s. And the government was much more ambivalent about rapid development in the far west than it is today, with some leaders prioritizing more paternalistic policies that would avoid radical cultural change as the best formula for assuring political stability in the region.

But in the last two decades, all of this has changed, leading to a sharp shift towards the building of huge dam projects in Yunnan and Tibet above all. The technical capacities and supporting infrastructure needed for capital-intensive projects in these areas are now available; the pressure to increase domestic supplies of energy (and other resources, including of course water) has become intense; and the regime has clearly decided that raising incomes in the far west is the best way to keep control and make use of those territories – even if the wrenching cultural changes, massive Han immigration, and severe inequalities accompanying this development increase conflict in the short to medium term. For better or worse, a kind of paternalism in western frontier policy dating back to at least the Qing (albeit one that has long been gradually weakening) is now being discarded quite decisively. Meanwhile, changes in the relationships among the central government, provincial governments, and private investors have helped create enormous opportunities to gain both power and profit through accelerated dam building.

Plans to "send western electricity east," with a particular focus on developing Yunnan hydropower for booming Guangdong, date back to the 1980s; seasonal deliveries of power began in 1993. Beginning in 2001, Guangdong officials began concluding deals for regular annual power purchases with Yunnan officials – and at the same time, officials in Beijing began vetoing plans for additional coal-fired power plant construction in Guangdong, which made reliance on hydropower an absolute necessity for the rapidly growing Pearl River Delta. It is not clear, at least to me, exactly what the relationship between provincial and central government power is in this story. One can see wealthy Guangdong reaching out to secure its own energy supplies here; but complaints from Guangdong about Beijing preventing the construction of power plants in the province, and about power shortages emerging when sufficient hydropower failed to come online on time, suggest that new inter-provincial agreements may often be shotgun weddings imposed by the center: a center for which creating these configurations is both a means of maintaining leverage over coastal boom areas and of integrating peripheral regions more deeply into Beijing's vision of a national political economy.

More generally, the "corporatizing" of the electrical power industry has created complex webs of public and private actors with strong interests in Southwestern hydro development. In 2002, the government-owned State Power Corporation of China was broken into 5 corporations, each of which was given exclusive development rights in particular watersheds. (There is also a sixth, connected to Three Gorges, which is directly under the State Council.) These companies were 100% state-owned, but have created partially-owned subsidiaries which sell shares to private parties (on the Shanghai, Hong Kong and New York stock exchanges), thus raising capital while retaining control. (For investors, meanwhile, power generation stocks provide a way to bet on the growth of the Chinese economy in general without needing lots of reliable information on the factors that might cause a particular manufacturer to succeed or fail.) And these subsidiaries, in turn, have combined with other subsidiaries of the big 5 and/or companies established by provincial governments to establish still other companies that undertake particular projects.

While this organization allows dam-builders to take advantage of private capital markets and corporate organization, their links to the state remain crucial. Huaneng Power Group, which holds development rights for the Lancang (Upper Mekong), was until recently headed by Li Xiaopeng, son of former Premier (and chief advocate of the Three Gorges project) Li Peng. (The younger Li, who like so many other Chinese leaders has a background in engineering, has since moved on to become deputy governor of Shanxi, with responsibility for industry and coal mining.) His sister, Li Xiaolin, is the CEO of Huaneng's most important subsidiary, China Power International Development Ltd. (a Hong Kong corporation). The transactions which create subsidiaries often involve the parent company giving the subsidiary some important asset (such as generators, transmission lines, or development rights) in return for a large stake in the new company; since there are rarely well-developed markets for these assets and the state-owned parent company does not face the same pressures to be profitable as the subsidiary, the prices at which these assets are transferred can be easily manipulated to artificially lower the costs (and increase the profits) of the subsidiary and its investors. And since all of these companies continue to do business with each other (sending power over somebody else's lines, for instance), there are many opportunities to transfer costs back and forth between entities that need to show a profit and others that do not (or that are less favored by powerful actors).

Powerful government connections also make it all the more likely that these companies will be able to avoid acknowledging (much less bearing) the full social and environmental costs of their work. Last but not least, the large and sometimes unpredictable fluctuations in water volumes far upstream mean that the turbines will not always be fully utilized, so that the actual amount of power generated may be much less impressive than is suggested by the enormous figures for "installed capacity" that are listed for these projects: uncertainties which holders of development rights seeking either investment partners or permission to build have no incentive to highlight. This does not mean, of course, that dams – including large dams – may not make economic and even environmental sense in many cases, given China's limited options. It does mean, however, that both political motives and profit seeking by politically-connected people are almost certainly causing dams to be built in a number of additional cases, where even a narrowly economic analysis would not justify them.

Implications for Tibet and Tibetans

Even many projects that will genuinely help millions in northern and eastern China – and perhaps others that will curb China's carbon emissions and its future food imports — have serious implications for people who live near the projects. Tibetans and other ethnic minorities in the far Southwest are likely to be the most affected. An unconfirmed report by the Tibetan government-in-exile says that at least 6 Tibetan women were recently shot by security forces as they protested a hydro project on the Tibet/Sichuan border.

First, there is the question of human tampering with sacred lakes and rivers. A good deal of this has already happened in Tibet (as with the large dam at Yamdrok Tso). A massive dam proposed at the great bend in the Yalong Zangbo (Yarlong Tsangpo) – 40,000 megawatts, or almost twice the capacity of Three Gorges — would again dramatically change a sacred site, to create power and water supplies that would mostly go to Han Chinese very far away. Meanwhile, the project poses serious risks for the traditional livelihoods of many people. Road-building and railway-building – particularly the Qinghai-Tibet highway and the railroad that runs near it, completed in 2006 – seem to have substantially damaged the permafrost layer in adjacent areas; the permafrost, in turn, protects a series of underground lakes, so that damaging it is likely to exacerbate an already worrisome drying trend in the region. (A Chinese surveying team recently reported that some of the sources of the Yangzi itself are drying up, and the area turning to desert.) Wetlands and grasslands that are important to the large numbers of livestock herders in Tibet have already shrunk quite significantly; this is likely to make them shrink faster. (A video on the Asia Society website covers some of these issues very well.) Dams in Yunnan appear to be interfering with local fisheries, and new ones pose significant threats to China's greatest concentration of biodiversity. And since much of this region is seismically quite active, the risk of an earthquake precipitating a catastrophic dam failure and sudden floods cannot be dismissed.

The Other Side(s) of the Mountains: Pakistan, India, Nepal, Burma, Vietnam

Of course, people and governments further downstream also use rivers that start in the Himalayas – and many have plans to do so much more intensively. Many of them are very worried about Chinese initiatives that may preempt their own current or future water usage.

On December 9, 2008, *Asia Times Online* reported that China was planning to go ahead with a major hydroelectric dam and water diversion scheme on the great bend of the Yalong Zangbo River in Tibet. The 40,000 megawatt hydro project itself raises huge issues for Tibetans and for China. But what matters most for people outside China is that the plan not only calls for impounding huge amounts of water behind a dam, but also for changing the direction that the water flows beyond the dam – so that it would eventually feed into the South-North diversion project. The water that would be diverted currently flows south into Assam to help form the Brahmaputra, which in turn joins the Ganges to form the world's largest river delta, supplying much of the water to a basin with over 300 million inhabitants. While South Asians have worried for some time that China might divert this river, the Chinese government had denied any such intentions, reportedly doing so again when Hu Jintao visited New Delhi in 2006. However, rumors that China was indeed planning to begin such a project soon continued to circulate. (As we will see later, some Indian essays published in 2007 already assumed that China would make a major diversion from the Brahmaputra, citing this as a reason for India not to proceed with its own plan to transfer water from the Brahmaputra to other river basins south and west of it.) Indian Prime Minister Singh reportedly raised the issue during his January 2008 visit to Beijing, but a December, 2008 report from *Asia Times Online* said that China provided no assurances this time, and is in fact planning to divert the river. (No public statement was made at that time, but fewer official denials have been issued; the latest came former water minister Wang Shucheng on May 26, 2009.) Chinese Prime Minister Wen Jiabao has said that water scarcity is a threat to the "very survival of the Chinese nation." Interestingly, unconfirmed reports back in 2000 had suggested that Beijing had already decided to go ahead; but not until 2009, when the Three Gorges would be completely finished.

Water is indeed a matter of survival – not only for China, but for its neighbours. Most of Asia's major rivers – the Yellow, the Yangzi, the Mekong, Salween, Irrawaddy, Brahmaputra, Ganges, Sutlej, and Indus – draw on the glaciers and snowmelt of the Himalayas, and all of these except the Ganges have their source on the Chinese side of the border in Tibet. In many of these cases, no international agreements exist for sharing the waters of those rivers that cross borders, or even sharing data about them.

There are water problems throughout South and Southeast Asia, but not the same ones in all places. Very crudely, the nature of the most pressing current problems varies with longitude. Pakistan and much of India (especially in the North and West) face very serious shortages of water for agriculture and for daily domestic use, as well as serious rural power shortages. The latter problem intensifies the former for many people, as it makes the operation of deep wells increasingly impractical; but in the longer run easing the power shortage without solving the water supply crisis will just intensify future shortages. In most of Southeast Asia, by contrast, there is plenty of water for now, but electricity is in short supply, and plans to alleviate that problem through hydropower threaten delicate riverine ecosystems.

Starting in the West, Pakistan may depend more on irrigation than any other large country on earth. Over half of the country receives less than 8 inches of rainfall per year; by way of comparison, Phoenix averages 8.4 inches. Only 8% of the country gets over 20 inches per year – the amount that falls in Tel Aviv. Yet the country is predominantly agricultural, and almost 80% of farming requires irrigation. As recently as 1990, irrigation accounted for a stunning 96% of water use. Meanwhile, much of the groundwater is brackish and/or badly polluted – partly due to current pollution, but also in part a legacy of past irrigation projects; some of the brackishness results from salination and waterlogging that goes back to colonial era projects.

Consequently, people often rely on diversions from irrigation canals to get water for their daily needs. (Since increased use of drip irrigation would reduce the availability of water in surface canals, this may be another way in which more "efficient" technologies, though very helpful in some ways, could intensify the problems of certain people — in this case, some particularly vulnerable ones.) Agriculture remains central to the economy, and there are even plans, backed by foreign investors, to sharply increase grain exports (mostly to the Middle East). Efforts to increase irrigation efficiency are underway, but the government is also looking for ways to engineer large increases in supply.

Northern and Northwestern India are not quite as dry as Pakistan, but nonetheless have millions of farmers, several arid regions, and highly irregular, often inadequate rains elsewhere. For India as a whole, the per capita water supply is about ¼ of the global average – as it is for China. Moreover, half the annual rainfall comes in 15 days, and 90% of total river flow comes during 4 months. Yet India has built only 1/5 as much water storage capacity per capita as China (and about 1/25 as much as the US or Australia). Canals for surface irrigation were built on a large scale in some areas under the British, and on a considerably larger scale after Independence; but many have been poorly maintained and/or not run to serve those who lack political influence. So in north and northwest India (and some other regions), probably even more than in northern China, well-digging has been essential to enabling farmers to survive, and to a "green revolution" that raised agricultural yields enough to keep up with the enormous population growth of the last half century. (As in many other cases, the high-yielding hybrid wheat, rice, and cotton seeds all required more water than older varieties.) Groundwater now provides 70% of India's irrigation water, and close to 80% of water for domestic use.

This extremely aggressive exploitation of groundwater is unsustainable. Well water is free to any farmer who can reach it by drilling down from his land, and the electricity to run the pumps is heavily subsidized, greatly straining the budgets of many Indian states. Even at heavily subsidized prices, however, energy costs have become a huge burden for many small farmers as water levels drop and pumps must work harder; moreover, the irregular way electricity is provided, with frequent spikes and interruptions, often ruins pumps, wreaking sudden devastation on unfortunate farmers. The large inequalities in landholding within many Indian villages are a further complication which is much more pronounced than in any part of rural China. Richer farmers have every reason to drill deeper wells, take more water from aquifers, and re-sell whatever they don't use themselves at high mark-ups to people without wells for their domestic use; indeed, this is often more profitable than using the water to raise crops. Other people then also need to drill deeper in response; a sort of tube well race has developed, depleting aquifers ever faster. Suicides of farmers who cannot get enough water to continue planting have become common events in recent years, including instances of protest by mass suicide. (Some of these protests are aimed at state governments which have been raising electricity prices to farmers; these rates are still far below those charged to urbanites but too high for many farmers nonetheless. Some protests are also aimed at corporate users and polluters of water; Coca Cola has been a particularly popular target.) Meanwhile, there is increasing concern that water scarcity and pollution could create dangerous shortfalls of agricultural output, especially in Punjab – which produces India's largest agricultural surpluses, including roughly half the wheat and rice procured by the central government pool that aims to stabilize supplies and prices – and in neighboring Pakistan. The pollution in question, which is bad enough to cause large increases in birth defects and cancer, has many sources, including the legacy of years of intensive irrigation, fertilization, and use of pesticides; salination and water-logging (with the latter problem also increasing the incidence of malaria) have in fact been mounting problems in the Punjab since the introduction of year-round irrigation by the British at the end of the 19th century. It is estimated that in East Punjab today, 50% of groundwater is recycled water from irrigation canals; in West Punjab, 80%. Near Karachi, where it reaches the sea, the Indus now often fills only a small fraction of its bed; fishing has disappeared, an invasion of seawater is harming agriculture, and water for domestic use is desperately short.

In this crisis, plans for new water projects have sprouted in large numbers. Though people are well aware that past projects often had unexpected effects that have led to current difficulties, the prospect of losing the agricultural output gains achieved through irrigation is terrifying, and possibilities for alleviating serious electricity shortages (which, among other things, inhibit manufacturing growth that could reduce reliance on agriculture) seem very tempting. And, ironically, the loss of water storage capacity that has occurred as some old dams have silted up has become an argument for more dam building.

While many of these plans are driven by very real needs, China is hardly the only country where political and economic interests create incentives to build some mega-projects that are incomprehensible in terms of overall costs and benefits. In India, for instance, the central government's inability to enforce water-sharing agreements among the states has led some upstream states to build extra water storage in order to keep for themselves water that is at least as badly needed downstream; meanwhile, some downstream states, despite desperate shortages, have balked at implementing water-saving measures that might weaken their claims to need a larger allocation from rivers flowing through multiple states. And since only direct human uses of water count as "needs" in these allocations, any other uses – e.g. releasing water to help maintain estuarial eco-systems – count as "waste" that might weaken future claims, and are thus discouraged. (Somewhat surprisingly, water-sharing agreements between India and Pakistan have thus far been more consistently observed than have those among Indian states, despite decades of hostility between these countries.)

The most ambitious new plans are, not surprisingly, found amidst the highest mountains. Pakistan, India, Bhutan, and Nepal all have plans for huge dams in the Himalayas. Planned construction over the next decade totals 80,000 megawatts (versus 60-64,000 in all of Latin America); India alone plans to add a further 67,000 MW in the following decade. India, like China, exploited the hydropower in its less mountainous areas first, and has only 11,000 MW of non-Himalayan potential left; potential Himalayan capacity (not counting China) is a staggering 192,000 MW, almost half of it in India. (The entire world currently has about 675,000 megawatts of installed hydroelectric capacity.) Meanwhile, India's 2001 census reported that 44% of households had no access to electricity; the figure is about the same in Bhutan and closer to 60% in Nepal. Interest in dam building is just as intense in Pakistan, though there irrigation is a higher priority than electricity. However, the estimated cost of the projects planned for the next 10 years is roughly $90 billion, much of which remains unsecured. (India has financing for a bit over half of its planned dam construction through 2012, but much less for needs through 2017.) Pakistan has recently turned to Chinese financing and technical expertise for its Diamer Bhasha dam, a $12.6 billion project which was announced in 2006, but had trouble attracting capital. There has also been some financial support from Middle Eastern sources and various international development banks.

Meanwhile, other foreign-backed plans will place additional strains on Pakistan's water supply. Investors from various wealthy but arid Middle Eastern states have recently been making large purchases of farmland, both in Pakistan and elsewhere in Asia and Africa. (South Korea and China have also been doing this, though not, as far as I know, in Pakistan.) The Pakistani Minister of Investment, seeking to dispel any fear that local farmers will be displaced, has said that all of the 6 million acres (equal to roughly 10% of the country's current cultivated acreage) up for sale or lease to foreigners was currently unused. If true, this means that any water devoted to it will represent an addition to existing demand. Indeed, a recent story in The Economist noted that many of these land purchases seem to be aimed above all at the water rights that go with the land; it quotes the chairman of Nestlés referring to these purchases as "the great water grab."

India, like China, has both extremely dry areas and some with plenty of water; and, as we have seen, it is also like China in that it is currently mining groundwater to produce important grain surpluses in some of these dry areas. So it may be no surprise that, like China, it is also contemplating a major scheme for diverting water from some river basins to others. The most ambitious, Himalayan, part of its Interlinking of Rivers Project would move water from the upper parts of the Ganges, Yamuna (a major tributary of the Ganges) and Brahmaputra Rivers westward, ending in the Luni and Sabarmati Rivers in Rajahstan and Gujarat. (Other Northwestern areas that would receive water are in Haryana and Punjab; a second, Peninsular, part of the project would mostly direct water to dry parts of Orissa and Tamil Nadu.) And just as China seems to be retreating from its earlier representations to India that it had no plans to divert water from the Yalong Zangbo/Brahmaputra, so this project suggests that India is hedging on its formal promises to Bangladesh (including a written understanding from 1996) that no water would be diverted away from the Ganges above the barrage at Farakka (a few kilometers from the India/Bangladesh border).

Some of the intermediate links would create shipping channels, and the project also aims to reduce seasonal flooding problems on the Yamuna (especially near Delhi). The project is also supposed to generate 30,000 megawatts of net hydropower (i.e. power available for other uses after subtracting the energy it would use for moving water). The main purpose, however, would be to provide large amounts of additional irrigation water, mostly in Western India; official plans claim it could increase total irrigated area by as much as 35 million hectares. Official cost estimates for the total project, with 260 links between rivers, was estimated at $120 billion, which would make it larger than any construction project in history so far, and even bigger than China's planned river diversions; based on subsequent comments by members of the task force that drafted the plan, one study has suggested a revised price tag of $200 billion.

Plans for the project have been shrouded in a degree of secrecy unusual for India – even more so, it appears, than with China's river diversion projects; among other things it is hard to get an estimate of the number of people likely to be displaced, though two scholars put the number as high as 5.5 million. Many of the parts of the plan that have been revealed have been sharply criticized on a number of grounds, and it is unclear which parts will actually wind up being built. Aside from a number of technological and ecological questions about specific parts of the projects, both domestic critics and a World Bank study have noted that the transfers being contemplated are only politically feasible if enforceable legal agreements can be reached on allocating the waters and compensating the "givers," and such agreements have generally not fared well in India. There is also widespread agreement that Indian governments need to put more of their water conservancy money into improving maintenance and management of existing facilities (many of which are decaying quickly), rather than further construction. Indeed, even one scholar who is largely supportive of the project estimates that net water availability could be increased as much by improving the current efficiency of water utilization by 20% as by building this project (though he favors doing both, and points to hydropower and other benefits of the project besides increased water supply). Some opponents, on the other hand, have suggested that building this project would so deplete resources for other water works that the latter might have to be privatized to raise cash, at considerable risk to poorer customers.

We will turn momentarily to some of the environmental risks associated with these new and proposed water projects. First, though, it is worth noting that in the case of large dams, environmental uncertainties not only represent risks to others, but financial risks for the dam builders themselves. Big dams have huge construction costs, but very modest operational costs once they are finished; thus they can become big cash cows once they are generating power while incurring very low additional costs (especially if, as seems very likely in this part of the world, demand for electricity continues to rise). Profitability is therefore very much dependent on how long they continue producing after completion. That period can be cut short by many factors, of which sedimentation may be the most common. Sanmenxia dam on the middle Yellow River, completed in 1962, is a particularly notorious example — not only because it failed quickly and expensively, but because many of the problems were in fact predicted. (The project went ahead anyway, in part it seems because in the aftermath of the withdrawal of Soviet technical experts, China wanted to prove that it could build such a dam without outside help.) Because interest must be paid on the construction costs, profitability is also very much affected by how much time elapses between the beginning of the project and the beginning of this revenue stream; thus mega-projects that take a long time to complete are especially vulnerable, economically speaking, to any shortfall in power generation.

In the case of Himalayan dams, at least three factors could well make the lives of these projects shorter than anticipated. First, the Himalayas are relatively young mountains with relatively high rates of erosion, and their upper reaches have relatively little vegetation to hold soil in place. (There has also been a lot of deforestation in recent decades.) This tends to make for high sediment burdens in rivers descending from the Himalayas. In Tibet, for instance, a 1986 study found that almost 40 percent of the small hydrodams built since 1949 had become defunct or unusable by being silted up; similar problems have developed on a number of Pakistani dams (which have not only lost their utility for generating power but for seasonal water storage and irrigation). Second, any errors in predicting future river flow can also have dramatic effects on the durability of a dam, sharply reducing profitability. In many of the Himalayan cases, there is not a very long run of data available (particularly since the Chinese government has not been very forthcoming about sharing the data that it has assembled), and there are reasons (mostly connected with climate change) to think that the future may be drier than the last few decades, especially in the Western Himalayas (though there are also some reasons to believe the opposite). And, as hard as it is to model future river flows in any case, it becomes exponentially harder when a great many large projects are being planned on the same set of rivers and tributaries. Several analysts have questioned whether the Brahamaputra basin – a critical water source for this plan – can be meaningfully considered to have a water "surplus" even now; some add that the likelihood (in their view) of a major Chinese diversion upstream and of glacial retreat from global warming make the idea that any "surplus" is available to be transferred extremely dubious.

A World Bank study of India's water future argues that the Himalayas offer one of the world's "most benign environments" for dam building. The basis of this estimate is simple: a calculation of people to be displaced and acreage to be submerged per megawatt generated. Given the huge power potential in the denominators of these projects and the sparse population of many highland areas, these ratios are not surprising, and they deserve to be taken seriously. But they are by no means a complete measure of the costs and risks involved.

Like all dams, those planned for the Himalayas would submerge significant amounts of land – including forests and grazing lands important to a number of the remaining migratory people in the region. Several involve diverting parts of rivers through underground tunnels, creating large dry regions, with serious local impacts on fisheries and on farming. Moreover, the Himalayas – though we don't often think of them this way – are a major and fragile hotspot of biodiversity. Their rapid rise from 500 meters to over 8,000 meters creates a remarkable range of ecosystems within a relatively small space; Conservation International reports that of an estimated 10,000 plant species in one Himalayan sub-region, over 3,100 are found nowhere else. And here, too, as in Tibet and Yunnan, there are significant risks of major disasters from earthquakes and/or glacial lake outbreak floods.

Perhaps most surprising, it is no longer clear that large hydrodams are even a consistently climate-friendly source of energy. While hydro-electricity can clearly be a substitute for fossil fuel consumption that produces carbon dioxide, the reservoirs behind large dams often include large amounts of rotting vegetable matter, and thus are potent sources of methane – a much more potent greenhouse gas. (This is not an issue for "run of the river" dams, which have no reservoirs, but these make up a very small percentage of big projects.) These emissions are larger in tropical and sub-tropical climates, where vegetation both grows and decays faster. A 2007 study suggested that methane from dam reservoirs actually accounted for 19% of India's greenhouse gas emissions, while hydropower accounts for only 16% of the country's electricity (and thus a much smaller percentage of its total energy use). These figures are still preliminary estimates; moreover, methane emissions might well be lower than average for dams high in the Himalayas, which is not an area where plant matter grows and decays rapidly. And there may well be ways to mitigate these effects by capturing and burning the methane to generate more power. But they do raise questions about the common assumption that despite their environmental risks, large dams are a clearly "greener" energy source than the most common alternatives; the non-trivial greenhouse emissions involved in creating huge amounts of concrete and steel further complicate the picture.

Further east, the plans are not quite as ambitious, but they still portend dramatic changes for millions of people. The Salween (called the Nu River in Eastern Tibet and Yunnan) is shrouded in the most mystery, since for most of its length it is either in China or Burma (elsewhere it forms the Burmese-Thai border); neither regime welcomes publicity. Because the Salween still runs within steep mountain gorges for many miles after crossing into Burma (it drops quite suddenly just before reaching its delta), there is enormous hydro potential here, and much less domestic demand. To date, the Salween has not been tapped very much for human use; it remains one of the few large free-flowing rivers left in Asia. A major dam on the Chinese side of the border was stopped in 2004 for environmental reasons, and work has recently been suspended again. However there are now a number of dams planned and/or underway, in both China (where the maximal program calls for a staircase of 13 dams) and Burma, with the expectation that the power generated in Burma will be exported to Thailand, Vietnam, and perhaps China. A number of the Burmese projects are being built by Chinese companies (and will be operated by them for the first several years after completion). Many are located in highland areas of Burma's Shan state, where the government has been trying for many years to gain fuller control over ethnic minority populations; activists have charged that the regime is taking advantage of the relocation of people which dam building requires and of providing security to the builders to further its political and military aims in the area. Another planned dam would be built in what is essentially a war zone in the Karen minority area near the Burmese-Thai border; much of the area is theoretically a wildlife sanctuary, but it has been heavily logged in recent years (particularly after Thailand banned logging on its side of the border) and roads are now being built through it to facilitate dam construction (and control).

Given the difficulty of visiting these areas, and the absence of information on exactly what projects are at what stage, it is hard to even guess at the likely social and environmental impact of the projects. And since the Salween watershed, with 6-7 million people, is far less populated than the Mekong to its east (around 70 million people)—not to mention the Ganges/Brahmaputra to the west, or the major Chinese rivers to the north—it has not gotten as much attention as these other rivers. Nonetheless it raises the full range of complex issues and trade-offs, with fears about endangered species, fish and other resources that local people rely on, forced relocations (and according to some forced labor) on one side and pressures for development in an exceptionally poor country on the other.

The larger and more densely populated Mekong basin raises all these issues and more. Here both physical and political geography create an important divide more or less at the Chinese border. For one thing, the vast majority of the river's hydropower potential is on the Chinese side of the border. The river starts 5,500 meters up on the Tibet-Qinghai plateaus, and is down to 500 meters above sea level when it leaves China. Its hydro potential within Yunnan alone almost equals its potential in Burma, Laos, Thailand, Cambodia and Vietnam combined – though the latter is far from trivial – despite the fact that Yunnan accounts for just a bit over one-third of the river's descent within China. China has thus far completed three hydro dams on the Mekong, and has at least two more under construction; the complete plan appears to call for a cascade of at least eight and perhaps as many as fifteen large hydrodams.

Planning for the lower Mekong began under a U.S. and U.N.-backed Mekong River Committee in the 1950s; China and the Democratic Republic of (North) Vietnam were excluded, and Cambodian participation was also intermittent as its relations with the U.S. fluctuated. While Lyndon Johnson, among others, spoke frequently of a major Lower Mekong Project modeled on the U.S. Tennessee Valley Authority, no substantial work was done during the war years; what were apparently private U.S. promises to help build Mekong dams as part of postwar reconstruction aid for Vietnam were never implemented either. Only in the late 1980's did a new Mekong River Commission emerge, with Vietnam and Cambodia now full members. The Commission is relatively weak, however, and the riparian states are mostly developing their own projects, often in partnership with China, Japan (especially through the Asian Development Bank) or U.S. partners.

Moreover, China has remained largely outside even the limited coordination generated within the Commission framework. Today, it sometimes sends representatives to attend meetings, but neither it nor Burma is a member. So far China's main interest in the Lower Mekong has been in navigation. A series of projects have been carried out since 2000 to facilitate this, and traffic appears to have increased quite significantly in the last 3-5 years, along with quite a bit of road construction linking Yunnan province with Burma, Thailand and Laos. It is not clear just how important a shipping artery China hopes to develop along the Mekong; while one Chinese official spoke of Middle East oil shipments coming up the Mekong to China in case the U.S. Navy blocked the Straits of Malacca in some future conflict, it seems implausible that such shipments could ever be large enough to matter much. (Nonetheless, the idea of moving oil on the Mekong – with the possibility of toxic spills – is a matter of great concern to farmers and fisher-people who rely on the river.)

While the hydro potential of the Lower Mekong may not match that of the Upper Mekong, it remains large – and all the more tempting given the severe poverty of the Greater Mekong Sub-region, where per capita income is estimated at one U.S. dollar per day. At least 11 large hydropower dams are currently planned for the mainstream of the Mekong in Southeast Asia, mostly in Laos. While there are widespread concerns that these dams could harm agriculture and fishing in the Lower Mekong – both of which are absolutely essential to the lives of its almost 70 million residents – regimes thinking in terms of industry, cities, and "modern" development may give electricity a higher priority. Meanwhile, the rather weak coordination among lower Mekong states (despite the existence of the commission) and the absence of any real control on what China does may well create a "prisoner's dilemma" that encourages dam construction: if others may well take actions that will mess up the river's ecosystem anyway, why not at least get some electricity for oneself out of it?

An obvious but nonetheless important point here is that there is no such thing as the ideal state of a river divorced from any point of view or set of interests. For instance, if Chinese projections about the effects of the three existing dams and two further dams currently underway on the Lancang/

Upper Mekong are correct, the results would be a much greater flow downstream in the dry season, and lesser flow in the wet season, with no change in overall annual flow. (The claim that these dams will have only limited effects is far from universally accepted – in fact many in Southeast Asia blame the Chinese dams already completed on the Lancang for the huge Mekong floods of 2008.) This would be good for navigation, for power generation, and perhaps for irrigation as well. Projects designed to aid navigation also generally aim to even out seasonal water flows. But even if this is true, dams on the Lancang could nonetheless have a serious impact on lower Mekong fisheries, for at least two reasons. First, dams inevitably trap some nutrient-rich sediment that would otherwise flow through to the Delta; this has been a problem with big dams elsewhere, appears to already be happening in parts of Yunnan affected by the first three Lancang dams, and is expected to happen on the lower Mekong as well. Second, many species of fish respond to subtle seasonal variations in water flow to know when to migrate and spawn; changes in the seasonal timing of peak flow after the completion of the Three Gorges Dam has, for instance, had a devastating effect on four species of Yangzi River carp. The United Nations estimates that 40 million people are active in Lower Mekong fisheries, and one report estimates that local fishing provides 80% of the protein for people living in the Lower Mekong region as well as significant export revenues. Thai and Lao fishermen claim that the Chinese dams already in existence on the Upper Mekong have begun affecting their catches, while spokesmen for the dam-builders claim these projects have had no significant impact on the Lower Mekong. There are also claims that reduced water flow at some times of year has led to greater invasion of the Delta by salt water, harming agriculture.

Dams on the Middle and Lower Mekong could have the same effects, and others as well. They will interfere with fish migration, which is concentrated on the lower and middle (especially lower) parts of the river. Mitigating technologies to allow for fish passage have proved only partially effective even on low dams in North America and Europe, and the Mekong poses a vastly more challenging problem: the amount of fish biomass is perhaps 100 times what it is on the Columbia (where fish ladders have achieved some positive results), and the number of species several times greater. (The more diverse the species, the more different times and places involved in migrations.) The territory that the Middle and Lower Mekong passes through is also much less steep and even more biodiverse than the Upper Mekong; and being lower and more tropical, would probably have higher methane emissions from any reservoirs. In various ways, then, downstream dams on the Mekong may be more dangerous than upstream ones, and they would be far more expensive per kilowatt generated. But their benefits would accrue mostly to people in the same countries that will suffer their probable harms – and that might be all that matters to planners thinking in terms of national interests.

But while everybody is looking to dam the rivers descending from the Himalayas, China's position is unique. It is not only that most of the rivers in question start on China's side of the border, so that their claims cannot be pre-empted by actions further upstream. A second crucial difference is that they alone, of the countries involved, can finance any project they choose without recourse to international lenders. And while the World Bank, Asian Development Bank and big private banks are not among the world's most ardent environmentalists, they have – either for their own reasons or because of pressures from third parties – refused to support some particularly controversial projects. China's domestic dam-building industry is also increasingly technically sophisticated, and is in fact now exporting its engineering know-how in this area. Thus, the only constraints Chinese dam-building faces are those generated within the country – and these are often (though not always) fairly weak.

Late in January, Jiang Gaoming of the Chinese Academy of Sciences released a sobering piece (China Dialogue, January 22, 2009, link) about how accelerating the construction of dams in China's Southwest – part of the P.R.C.'s ambitious stimulus package to fight the global recession – is worsening the already considerable environmental and social risks involved, with some projects beginning before any Environmental Impact Assessments have been completed. Protests against Three Gorges by some leading scientists and engineers did not stop that project; it remains to be seen whether they will have more effect in the future. Recent reports that some poorly built dams on the Yellow River in Gansu – and perhaps many others elsewhere in China – are in dire need of repair — may strengthen people, both within and outside the government, who are urging a more cautious approach to further mega-projects, but the outcome of such arguments remains unclear.

In short the possible damage to China's neighbours from this approach to its water and energy needs is staggeringly large – and the potential to raise political tensions is commensurate. Previous water diversion projects affecting the source of the Mekong have already drawn protests from Vietnam (and from environmental groups), and, as noted above, a project on the Nu River (which becomes the Salween in Thailand and Burma) which was suspended in the face of significant domestic and foreign opposition in 2004 and then re-started, has recently been halted again by order of Prime Minister Wen Jiabao. But some projects now underway or being contemplated have considerably larger implications, both for Chinese and for foreigners. The diversion of the Yalong Zangbo – if that is indeed on the agenda – would have the largest implications of all. If the waters could arrive in North China safely and relatively unpolluted – by no means sure things — and having generated considerable power along the way, the relief for China's seriously strained hydro-ecology would be considerable.

On the other hand, the impact on Eastern India and Bangladesh, with a combined population even larger than North China's, could be devastating. The potential for such a project to create conflicts between China and India –and to exacerbate existing conflicts over shared waterways between India and Bangladesh – is gigantic.

LANDMARK RULING IN SOUTH CHINA SEA ARBITRATION

The wait is over: a judgment has been issued in the *Philippines v. China*South China Sea arbitration. A five-judge tribunal constituted under the Permanent Court of Arbitration (PCA) in The Hague has released its much-anticipated Award concerning the Philippines' challenge to a number of China's maritime claims and activities in the region. The Philippines initiated the arbitration in January 2013 under the dispute settlement procedures of Annex VII to the 1982 United Nations Convention on the Law of the Sea (UNCLOS).

Summary of Key Claims and Holdings

The Philippines' claims fell into four general categories. The ruling of the Tribunal on each category of claims is summarized below: The broadest claim was a challenge to China's "nine-dash line" covering most of the South China Sea. China has never clarifiedwhether the line represents a claim to the islands within the line and their adjacent waters; a boundary of national sovereignty over all the enclosed waters (including, but not limited by, the land features inside the line); or a "historic" claim of sovereignty or some other set of historic rights to the maritime space within the line. The Philippines sought a declaration that the countries' respective rights and obligations regarding the waters, seabed, and maritime features of the South China Sea are governed by UNCLOS. As such, China's claims based on any "historic rights" to waters, seabed, and subsoil within the nine-dash line are contrary to UNCLOS and invalid.

Holding: UNCLOS "comprehensively" governs the parties' respective rights to maritime areas in the South China Sea. Therefore, to the extent China's nine-dash line is a claim of "historic rights" to the waters of the South China Sea, it is invalid.

Reasoning: Whatever historic rights China may have had were extinguished when UNCLOS was adopted, to the extent those rights were incompatible with UNCLOS.

The Philippines sought a determination as to whether certain land features in the Spratly Islands claimed by both China and the Philippines are properly characterized as islands, rocks, low tide elevations (LTEs), or submerged banks. Under UNCLOS, an "island" generates both a territorial sea of 12 nautical miles and an exclusive economic zone (EEZ) of up to 200 nautical miles, subject to delimitation of a maritime boundary with any other countries' overlapping territorial seas or EEZs. A "rock" is entitled to a territorial sea no greater than 12 nautical miles, but not an EEZ. LTEs and submerged banks do not generate any such entitlements.

Holding: None of the features in the Spratly Islands generates an EEZ, nor can the Spratly Islands generate an EEZ collectively as a unit. As such, the Tribunal declared certain areas are within the Philippines' EEZ and not overlapped by any possible Chinese entitlement.

Reasoning: The baseline of analysis is what the features can sustain in their "natural condition" (i.e., not after construction of artificial islands, installation of desalination plants, etc.). Based on historical evidence, none of the features in the Spratly Islands can sustain either a stable community of people or economic activity that is not dependent on outside resources or purely extractive in nature. The current presence of personnel on the features is dependent on outside support and does not reflect the capacity of the features in their natural condition.

The Philippines sought a declaration that China violated UNCLOS by interfering with the Philippines' rights and freedoms within its EEZs. This includes preventing Philippine fishing around Scarborough Shoal, violating UNCLOS's environmental protection provisions through construction and fishing activities that have harmed the marine environment (including at Scarborough Shoal, Second Thomas Shoal, and Mischief Reef), and by dangerously operating law enforcement vessels around Scarborough Shoal.

Holding: China violated the Philippines' sovereign rights in its EEZ. It did so by interfering with Philippine fishing and hydrocarbon exploration; constructing artificial islands; and failing to prevent Chinese fishermen from fishing in the Philippines' EEZ.

China also interfered with Philippine fishermen's traditional fishing rights near Scarborough Shoal (without prejudice to the question of sovereignty over Scarborough Shoal). China's construction of artificial islands at seven features in the Spratly Islands, as well as illegal fishing and harvesting by Chinese nationals, violate UNCLOS obligations to protect the marine environment. Finally, Chinese law enforcement vessels unlawfully created a serious risk of collision by physically obstructing Philippine vessels at Scarborough Shoal in 2012.

Reasoning: This set of holdings depended on the Tribunal finding that certain areas are within the Philippines' EEZ and not subject to possible overlapping Chinese entitlements. It also depended on finding that activities such as island construction are, *in accordance with China's own public statements*, not "military activities" and therefore not excluded from jurisdiction under UNCLOS. Once this was established, the Tribunal considered Chinese activities in the relevant areas and found that China had (a) interfered with Philippine petroleum exploration at Reed Bank, (b) purported to prohibit fishing by Philippine vessels within the Philippine EEZ, (c) protected and failed to prevent Chinese fishermen from fishing within the Philippine EEZ at Mischief Reef and Second Thomas Shoal, and (d) constructed artificial islands/ installations at Mischief Reef without the Philippines' authorization. As for Scarborough Shoal, regardless of who has sovereignty, both Philippine and Chinese fishermen have "traditional fishing rights" at the Shoal that were not extinguished by UNCLOS, and China violated the Philippines' rights by entirely preventing Filipino fishermen from fishing near Scarborough Shoal after May 2012. In addition, Chinese artificial island construction has caused "severe harm to the coral reef environment" and China has failed to stop its nationals from engaging in "harmful" and "destructive" harvesting and fishing of endangered sea turtles, coral, and giant clams in violation of UNCLOS. Finally, Chinese law enforcement vessels violated maritime safety obligations by creating a serious risk of collision on two occasions in April and May 2012 during the Scarborough Shoal standoff.

The Philippines sought a declaration that China's recent actions, specifically its land reclamation and construction of artificial islands in the Spratly Islands after the arbitration was commenced, violated the obligations UNCLOS places on states to refrain from conduct that "aggravates and extends" a dispute while dispute resolution proceedings are pending.

Holding: China has aggravated and extended the disputes through its dredging, artificial island-building, and construction activities.

Reasoning: While these proceedings were pending, China has built a large island on Mischief Reed, an LTE within the Philippines' EEZ; caused irreparable harm to the marine ecosystem; and permanently destroyed evidence of the natural condition of the features at issue.

Initial Takeaways

1. Not many people predicted that the Philippines would all but run the table in this case. It's hard to imagine a much more favorable outcome for their legal team.
2. One of the ironies of the Award is that China has vociferously argued in public statements that it is not "militarizing" the South China Sea

and that its actions there are for civilian purposes. Those claims turned out to be crucial to the Tribunal's conclusion that it had jurisdiction to consider the legality of certain Chinese actions such as construction of artificial islands in the South China Sea, because Article 298(1)(b) of UNCLOS excludes disputes concerning "military activities" from compulsory dispute settlement. Despite China's non-participation in the proceedings, the Tribunal went out of its way to review the December 2014 position paper issued by China's Ministry of Foreign Affairs as well as numerous public statements of Chinese leaders. This was an example of where those public statements worked against China's legal interests in the arbitration.

3. The Tribunal rejected the possibility that China could claim the entirety of the Spratly Islands as a single archipelagic feature, as suggested in recent statements by the Ministry of Foreign Affairs as well as a white paper issued last month by the Chinese Society of International Law. As Julian noted earlier, this was a bit of a preemptory legal strike against "any Chinese attempt to draw 'straight baselines' around the Spratlys and thus treat the whole area as a single entity for generating maritime rights."
4. Of all the rulings on the status of features in the Spratly Islands, perhaps none will generate more discussion than the conclusion that Itu Aba (Taiping Island) is a rock and not an island. Many observers thought that Itu Aba, the largest naturally occurring land feature in the Spratly Islands, had the strongest claim to being deemed an island entitled to both a territorial sea and an EEZ. The concepts the Tribunal employed to determine what makes something a "rock which cannot sustain human habitation or economic life of [its] own" are likely to guide future legal determinations of this character.

It will take time to digest this portion of the opinion, but the Tribunal's "habitability and economic life" factors seem to include:

- The objective capacity of the feature in its natural condition (i.e., "without external additions or modifications" and without outside support), to sustain, over an extended period of time, either
  - (a) a stable community of people for whom the feature constitutes a home and on which they can remain, or
  - (b) economic activity that is not
    - (i) dependent on outside resources, or
    - (ii) purely extractive in nature without the involvement of a local population.

- Factors contributing to the natural capacity of a feature to do so "include the presence of water, food, and shelter in sufficient quantities to enable a group of persons to live on the feature for an indeterminate period of time."
- In assessing these "capacity" factors, the Tribunal stated, "the most reliable evidence of the capacity of a feature will usually be the historical use to which it has been put." Applying that standard here, the Tribunal saw "no indication that anything fairly resembling a stable human community has ever formed on the Spratly Islands. Rather, the islands have been a temporary refuge and base of operations for fishermen and a transient residence for labourers engaged in mining and fishing."

Given its sweeping conclusions favoring the Philippines, the Award may seem to have nothing positive in it for China. But the Tribunal offered an important qualification to its judgment, and perhaps a bit of an olive branch toward the end of a decision it knew would not be well received in Beijing.

We should not assume, said the Tribunal, that these disputes are the product of *bad faith* on the part of the PRC; rather, they are the result of basic disagreements about respective rights and obligations and the applicability of UNCLOS. From paragraph 1198 of the Award:

"The root of the disputes presented by the Philippines in this arbitration lies not in any intention on the part of China or the Philippines to infringe on the legal rights of the other, but rather—as has been apparent throughout these proceedings—in fundamentally different understandings of their respective rights under the Convention in the waters of the South China Sea. In such circumstances, the purpose of dispute resolution proceedings is to clarify the Parties' respective rights and obligations and thereby to facilitate their future relations in accordance with the general obligations of good faith that both governments unequivocally recognise."

Where does this leave us? China's position all along with respect to these proceedings can be summed up as "no acceptance, no participation, no recognition, and no implementation." The PRC Ministry of Foreign Affairs predictably wasted no time releasing astatement declaring that "the award is null and void and has no binding force."

The Philippine Foreign Affairs Secretary welcomed the decision, stating: "The Philippines strongly affirms its respect for this milestone decision as an important contribution to ongoing efforts in addressing disputes in the South China Sea." No surprises here, especially given that the Tribunal resolved virtually all the key issues in favor of the Philippines. For its part, the U.S. State Department issued a measured statement remarking that "[t]he decision today by the Tribunal in the Philippines-China arbitration is an important contribution to the shared goal of a peaceful resolution to disputes in the South China Sea."

As these statements suggest, the issuance of this Award by no means puts to rest the disputes or the tensions in the South China Sea. The arbitration was never going to resolve issues of sovereignty over the islands and rocks in the South China Sea, because disputes over territorial sovereignty are beyond the jurisdiction of an UNCLOS Tribunal.

And since the Tribunal has no power to enforce its nominally binding decision, questions now turn to what any form of "implementation" might look like and the effect this ruling will have on future negotiations over territorial sovereignty.

China, the Philippines, ASEAN countries, and the United States face a range of strategic questions about the best way forward. Will Beijingdemonstrate its disregard for the decision by engaging in land reclamation at Scarborough Shoal or declaring an Air Defense Identification Zone in the South China Sea, as some have predicted? Will it continue to insist on conditioning any future bilateral negotiations with the administration of new Philippine President Rodrigo Duterte on his government's rejection of the Tribunal's Award? Will it worry that some of these behaviors will push the Philippines and other ASEAN nations closer to the United States? Will we see the U.S. Navy conducting "pure" freedom of navigation operations (FONOPs) within 12 nautical miles of the Spratly Island features the Tribunal says are not entitled to a territorial sea?

THE SOUTH CHINA SEA MOMENT OF TRUTH IS ALMOST HERE

The Philippines' lawfare strategy in the South China Sea disputes is inching closer to a moment of truth. In coming weeks, an arbitral tribunal, formed under the aegis of the United Nations Convention on the Law of the Sea (UNCLOS), is set to pass a final judgment on the ongoing maritime spats between China and the Philippines. For the first time, a team of impartial, top-caliber legal experts will officially weigh on the validity of China's expansive claims and growing footprint across arguably the world's most important waterway. What is at stake is preventing China from fulfilling a Seldenian Closed Sea (*Mare clausum*) in favor of preserving a Grotian Free Sea (*Mare Liberum*) at the heart of the Western Pacific.

Astonishingly, Duterte has even expressed reservations concerning the wisdom ofongoing efforts to bolster the Philippines' minimum deterrence capability. "Fighter jets are good only for ceremonial flybys. I'm not in favor of building up external defense, I will not got to war with China," Duterte recently told reporters. Though known as often mercurial, he was actually consistent with his earlier stance during the campaign trail, when he dismissed the purchase of much-needed jet fighters as a "waste of money." For the incoming president, what matters is internal security operation, especially in light of the worrying resurgence of extremist groups, tied to Islamic State, in the southern island of Mindanao.

Duterte, meanwhile, has expressed growing interest in reviving long-frayed bilateral investment relations with China, even though this may come at the expense of a compromise on sovereignty disputes in the South China Sea. During his meeting with Chinese ambassador Zhao Jian, among the first dignitaries who met the president-elect shortly after the elections, Duterte and the Chinese envoy apparently went down to business right off the bat, discussing prospects for massive Chinese infrastructure investments in the Philippines. Obviously delighted by the cordial exchanges, with large-scale Chinese investments hanging in the balance, Duterte went so far as to praise Chinese President Xi Jinping as a "great" leader.

Duterte has also expressed doubts as to the utility of the Philippines' arbitration case against China, which has boycotted the proceedings and questioned the jurisdiction of the arbitral tribunal to oversee the South China Sea disputes. Encouraged by convivial exchanges with the incoming Philippine leadership, China recently reiterated its call on thePhilippines to entirely drop the arbitration case as a sign of goodwill. After all, the verdict is expected to be released a week after Duterte officially assumes power, so technically the case could still be dropped. And as Columbia University professor Matthew C. Waxman succinctlyexplains, much is also at stake for the whole international law regime, which may explain the curious timing of the expected release of the arbitration judgment.

The Trial of the Century

"For the UNCLOS system—as a body of rules and binding dispute settlement mechanisms—prominence and credibility are at stake," Waxman explains. The arbitration body faces the risk of "being ignored, derided and marginalized by the biggest player in the region."

Last October, the arbitral tribunal (formed under Article 287, Annex VIIof UNCLOS) decided that it would indeed exercise jurisdiction on almost half of the items in the Philippines' *memorial* (official complaint), with the remaining items subject to simultaneous examination in terms of both jurisdiction and merit. In a ten-page summary, the judges argued that the Philippine-initiated arbitration case "was properly constituted" and that the "act of initiating this arbitration did not constitute an abuse of process [as asserted by China]."

The judges reiterated that "China's non-appearance in these proceedings does not deprive the Tribunal of jurisdiction," and "international law does not require a State to continue negotiations when it concludes that the possibility of a negotiated solution has been exhausted." The Tribunal, which has no mandate to decide on questions of sovereignty, decided that it can nonetheless exercise jurisdiction on determination of the nature of disputed features, particularly the Mischief, Gaven, McKennan, Hughes, Johnson, Cuarteron and Fiery Cross Reefs, as well as Scarborough Shoal.

It can also exercise jurisdiction on allegedly aggressive maneuvers by China against Philippine vessels operating close to Scarborough Shoal, as well as the ecological impact of China's reclamation activities near Scarborough and Second Thomas shoals. But key items such as the validity of China's sweeping nine-dashed-line claims anddubious doctrine of "historical rights" were left for further deliberation. Meanwhile, China continuously ignored opportunities, in accordance to Article 5, Annex VII, to formally participate in the proceedings.

Thus, the arbitration body effectively demolished China's longstanding claim that (1) UNCLOS and arbitration bodies under its aegis have no mandate to arbitrate disputes concerning the South China Sea disputes; (2) the Philippines has yet to exhaust bilateral negotiations before resorting to compulsory arbitration; and (3) China, under Article 298, has exempted itself from such arbitration procedures.

This isn't just some legal hairsplitting. There are huge strategic implications. First of all, it means that not only the Philippines, but also other claimant countries could resort to a similar lawfare strategy to pressure and extract concessions from China. In effect, the Philippines' arbitration case could create a "lawfare multiplier." So far, Indonesia, which is inching closer to dropping its neutrality status in the South China Sea disputes, and Vietnam, which has ramped up defense ties with America, have threatened to go along the same path if China continues to press its advantage in adjacent waters.

Secondly, and more importantly, the arbitration verdict could provide a perfection legal justification for not only America, but also other key naval powers such as Japan, to launch sustained, multilateral Freedom of Navigation Operations in the South China Sea. Coordinated and multinational FONOPs by America and its key allies hold the promise of creating just enough pressure to force China to recalibrate its posturing in disputed areas.

Hard Choices

What is clear is that the Duterte administration will not drop the arbitration case, which is in its final phase. This is just politically impossible, given the amount of domestic and international support the Philippines' lawfare has generated.

In fact, incoming foreign affairs secretary Perfecto Yasay made it clear that the Duterte administration will "not pursue any bilateral talks [with China] at this time until we hear, or wait for, the outcome of the decision of the arbitral tribunal to come out."

Of course, there is a possibility, albeit minimal, that the Philippines will lose on all key items in its arbitration case. For instance, the arbitral body may resort to indefinite legal semantics to avoid giving an impression of openly scolding China.

It could also shun exercising jurisdiction on key items like the validity of China's nine-dashed-line claims, while partially censuring China on other more minor items.

This would surely be a disaster for the Philippines and likeminded countries, which are eager to leverage international law against China, but still leaves Duterte the option of distancing himself from the potential debacle by dismissing it as nothing but a foolhardy maneuver of his predecessor.

UNSUSTAINABLE WATER USE IN UZBEKISTAN'S COTTON INDUSTRY

For generations cotton has remained the driving force behind Uzbekistan's agricultural economy that has made the country the world's 3nd largest exporter of cotton, creating a wealth of foreign exchange for the Uzbek government. Much of the cotton exports are destined for Europe. However, the cotton industry has not prospered without a deep cost, with the legacy of demise of the Aral Sea directly linked to irrigation projects built during the later stages of the Soviet era. Uzbekistan's large "monoculture" cotton industry has come under fire from a variety of international critics for its labor practices, especially is use of child labor, as well as for using cotton revenues to enrich the entrenched regime. The country has also bee criticized for resisting major land reform that could give Uzbek farmers more freedom to prosper from access to international markets. Instead the Uzbek government has only modified the state driven system of agriculture it inherited from the Soviet Union.

Cotton and other agricultural goods in Uzbekistan are threatened by a series of environmental and infrastructure risks that will put future rural prosperity and development at risk. The large irrigation system is literally falling apart due to neglect and gross mismanagement. Farmers must struggle to get enough water as leaks and illegal water diversions prevent half of the irrigated water from reaching its intended destination. Crop yields are also suffering from increasing salinization of the soil and flooding of fields and rising groundwater known as water logging. When combined with the future impact of climate change, worsening soil conditions will make farmers' lives increasing difficult in the naturally arid climate. This is an example of a mismanaged water system, and its consequences for regional cooperation and environmental sustainability.

State Run Industry

Unlike several of its Central Asian neighbors, Uzbekistan has held onto much of the Soviet era agricultural system, with centrally directed production quotas and government owned enterprises that control the marketing of cotton to international traders. The system is tightly run from top officials making it subject to many abuses, and international civil society groups have brought complaints of child labor and forced labor used to pick the annual fall cotton crop.

After independence, Uzbekistan moved from the Soviet system of collective farms to a cooperative setup where former state workers owned a share of the new company. Over time little changed in terms of farm management and the leases to the land are still owned by the state.

Likewise, production quotas for cotton still come from the central state officials, and failure to deliver on crop production quotas could lead to severe sanctions. The Uzbek government has only made limited efforts at land reform and developing private farms.

Despite its strategic importance to Uzbekistan, the cotton industry is in relative decline along with the broader agricultural sector. In the first decade of independence cotton production fell by 16 percent. The number of hectares of land committed to cotton has been more than cut in half since Soviet days and crop yields also fell by 17 percent in 2003, as a result of a drought in 2001, according to data from the Food and Agriculture Organization.

Irrigation accounts for 90 percent of Uzbekistan's agricultural production, and uses 85 percent of all water resources in the country, water that is coming from upstream countries via the Syr Darya and Amu Darya river basins. Water use for Uzbek cotton is extremely wasteful as it takes nearly twice the global average of water to grow a kilogram of cotton harvested, due to poor irrigation practices. The irrigated cotton crop has also been a source of tension between Tajikistan and Uzbekistan. Upstream country Tajikistan insists its downstream neighbor must abandoned cotton in favor of less water intensive crops like wheat, corn and vegetables. Uzbekistan argues it has reduced its cotton acreage as far as it can, and moreover that cotton provides its poor rural population with jobs and income. The country also emphasizes that cotton and irrigated agriculture is a vital element in Uzbek culture and ought to be preserved.

Recent droughts during the last decade have raised the question of water use and its intensity for the cotton crop. However, lack of management controls makes monitoring water use at the farm level largely a mystery. German researchers made an estimate water use for crops like cotton, wheat and rice. The study projected major losses of water in cotton fields. Overall, water irrigation on Uzbek farms was viewed as inefficient with water losses approaching 30 percent.

The Asian Development Bank is helping with an overhaul of Uzbekistan's water sector. The bank has identified major water management flaws such as overloaded water drainage and high groundwater levels which can damage agricultural land with high salt levels.

ADB identified a number of key reforms including a national program to measure water irrigation and establishment of water use fees as an incentive to efficient water use. Uzbekistan says it has experimented with using new drip irrigation technology that is far more water efficient. But to revamp the system for the 1.1 million hectares of cotton could cost $8 billion, far beyond the country's capacity to finance a transition.

Irrigation System in Rapid Decay

The water irrigation and drainage infrastructure is crumbling quickly across Central Asia Construction practices during the Soviet era were inferior and countries failed to pay for the maintenance of the system and farmers are too poor to pay for major repairs.

Making significant repairs to the current irrigation system would cost nearly $24 billion according to a 2000 World Bank estimate. Uzbekistan must find financing from the international community and an early proposal to fund repairs through the state budget was rejected by donor countries. A World Bank field assessment in 2001 found canals were in rapid decline. Many of the irrigation canals and bridges have become structurally unsound. Irrigation infrastructure had deteriorated the most in at the end of canal systems, where farmers struggle to get adequate water and suffer from high salt levels in the water, which destroys the productivity of the soils. Drains are often overgrown and not been repaired for many years.

In Uzbekistan, political influence plays a role in who get enough water for crops. Smaller farmers believed the wealthier farms and cooperatives get the water first. This is mostly because the state managed cooperatives grow the strategic crops of cotton and wheat and get top priority in water distribution. Private farmers, who grow a more diverse number of crops are a lower priority for water and suffered during droughts and water shortages. Poor environmental management of the water system has led to salinization of the soil, which harms crop productivity. Higher salt levels come from the irrigated water in downstream countries and higher groundwater levels associated with water logging The Asian Development Bank has noted nearly half of all land in Uzbekistan has become salinized. Cotton yields can fall from a range of 20 percent to 80 percent on highly salinized land. Crop land also been abandoned in growing numbers because it simply become unproductive. A quarter of all farmland in some districts has been taken out of production due to increasing salt levels. Aggressive production targets have also contributed to salinization and lost income for farmers in Uzbekistan. Farmers with degraded soils have trouble meeting state quotas for cotton and wheat. They lose income as yields fall. Meanwhile government production quotas did not change, and sometimes were increased from year to year.

International institutions like the Asian Development Bank and the Global Environmental Facility have responded to the growing crisis of land degradation in Central Asia. A regional strategy was established in 2006 under the Central Asian Countries Initiative for Land Management (CACILM). It aims to boost rural incomes through investments in soil conservation and improved land management. Uzbekistan got a $3 million grant for land rehabilitation for salt damaged areas and improved conservation practices.

COLD WAR IN THE PACIFIC: CHINA ESCALATES TENSIONS WITH NEIGHBOURS

If it were only a matter of distance, the solution to a dispute over a small group of hotly contested islands in the East China Sea would be simple. Taiwan, which is just 200 kilometres (125 miles) away from the islands, would take the prize. The Chinese mainland is farther off, at 330 kilometres away, and the Japanese island of Okinawa even more distant, at 400 kilometres. Why then shouldn't small Taiwan take control of the five uninhabited islands and three rock outcroppings, known as the Diaoyu in China and Senkaku in Japan?

While Taiwan does lay claim to the islands, so do its more powerful neighbours, China and Japan. And the dispute is, unfortunately, not about distance.

It has to do with influence and natural resources, with hegemony and nationalism, and with bitter historical memories and fresh, global aspirations — in short, it's a toxic mixture of geopolitics. In fact, a military crisis is brewing in East Asia — one that is being played out hundreds to thousands of kilometres away from these desolate islands.

A NEW AIR DEFENCE ZONE

In Beijing, 1,600 kilometres to the northwest of the islands, the Defence Ministry announced a surprise decision a week ago Saturday to establish an air defence identification zone in the East China Sea. The ministry said all aircraft that fly into the defined area will now be required to declare their intentions and adhere to the orders of Chinese air traffic controllers.

Two days later in Washington, 12,500 kilometres to the east of the disputed islands, US President Barack Obama challenged the Chinese move by sending two unarmed B-52 long-range bombers into the new zone. The aircraft took off from an air force base on the American island of Guam and, a few hours later, penetrated the Chinese surveillance zone without notifying Beijing. B-52s are designed to carry nuclear bombs to their targets. It was a strong signal.

When news of these US flights broke, it boosted confidence in Tokyo (1,800 kilometres away from the islands) and in Seoul (1,400 kilometres away). Since then, Japan and South Korea have also dispatched military aircraft into the Chinese zone. China responded by placing its air force on alert and sending up fighter jets to escort Japanese and American planes. The situation begs an obvious question: What happens if a foreign fighter jet and a Chinese interceptor meet and one of the pilots loses his nerve?

Strategic Obsession

All of the players involved — except China — have concluded that Beijing's actions could jeopardize peace in East Asia. All it takes is for someone to make a sudden move. According to the *Financial Times*, retired Admiral William Fallon, the former commander of US armed forces in the Pacific, called the dispute "absolutely unnecessary," adding that "If you send up fighters, it is another opportunity for people to screw up."

His comment was apparently aimed at all the parties involved: the Chinese, the Japanese, the South Koreans and the Americans.

This week, US Vice President Joe Biden is set to visit Beijing. This was initially intended to be a relaxed meeting with President Xi Jinping, whom Biden knows well.

But instead Obama's deputy now has to consider some serious questions: Could the Far East actually stumble into a war? What is driving the parties involved in this island dispute, which has been smoldering for decades, and is now threatening to become extremely dangerous? And what can the US do to avert an escalation?

China's motives in this conflict are clear: One year ago, the country surpassed the US as the world's largest trading nation, and 90 percent of Chinese exports are shipped by sea.

At the same time, the rapidly growing country has been racing to establish its naval presence, just as the German Empire did over 100 years ago. Yet it bothers Beijing's military leaders that Chinese access to the Pacific is blocked by a chain of islands and peninsulas that are controlled by American allies. The so-called "first island chain" has become a strategic obsession for the Chinese. China's navy celebrates maneuvers in which its ships sail out into the Pacific — as the aircraft carrier *Liaoning* did last week — as the "breakthrough" of this chain. Right in the middle of this chain, only 600 kilometres from the bustling port of Shanghai, lie the Diaoyu/Senkaku islands.

In the eyes of China's military, logic dictates that the country should gradually expand its airspace to include these islands; they view all objections from competitors as pure envy. "America is applying a double standard," says Chinese Major General Lou Yuan.

"The US has surrounded itself with exclusion zones and demands of others that they identify themselves. Yet their aircraft refuse to call in. This is totally overbearing!"

The strategic fixation with the islands has also become a political one that extends beyond the narrow sphere of the military. Many mainstream bloggers in the country also vehemently criticize China's biggest rival, while supporting China's alleged right to self-assertion. "The Americans are like spoiled teenagers," writes blogger Jiangchen-jc, who argues that "they have to challenge others in order to prove their uniqueness."

The timing is most convenient for China's new political leadership. By taking a hardline approach on foreign and defence policy, it can now silence critics who suspected that the government had become too liberal with recent sweeping economic and social reforms.

DEMONSTRATING CHINESE RESOLVE

China's simplest means of demonstrating its resolve in the current nationalistic climate in East Asia is to take a tough stance against Japan. Neither the perpetrators nor the victims have come to terms with the years of occupation — and the war crimes committed — by the Japanese on Chinese soil during World War II. It is easy for China's leaders to score political points against the Japanese in a bout of saber-rattling.

Meanwhile, Tokyo is reveling in the US show of strength in the Pacific, taking it as a sign of solidarity. From Japan's perspective, China's efforts to expand its air defence zone have backfired. Beijing's unilateral action instead forced the Americans to more declaratively take sides with the Japanese in the ongoing island dispute. The Obama administration had generally refrained from getting too deeply involved in the conflict. And even though the White

House left little doubt last week that the Senkaku islands fall under the protection of the US-Japanese military alliance, it also stopped short of overtly taking sides with Japan.

Furthermore, thanks to its own flyover, the US Air Force preempted a Japanese reaction, which Beijing might have responded to in a more aggressive manner. Japan, which maintains a strong, highly advanced army, would prove to be a significant opponent for China in the event of an outright military conflict. What's more, Japanese Prime Minister Shinzo Abe has expressed a desire to water down his country's strictly pacifist constitution.

US 'Pivots' to Asia

In 2011, Obama announced a "pivot" to the Asia-Pacific region, shifting the American approach to China. The move was seen as a way of not only continuing US cooperation with China, but also containing Beijing's power in the region. "As a Pacific nation, the United States will play a larger and long-term role in shaping this region and its future," Obama said.

US reengagement in the Asia-Pacific also referred to America's military presence. General Martin Dempsey, chairman of the Joint Chiefs of Staff and Obama's chief military adviser says, "The US military will be obliged to overtly confront China as it faced down the Soviet Union." By 2020, the Pentagon intends to station roughly 60 percent of its naval military forces in the Pacific, including six aircraft carriers and numerous destroyers, cruisers and submarines. In 2011, the US began to expand its military presence in Australia, the first US military buildup in the Pacific since the Vietnam War. In the future, up to four US warships will be allowed to moor in the city-state of Singapore. Since 2011, former wartime opponent Vietnam has allowed the US Navy to use the port of Cam Ranh Bay.

Meanwhile, the Philippines are likely to become America's most important partner in a separate, but similar, conflict over disputed islands in the South China Sea. Some 40 percent of international maritime trade passes through those contested waters.

Washington and Manila have been negotiating since August on stationing more US Marines in the country. Filipino Defence Secretary Voltaire Gazmin has already announced that the US will in the future inform his country's armed forces if Chinese ships enter territorial waters claimed by Manila. In exchange, US warships will soon be able return to Subic Bay, a Filipino naval station that the US Navy vacated in 1992.

Lessons from Europe?

The growing US military presence is intended to reassure America's closest Asian allies, but China views US encroachment in the region as a threat. When Vice President Biden travels through the region this week, he will have to maintain a delicate balance: He has to reassure US allies, yet at the same time caution them not to overreact. He also has to warn China over its provocative air defence zone, while maintaining an ongoing relationship between the two world powers.

After all, Europeans know all too well how quickly even rational foreign policy actors can find themselves enmeshed in irrational chain reactions in times of crisis. Historians and politicians have been discussing the similarities between China's current situation and the international stage prior to the outbreak of World War I for years.

American political scientist Robert Kagan says that Washington has taken on the role of the British Empire in East Asia, and the US must make it clear to Beijing — "which is the Germany of the time" — that it "will in fact respond if China behaves in a way that seems unacceptable."

In his bestseller "The Sleepwalkers," which describes how Europe entered the bloody catastrophe of World War I, historian Christopher Clark comments on today's global order: "Since the end of the Cold War, a system of *bipolar stability* has made way for a more complex and unpredictable array of forces, including declining empires and rising powers — a state of affairs that invites comparison with the Europe of 1914," he writes.

4

Water Crisis

When there is not enough potable water for a given population, the threat of a *water crisis* is realized. The United Nations and other world organizations consider a variety of regions to have water crises of global concern. Other organizations, such as the Food and Agriculture Organization, argue that there are no water crises in such places, but steps must still be taken to avoid one.

Causes of Water Crisis

There are several principal manifestations of the water crisis.

- Inadequate access to safe drinking water for about 884 million people
- Inadequate access to water for sanitation and waste disposal for 2.5 billion people
- Groundwater overdrafting (excessive use) leading to diminished agricultural yields
- Overuse and pollution of water resources harming biodiversity
- Regional conflicts over scarce water resources sometimes resulting in warfare

Waterborne diseases and the absence of sanitary domestic water are one of the leading causes of death worldwide. For children under age five, waterborne diseases are the leading cause of death. At any given time, half of the world's hospital beds are occupied by patients suffering from waterborne diseases. According to the World Bank, 88 percent of all waterborne diseases are caused by unsafe drinking water, inadequate sanitation and poor hygiene.

Water is the underlying tenuous balance of safe water supply, but controllable factors such as the management and distribution of the water supply itself contribute to further scarcity.

A 2006 United Nations report focuses on issues of governance as the core of the water crisis, saying "There is enough water for everyone" and "Water insufficiency is often due to mismanagement, corruption, lack of appropriate institutions, bureaucratic inertia and a shortage of investment in both human capacity and physical infrastructure". Official data also shows a clear correlation between access to safe water and GDP per capita.

It has also been claimed, primarily by economists, that the water situation has occurred because of a lack of property rights, government regulations and subsidies in the water sector, causing prices to be too low and consumption too high. Vegetation and wildlife are fundamentally dependent upon adequate freshwater resources. Marshes, bogs and riparian zones are more obviously dependent upon sustainable water supply, but forests and other upland ecosystems are equally at risk of significant productivity changes as water availability is diminished. In the case of wetlands, considerable area has been simply taken from wildlife use to feed and house the expanding human population. But other areas have suffered reduced productivity from gradual diminishing of freshwater inflow, as upstream sources are diverted for human use. In seven states of the U.S. over 80 percent of all historic wetlands were filled by the 1980s, when Congress acted to create a "no net loss" of wetlands.

In Europe extensive loss of wetlands has also occurred with resulting loss of biodiversity. For example many bogs in Scotland have been developed or diminished through human population expansion. One example is the Portlethen Moss in Aberdeenshire.

On Madagascar's highland plateau, a massive transformation occurred that eliminated virtually all the heavily forested vegetation in the period 1970 to 2000. The slash and burn agriculture eliminated about ten percent of the total country's native biomass and converted it to a barren wasteland. These effects were from overpopulation and the necessity to feed poor indigenous peoples, but the adverse effects included widespread gully erosion that in turn produced heavily silted rivers that "run red" decades after the deforestation. This eliminated a large amount of usable fresh water and also destroyed much of the riverine ecosystems of several large west-flowing rivers. Several fish species have been driven to the edge of extinction and some, such as the disturbed Tokios coral reef formations in the Indian Ocean, are effectively lost. In October 2008, Peter Brabeck-Letmathe, chairman and former chief executive of Nestlé, warned that the production of biofuels will further deplete the world's water supply.

Overview of Regions Suffering Crisis Impacts

There are many other countries of the world that are severely impacted with regard to human health and inadequate drinking water. The following is a partial list of some of the countries with significant populations (numerical population of affected population listed) whose only consumption is of contaminated water:

- Sudan 12.3 million
- Venezuela 5.0 million
- Ethiopia 2.7 million
- Tunisia 2.1 million
- Cuba 1.3 million.

According to the California Department of Resources, if more supplies aren't found by 2020, the region will face a shortfall nearly as great as the amount consumed today. Los Angeles is a coastal desert able to support at most 1 million people on its own water; the Los Angeles basin now is the core of a megacity that spans 220 miles (350 km) fromSanta Barbara to the Mexican border. The region's population is expected to reach 41 million by 2020, up from 28 million in 2009.

The population of California continues to grow by more than two million a year and is expected to reach 75 million in 2030, up from 49 million in 2009. But water shortage is likely to surface well before then.

Water deficits, which are already spurring heavy grain imports in numerous smaller countries, may soon do the same in larger countries, such as China and India. The water tables are falling in scores of countries (including Northern China, the US, and India) due to widespread overpumping using powerful diesel and electric pumps. Other countries affected include Pakistan, Iran, and Mexico. This will eventually lead to water scarcity and cutbacks in grain harvest. Even with the overpumping of its aquifers, China is developing a grain deficit. When this happens, it will almost certainly drive grain prices upward. Most of the 3 billion people projected to be added worldwide by mid-century will be born in countries already experiencing water shortages. Unless population growth can be slowed quickly, it is feared that there may not be a practical non-violent or humane solution to the emerging world water shortage.

After China and India, there is a second tier of smaller countries with large water deficits — Algeria, Egypt, Iran, Mexico, and Pakistan. Four of these already import a large share of their grain. But with a population expanding by 4 million a year, they will also likely soon turn to the world market for grain.

According to a UN climate report, the Himalayan glaciers that are the sources of Asia's biggest rivers – Ganges, Indus, Brahmaputra, Yangtze, Mekong, Salween and Yellow – could disappear by 2035 as temperatures rise. It was later revealed that the source used by the UN climate report actually stated

2350, not 2035. Approximately 2.4 billion people live in the drainage basin of the Himalayan rivers. India, China, Pakistan, Bangladesh, Nepal and Myanmar could experience floods followed by droughts in coming decades. In India alone, the Ganges provides water for drinking and farming for more than 500 million people. The west coast of North America, which gets much of its water from glaciers in mountain ranges such as the Rocky Mountains and Sierra Nevada, also would be affected.

By far the largest part of Australia is desert or semi-arid lands commonly known as the outback. In June 2008 it became known that an expert panel had warned of long term, possibly irreversible, severe ecological damage for the whole Murray-Darling basin if it does not receive sufficient water by October. Water restrictions are currently in place in many regions and cities of Australia in response to chronic shortages resulting from drought. The Australian of the year 2007, environmentalist Tim Flannery, predicted that unless it made drastic changes, Perth in Western Australia could become the world's first ghost metropolis, an abandoned city with no more water to sustain its population. However, Western Australia's dams reached 50% capacity for the first time since 2000 as of September 2009. As a result, heavy rains have brought forth positive results for the region. Nonetheless, the following year, 2010, Perth suffered its second-driest winter on record and the water corporation tightened water restrictions for spring.

THE RISKS ARISING FROM ASIA'S WATER STRESS

Water, the most vital of all resources, has emerged as a key issue that would determine if Asia is headed toward cooperation or competition. After all, the driest continent in the world is not Africa but Asia, where availability of freshwater is not even half the global annual average of 6,380 cubic metres per inhabitant.

When the estimated reserves of rivers, lakes, and aquifers are added up, Asia has less than one-tenth of the waters of South America, Australia and New Zealand, not even one-fourth of North America, almost one-third of Europe, and moderately less than Africa per inhabitant. Yet the world's fastest-growing demand for water for food and industrial production and for municipal supply is in Asia, which now serves as the locomotive of the world economy.

Today, the fastest-growing Asian economies are all at or near water-stressed conditions, including China, India, South Korea, Vietnam, and Indonesia. But just three or four decades ago, these economies were relatively free of water stress. Now if we look three or four decades ahead, it is clear that the water situation will only exacerbate, carrying major implications for rapid economic growth and inter-riparian relations.

Most Number of Dams

Asia is not just the global irrigation hub; it is also the world's most dam-dotted continent. China, the world's biggest dam builder, alone has slightly more than half of the approximately 50,000 large dams on the planet.

Most of the best dam sites in Asia already have been taken. Yet the numerous new dam projects in Asia show that the damming of rivers is still an important priority for policymakers. Such a focus on dam building has only intensified intrastate and interstate water disputes and tensions in Asia, with implications for regional security and stability.

The countries likely to bear the brunt of upstream diversion of waters are those located farthest downstream on rivers like the Brahmaputra, Mekong, and Tigris-Euphrates: Bangladesh, whose very future is threatened by climate and environmental change; Vietnam, a rice bowl of Asia; and Iraq, still internally torn.

Cross-border water appropriations from the Illy River threaten to turn Kazakhstan's Lake Balkhash into another Aral Sea, which is dying.

A Way Out

So, the big question is: How can Asian nations prevent the sharpening struggle for water resources from becoming a tipping point for overt conflict? To contain the security risks, Asian states must invest more in institutionalised cooperation on transboundary basin resources in order to underpin strategic stability, protect continued economic growth, and promote environmental sustainability.

The harsh truth is that only four of the 57 transnational river basins in Asia have a treaty covering water sharing or other institutionalised cooperation. These are the Mekong, Ganges, Indus and Jordan river basins. The absence of a cooperative arrangement in most Asian transnational basins is making inter-country water competition a major security risk, increasing the likelihood of geopolitical tensions and instabilities.

With its multitude of inter-country basins, Asia cannot continue to prosper without building political and technological partnerships to help stabilise inter-riparian relations, encourage greater water efficiency, promote environmental sustainability, take on practicable conservation strategies, and invest in clean-water technologies. If Asian states are to address their water challenges, they will need to embrace good practices on the strategic planning and management of water resources.

Rising Security Risks

With increasingly fierce intra- and inter-state water competition, the risk of water conflict is higher in Asia than elsewhere in the world.

Water is a new arena in the Asian Great Game. In fact, political, diplomatic or economic 'water wars' are already being waged between riparian neighbours in several parts of Asia, fuelling a cycle of bitter recrimination and fostering mistrust that impedes broader regional cooperation and integration. The resources of transnational rivers, aquifers and lakes have become targets of rival appropriation plans. Securing larger portions of shared resources has become a flashpoint in inter-country relationships; there is no incentive to conserve or protect supplies for users beyond national borders, unless there are specific water-sharing arrangements in place.

With a particular river or groundwater basin often tied into a country's identity and self-image, ownership and control over such resources can be perceived as crucial to national interest. This has helped give rise to grand but environmentally questionable ideas: China's Great Western Route to divert river waters from the Tibetan Plateau to its parched north; South Korea's politically divisive Four Rivers Project; India's proposal to link up its important rivers; and Jordan's plan to save the shrinking Dead Sea by bringing water from the Red Sea through a 178-kilometre-long canal (which is also to serve as a source for desalinated drinking water).

India's river-linking plan was conceived by a poet prime minister, which may explain why it never took off and was abandoned by the current government. In contrast, the Great Western Route plan was conceived by the engineers who dominate China's top political leadership.

Asia's water map fundamentally changed after the 1949 Communist victory in China. Most of the continent's important international rivers originate in territories that the People's Republic of China either forcibly annexed or reasserted Chinese control over. The annexed Tibetan Plateau, for example, is the world's largest freshwater repository and the source of Asia's greatest rivers, including those that are the lifeblood of mainland China and South and Southeast Asia. Other such Chinese territories contain the headwaters of rivers such as the Irtysh, Illy and Amur, which flow to Russia and Central Asia.

This makes China the source of cross-border water flows to more countries than any other upstream power in the world. Beijing now controls the headwaters of more than a dozen important international river basins. Yet China rejects the notion of water sharing or institutionalized cooperation with downstream countries. Whereas riparian neighbours in Southeast and South Asia are bound by water pacts that they have negotiated between themselves, China does not have a single water treaty with any coriparian country.

For example, it is a dialogue partner but not a member of the Mekong River Commission, suggesting a desire to listen to discussions among other basin states without agreeing to abide by the commission's rules or taking on legal obligations by becoming a party to the 1995 Mekong Treaty. Moreover, while promoting multilateralism on the world stage, China has given the cold shoulder to multilateral cooperation among river-basin states. The lower Mekong countries view China's strategy as an attempt to divide and conquer. It is hardly a surprise, then, that China is at the centre of much of the current water-related tension in Asia.

Although China publicly favours bilateral initiatives over multilateral institutions in addressing water issues, it has not shown any real enthusiasm for meaningful bilateral action. As a result, water has become a new political issue in the country's relations with neighbours such as India, Kazakhstan, Nepal and Russia. China deflects attention from its refusal to share water, or to enter into institutionalized cooperation to manage common rivers sustainably, by promoting the accords it has signed on sharing flow statistics with riparian neighbours. These are not agreements to cooperate on shared resources, but rather commercial accords to sell hydrological data that other upstream countries provide free to downriver states.

Beyond China, there are water tensions between India and Pakistan, among the Central Asian nations, between Turkey and its downriver neighbours, and between Israel and the Palestinians. But given China's unique riparian position and role, it will not be possible to transform Asian water competition into cooperation without its active participation.

Internal water disputes are also rife across the continent. The lopsided availability of water within some Asian nations (abundant in some areas but deficient in others) has given rise to plans for mega-dam projects or grand diversion structures, which have run into stiff grassroots opposition over issues of population displacement and submergence of land. To compound matters, governmental or commercial decisions on where to set up new manufacturing or energy plants are increasingly being influenced by local availability of adequate water resources.

Where availability is already low, a decision to establish a new plant often triggers local protests because it is likely to spur greater competition over scarce water resources. It has become virtually impossible to site nuclear power plants along freshwater bodies in water-scarce Asia, the centre of the so-called global nuclear renaissance. These water-guzzling plants must instead be built on coastlines where they can rely on seawater for their operations. Yet, Fukushima has served as a warning of the vulnerability of coastal nuclear facilities to extreme events, which are likely to become more common as the climate changes. Water conflict within nations, especially those that are multi-ethnic and culturally diverse, often assumes ethnic or sectarian dimensions, accentuating internal security challenges. Such intrastate water disputes rarely get the kind of international attention that interstate discords do, but as the internal conflicts in Yemen and Afghanistan show, recurrent drought and water scarcity can poison inter-ethnic or inter-sectarian relations and trigger bloodletting. Endemic local conflicts over water in some drought-ridden areas in Asia have even led villagers to engage security guards to protect their sources of freshwater, such as wells or water trucks. Asia's experiences over the past quarter century show that internal water conflicts tend to be more damaging and violent than disputes between countries.

WATER CRISIS IN CENTRAL ASIA

Freshwater is a vital element for human life and global civilization. River flows traveling between countries in a common basin has been a source of tension between states, but it has also contributed to unifying regions. The dualistic nature of transboundary waters carries a lesson of international cooperation in an increasingly globalized world. In 2001, former United Nations Secretary General Kofi Annan stated that "fierce competition for freshwater may well become a source of conflict and wars in the future," especially in politically volatile regions like the Middle East. However, many countries in politically unstable regions have found ways to cooperate and have created joint water management regimes to resolve tension over cross-boundary freshwater.

The Transboundary Freshwater Dispute Database (TFDD) at Oregon State University (OSU) has identified 263 water basins that cross national boundaries, which cover over 40 percent of the world's population. Since World War II, over 157 water treaties have been signed between riparian countries to cooperate and deal with complexities of joint water bodies. However, it often requires years of negotiations and support from the international community to craft these agreements. Over the years, effective agreements with processes to settle disputes have been put into effect in the Indus River (India-Pakistan) and the Mekong River Basin (Southeast Asia) and progress is being made in managing tensions between upstream and downstream countries along the Nile River in Africa.

The TFDD has cataloged more than 1800 water related events between countries over the last half century and findings suggest that most interactions between countries were mild and cooperative, rather than leading to open conflict. In fact, the last "water war" was in 2500 BC among rival city-states bordering the Tigris and Euphrates Rivers.Since World War II, two-thirds of water contacts between countries were cooperative and most were verbal, either supportive or negative without any government sanction involved.

Water is more likely to lead to localized conflict and violence on an intrastate level rather than between sovereign states. In the broad quantitative study of these events, OSU researchers found that water can act as an "irritant" to degrade relations between countries or as a "unifier" to create a more regional focus on water management in spite of wars and hostile relations between neighboring countries. Over time, effective water agreements share a number of important qualities. These include adaptive management structures, clear and flexible rules for water allocation and management, equal distribution of benefits, conflict resolution and enforcement mechanisms. Moreover, the trend shows that transboundary water agreements are negotiated in an atmosphere shifting from a "rights based" stance to a "needs based" practical approach. It has been crucial to identify shared benefits in transboundary water agreements as was accomplished in the agreement between the United States and Canada in the 1960s. This agreement established flood control for both neighboring states and gave Canada the right to divert water from the Columbia River for hydropower.

In order to govern transboundary waters, the international community needs a global framework convention, which has yet to be accomplished. In 1997, the United Nations General Assembly passed the Convention on the Non-Navigational Uses of International Watercourses. Yet, the convention was never ratified. It faced opposition from upstream countries like China and Turkey and many of its provisions were considered overly vague. Upstream and downstream countries were also conflicted about how it treated basic concepts of international law.

The UN Watercourses treaty was also overshadowed by the decision by the International Court of Justice in 1997, to uphold a twenty year old agreement between Hungry and Czechoslovakia in a case known at the Gabcikovo-Nagymaros Project. The court stopped the post-Communist governments of Hungary and Slovakia from abandoning a management agreement for a system of locks on the Danube River. The ICJ ordered the two riparian countries to increase cooperation including creating a joint regime to manage the project on the Danube River.

Nevertheless, a number of regional transboundary water agreements have emerged in recent years. Prominent examples of such treaties can be found in Southern Africa and Europe. In Europe, the Convention on the Protection and Use of Transboundary Watercourses and International Lakes was ratified by the United Nations Economic Commission for Europe (UNECE) and came into effect in 1996. This treaty is regarded as very robust. UNECE has also developed a number of new programs to increase cooperation, including the International Water Assessment Center, and National Policy Dialogues in former Communist countries.

Active engagement by the international community clearly makes a difference in advancing cooperation among countries over international waters. In a number of cases the World Bank and the Global Environment Facility have helped develop regional water sharing agreements, as have various UN agencies like the United Nations Development Programme (UNDP) and the United Nations Environment Programme (UNEP). It may take decades of engagement and active diplomacy, but the wide range of success in water cooperation has emerged in every corner of the globe. This is an encouraging sign in an age of climate change when water conflicts are likely to grow more combative, which in turn may increase the need for international mediation in water disputes worldwide.

GLOBAL EXPERIENCES IN MANAGING WATER CRISIS

It is alleged that the likelihood of conflict rises if the rate of change within the basin exceeds the capacity of institution to absorb that change. Although water crisis is closely related to regional tensions, history showed that acute conflicts over water are far less than the record of cooperation.

The key lies in strong institutions and cooperation. The Indus River Commission and the Indus Water Treaty survived two wars between India and Pakistan despite their hostility, proving to be a successful mechanism in resolving conflicts by providing a framework for consultation inspection and exchange of data. The Mekong Committee has also functioned since 1957 and survived the Vietnam War. In contrast, regional instability results when there is an absence of institutions to co-operate in regional collaboration, like Egypt's plan for a high dam on the Nile. However, there is currently no global institution in place for the management and management of trans-boundary water sources, and international co-operation has happened through ad hoc collaborations between agencies, like the Mekong Committee which was formed due to an alliance between UNICEF and the US Bureau of Reclamation. Formation of strong international institutions seems to be a way forward – they fuel early intervention and management, preventing the costly dispute resolution process.

One common feature of almost all resolved disputes is that the negotiations had a "need-based" instead of a "right–based" paradigm. Irrigable lands, population, technicalities of projects define "needs". The success of a need-based paradigm is reflected in the only water agreement ever negotiated in the Jordan River Basin, which focuses in needs not on rights of riparians. In the Indian subcontinent, irrigation requirements of Bangladesh determine water allocations of The Ganges River. A need based, regional approach focuses on satisfying individuals with their need of water, ensuring that minimum quantitative needs are being met. It removes the conflict that arises when countries view the treaty from a national interest point of view, move away from the zero-sum approach to a positive sum, integrative approach that equitably allocated the water and its benefits.

The Blue Peace framework developed by Strategic Foresight Group in partnership with the Governments of Switzerland and Sweden offers a unique policy structure which promotes sustainable management of water resources combined with cooperation for peace. By making the most of shared water resources through cooperation rather than mere allocation between countries, the chances for peace can be increased. The Blue Peace approach has proven to be effective in cases like the Middle East and theNile basin.

COLLECTIVELY ADDRESSING WATER SECURITY

Water security encompasses a society's ability to safeguard access to quality water to support livelihoods, health, power generation and industrial growth. Considering the unique geographic advantage of South Asia's many major river basins, most notably the Indus, Ganges and Tsangpo-Brahmaputra to name a few, water scarcity and security would not appear at first glance to be a source of a such raging debate. Nevertheless, the main challenges arise from the perennial gap between scarce supply and the demands of a massive population along with the transboundary nature of the water resources. The international Ganges-Brahmaputra-Meghna basin and the Indus basin drain approximately half of the region, and hence any and every solution towards mitigating the cascading effects of water stress must arise via collaborative management.

Despite shared concerns over the inevitable threat of water scarcity, neighboring — and historically adversarial — countries have found it difficult to collectively curate effective agreements over efficient water resource management within international river basins. In the absence of guiding frameworks, controversy plagues hydro-political relationships. Downstream countries frequently accuse their upstream counterparts of exploiting shared resources without any regard to the interest of their neighbors, perhaps most notably as Bangladesh has towards India's development of the Farrakah Barrage and the diversion of flows from the Ganges River. Conversely, upstream states dismiss such accusations on the grounds of exercising sovereign rights of usage. This has only exacerbated regional tensions and underlying security concerns.

The issue of water resource depletion and mismanagement is particularly acute in India and Pakistan. The region's aquifers number among the world's "most stressed," and the impacts of worsening climate change have engendered water supply uncertainties. Moreover, the problem is further aggravated by tense bilateral relationships and lackluster institutional responses. While certain joint mechanisms exist, such as the India-Pakistan Indus Waters Treaty of 1960 and India-Bangladesh Ganges Water Sharing Treaty of 1996, long-standing and seemingly intractable regional disputes have put a strain on these agreements.

For instance, there has always been a concern over the potential revocation of the Indus Water Treaty and Pakistan has time and again accused India of utilizing the water from Indus, Chenab and Jhelum for industrial activity in violation of the treaty, which in its present form only permits water usage of electricity generation. On the other hand, India continues to question the neutrality of certain arbitrating bodies working in favor of Pakistan's interests.

Water cooperation has also been a controversial issue between India and Nepal where a number of hydroelectric project agreements have been signed on major rivers, such as Kosi, Gandaki and Karnali yet there has been no execution.

THE WAY FORWARD

National governments and regional policy makers must address the incessant politicization of water resource management, and bring South Asia's water challenges to the forefront of what needs to be a strategic vision in order to make a measurable impact. Decades of geopolitical conflict—most prominently among India, Pakistan, and Bangladesh—have produced numerous obstacles which lie in the pursuit of this goal. A step-by-step approach in the necessary incremental process may be the most advisable solution. As such, the first step towards enabling effective hydro-political regimes to take root in South Asia would be for key regional players to ratify the United Nations Watercourses Convention (UNWC).

Upon gathering the requisite 35 ratifying signatures, the UNWC entered into force in 2014 and, as the first hydro-politically oriented United Nations treaty, codified numerous foundational legal principles regarding the utilization and allocation of transboundary water resources. In addition to functioning as a binding piece of international law for ratifying nations, the UNWC would also act as a depoliticized manual of legal best practices from which South Asia's riparian countries may draw in drafting fair and equitable multilateral and bilateral water sharing agreements.

While the UNWC has seen limited traction in the more water scarce and hydro-politically contentious regions, including the Middle East and South Asia, the treaty has already established several salient principles to which ratifying nations are held. Chief among these are the obligations to not "cause significant harm" to other watercourse states as well as the "reasonable and equitable use" of increasingly scarce water resources.

Building on this first step will not only give life to a more proactive sharing of transboundary hydrological data and information, but also empower accurate and effective risk and water sharing mechanisms. One such example would be the Integrated River Basin Management (IRBM) process. Advocated by the World Bank and World Wildlife Fund, IRBM encourages knowledge sharing, community mobilization and active stakeholder participation for transparent and fact based decision making towards water cooperation.

In addition to third party solicitation, equally essential are joint, information-based dialogues to enable a cooperative environment and productive outcomes for the region's collective interests. Frequent and targeted dialogues are necessary as way to help navigate and unpackage the range of complexities associated with water conservation and sharing, allowing decision makers to pool efforts, produce stronger consensus and determine synergies.

In sum and substance, addressing existing vulnerabilities and averting future water crises will require practical and clear strategies on all fronts. Such an undertaking will have positive spillover effects on overall regional welfare given the potential of hydro-political cooperation to serve as a mainstay of stability and trust-building between neighboring nations.

FRESHWATER TREATIES

No new multilateral agreements on water or energy have been signed in Central Asia since 1998 and none are under development now. Major existing agreements like the Almaty Agreement and the Syr Darya Framework Agreement are implemented poorly, largely due to the lack of co-ordination in national water policies and legislation across the region. Some of the Central Asian states (Kazakhstan, Kyrgyzstan and Tajikistan) have expressed a strong desire to develop new agreements that satisfy concepts of international watercourse law. However, there is still reluctance on the part of the major water using countries, Turkmenistan and Uzbekistan, to enter into discussions on this issue. One of the major problems in achieving regional co-operation in shared water resources in Central Asia will be to attract the attention of these countries to the ideas of international water law. In promoting consensus on principles of regional co-operation, a major role could belong to international donor agencies that may try to convince Uzbekistan and, in case of the Afghanistan situation in the Amu Darya basin, Turkmenistan that this is a serious problem that must be dealt with soon (McKinney, 2003).

River Boundaries

The border problem is among additional factors that could further worsen the water situation in Central Asia. The Soviet-made borders in Central Asia provide a continuous possibility for their redefinition (Gleason, 2001). There were several border incidents between Uzbekistan and its neighbours in the past when the former unilaterally commenced a survey of its border and moved its boundary posts, as happened in early 2000 when three hundred kilometres of Kazakhstan's territory suddenly appeared to be within Uzbekistan. After Kazakhstan objected, a bilateral demarcation commission was set up. As of early 2003, Uzbekistan's border disputes with Kazakhstan have been completely settled and border delimitation with Tajikistan and Kyrgyzstan was close to the end.

Particular problem in terms of border situation is Central Asia's two major rivers. Both Syr Darya and Amu Darya pass through several international borders, and in some parts the Turkmenistan border with Uzbekistan is defined by the watercourse of the Amu Darya. The border between Afghanistan and Uzbekistan is the Amu Darya, and one of the rivers that form the Amu Darya, the Pyandj, serves as the border between Tajikistan and Afghanistan. Toset, Gleditsch and Hegre (2000) define three types of relationship over the shared river resources: river boundary; mixed; and upstream/downstream. While the latter, in the authors' opinion, has a higher conflict potential, a river boundary situation, when a country on the left bank diverts water and a country on the right bank retaliates by taking water to its own side of the river, is no less serious. Navigation problems and transborder pollution add to the problem dramatically. It is argued that the longer the border, the more opportunities for potential contentious issues for conflict. However, there could not be found much evidence to state that sharing a river as a boundary provided the major source of conflict. In the Amu Darya case, a common border lying along the river watercourse may contribute to the generally tense relations both between downstream (Turkmenistan/Uzbekistan) and upstream (Afghanistan/Tajikistan) riparians.

Trade Complications

Trade issues between Tajikistan and Uzbekistan further complicate the relations between the two countries. Trade in staple goods like cotton, water, natural gas, and oil is conducted by state agencies. Thus, in case of failure to pay or any other irritation it is very convenient to suspend deliveries temporally, close border or increase visa requirements, as happened more than once. Furthermore, transborder trade, traditional and supporting many families in this area, is subject to now thawing, now frosting regional affairs. No single transborder trade regulatory regime exists between the Amu Darya riparians.

Sarez Lake: A Natural Threat to the Basin's Stability

On 6 February 1911, a powerful earthquake in the Pamir region of Gorny Badakhshan, in what is now Tajikistan, caused a 2.2 cubic kilometre piece of the Muzkol Range to collapse, sealing off the Murgab Gorge and creating a 500-metre natural dam. The new canyon became soon filled with water and formed the Sarez Lake, 75 kilometres long and 505 metres deep and containing 17 cubic kilometres of glacial water. Experts say that this unstable natural dam called the Usoy Obstruction after the name of a village buried under it could break as a result of an earthquake or landslide and release the water into the Pyandj. This would endanger millions of people in Tajikistan, Uzbekistan, Turkmenistan and Afghanistan. So far, efforts by the Tajik government to install the early warning system components on the dam, along the lake and downstream under the terms of an international tender were sustained locally, without getting other riparians involved. Rather relative stability in the Tajik mountains that still remember a devastating civil war in the 1990s call many good plans in question. The weakest point in any strategy concerning the Sarez Lake is funding which might be very significant. Tajikistan alone would never afford million-dollar project costs. Yet none of the Amu Darya riparians concerned is willing to consider the problem of the Sarez Lake its own.

Impact of International Law

With the advent of independence, Central Asian states have quickly become the parties, and in some cases ratified, the international environmental agreements and conventions such as the Convention on Biological Diversity, the Convention to Combat Desertification, and the United Nations Framework Convention on Climate Change. However, no international convention related in either event to water has been acceded to, even to the Convention on Wetlands of International Importance Especially as Waterfowl Habitat, not to mention the Convention on the Law of the Non-Navigational Uses of International Watercourses. Only Kazakhstan is a party to the Convention on the Protection and Use of Transboundary Watercourses and International Lakes (Sievers, 2002).

Vinogradov and Langford (2001) argue that some regional water treaties (the 1998 Syr Darya Framework Agreement) do address the particularly sensitive issue of the water utilisation in the region and proceed from the interest in joint use of water resources to seeking common definitions and to acknowledging international legal principles relevant to the use of transboundary water resources, such as the provision referring to the joint management clause based on the "basin principle which provides for the equality of the parties' rights to use and responsibility to ensure rational utilisation and protection of the "common and integral water resources of the region. While this provision is certainly an improvement over earlier arrangements based on the concepts of water apportionment and "maximum utilisation, the principle of "equitable and reasonable utilisation and participation, in accordance with Article 5 of the UN Convention on the Law of the Non-Navigational Uses of International Watercourses, should be recognised. This principle takes into consideration such factors as geography, hydrographic, hydrological, climatic, ecological and other factors of a natural character; social and economic needs of a watercourse; the population dependent on the water resources; existing and potential uses; conservation, protection, development and economy of water resources use; and the availability of alternatives to a planned or existing use (UN, 1997).

Of particular importance for Central Asia's water resources are the principles of the 1997 UN Convention which include the obligation not to cause significant harm to other watercourse states (UN, 1997, art. 7); the general obligation to co-operate through joint mechanisms or commissions (Ibid., art. 8); to exchange information on a regular basis (Ibid., art. 9); and to provide timely notification of planned measures and emergency situations which may have a significant adverse effect upon other watercourse states (Ibid., arts. 12,28). Where significant harm nevertheless is caused to another state, the party responsible for causing such harm is obliged, in consultation with the affected state, to eliminate or mitigate such harm, and where appropriate, to discuss the question of compensation. However, none of Central Asian countries have ever acceded to the 1997 UN Convention.

Vox Populi?

Broad public participation and access to environmental information are essential in forming meaningful local water and environmental policy. The participation of non-governmental organisations (NGOs) who play important role in informing citizens of their opportunities to participate requires access to accurate and timely information. When the information about the state of the environment is available to citizens, they can express public opinion regarding various issues, particularly water use and environmental protection (McKinney, 2003). It is not a case, however, for the sealed societies such as Turkmenistan and Uzbekistan where access to any information, let alone environmental one, is severely restricted. Not surprisingly, these two states are not the parties to the 1998 UNECE Convention on Access to Information, Public Participation and Access to Justice in Environmental Matters (the Aarhus Convention), although other three Central Asian countries have acceded to it (Kyrgyzstan, Tajikistan) or ratified it (Kazakhstan).

Summing up Results

Six indicators used in the analysis were not sufficient to identify with exact accuracy a level of potential conflict over water in the Amu Darya Basin, yet some results.

Potential for conflict over water resources in the Amu Darya Basin remains to be high, despite one of the six indicators (population density) tends to run counter to this conclusion. This allows for the possibility to say that population density can be indicator of conflict only in such overpopulated places as the Ferghana Valley which has already seen outbreaks of violence in the past. On the country level, it is overall unfriendly relations fuelled by the leaders' personal competition, as well as rapid institutional change that could account for worsened water affairs in the region.

Over the last years, several new points of contention have arisen, particularly in the continuing tensions between Uzbekistan and Tajikistan over the Rogun Dam and between Uzbekistan and Turkmenistan around Golden Century Lake. Not in the nearest future though, the potential for further internationalisation - rapid rise of Afghanistan as a state and possible Karakalpakstan's claim for independence - could contribute to these tensions seriously and disintegrate the basin even further. In absence of solid legal base relevant to the international water law and mechanisms responsible for enforcing it, the region's tensions are deepening and threaten to destabilise not only Central Asia, but also neighbouring countries. The role of indicators of water conflict in identifying and, in future, measuring a basin's conflict proneness is critical for those who will be involved in resolving disputes over river freshwater. The water conflict indicators allow for identifying specific tasks to concentrate efforts on, such as legal and institutional aspects of Central Asia's water disputes, and pinpoint potential "apples of discord, such as big water infrastructure projects.

CONCLUSIONS AND RECOMMENDATIONS

While wasting water several times more than in the Middle East, people in Central Asia do not account for huge water diversions. In fact, it is agricultural sector and, more specifically, cotton growing that is to blame for the major anthropogenic loss of water from the Amu Darya. Downstream riparians – Uzbekistan and Turkmenistan, the region's major cotton producers, are unable to abandon cotton production because it is perhaps the only hard currency earning sector for them, in the absence of developed small sector regulations and, in case of Uzbekistan, of hard currency convertibility. With upstream riparians claiming the old Soviet water allocation schemes to be limiting the development of their own agriculture, downstream countries should reconsider their attitudes towards cotton and rice irrigation and embark on a real reform of small and medium sector, including farmland privatisation. Cotton is a root of evil in Central Asia, not its saviour from hardships of economic underdevelopment.

Central Asian governments did not give up their plans to develop the Soviet-style giant projects which are costly and environmentally devastating. It is fair to say that these would offer only short-term relief and would destabilise already fragile situation.

Tajikistan should terminate the contract with the Baltic Construction Company for the construction of the Rogun Dam. Turkmenistan should abandon the marantic idea of building the Golden Century Lake which is being built in the desert where water will simply evaporate. Any idea of diverting Siberian rivers to Central Asia should be immediately shelved as environmentally dubious and hugely expensive. It is time for Central Asia to think globally while acting locally.

Whereas Karakalpakstan is unlikely to secede from Uzbekistan today, this in no way lessens such a potential for the area in future. Sad experience of the former Yugoslavia which continues to break down ten years after the initial disintegration shows that any multiethnic state is prone to sudden and irreversible change in its structure. This is especially indicative of the former Soviet Union on which territory there are still several unrecognised statelets claiming their independence, and there will be more, as a result of arbitrary Soviet boundary planning. The priorities of people of Karakalpakstan should be taken into account when it comes to the water allocation and use, and a real Karakalpak autonomy enshrined in the Constitution of the Republic of Uzbekistan should be given to the region. Nonetheless, existing repressive regime in Uzbekistan is very unlikely to loose its grip on the Karakalpaks and tensions are expected to grow.

Given that Afghanistan's rehabilitation is unlikely without increasing its intake from the Amu Darya, Afghanistan's water demands will have to be taken into consideration when negotiating the water situation in the Basin. In promoting consensus on principles of regional co-operation, a major role could belong to international donor agencies that may try to convince Uzbekistan and Turkmenistan that the Afghanistan situation is a serious problem that must be dealt with soon. Interstate legislative co-ordination for the Amu Darya water resources should be tailored to fit sustainable development of the Amu Darya Basin before proceeding with reconstruction assistance in Afghanistan.

Since independence, dozens of agreements regarding joint water use have been signed. However, fewer agreements are implemented. Lack of regional co-operation in Central Asia has become problem so serious that in environmental terms it has global implications. Fearful of disrupting existing patterns of water use in their agricultural policies, two most stubborn riparians, Turkmenistan and Uzbekistan, claimed their commitment to bilateral relations.

One of the major problems in achieving regional co-operation in shared water resources in Central Asia will be to attract the attention of these countries to the ideas of international water law and to a multilateral approach. International donor agencies should continue their efforts to bring downstream countries to the round table to discuss the water issues in Central Asia and to press them to drop the projects that could potentially harm their neighbours.

That is possible only if adequate and sufficient information on the environment is available to any party concerned. Unless single information network regarding the state of the environment exists in Central Asia, with the reference to the Aarhus Convention, local repressive regimes will be certain about their last word in the never-ending story of Central Asian water crisis.

5

India and Pakistan Squaring Off Over Their Rivers

India's Wular Lake, a popular picnic and tourist spot nestled in the Kashmir Valley, is an unlikely site for conflict. But India's plan to build a structure on the Jhelum River at the mouth of the lake that will allow it to release water during the river's lean winter months has outraged neighboring Pakistan, which believes the project will give India the power to control how much water flows downstream to its farmers. After two and a half decades of deadlock and 15 marathon rounds of bilateral talks — the most recent occurring in late March — the countries appear a long way from finding common ground.

The dispute isn't the first of its kind, nor will it be the last. The waters of the Indus River and tributaries like the Jhelum — and the dams built on them by India — have long been one of the main points of contention between the rival neighbors, along with the disputed region of Kashmir itself and cross-border terrorism. Pakistan, whose agriculture-dominated economy is heavily reliant on the Indus and its tributaries, fears upstream dams allow India to manipulate the flows of water as it sees fit. Many in Pakistan accuse New Delhi of wantonly exacerbating the country's dire water shortages, choking its agricultural production and ruining livelihoods.

India dismisses these accusations as paranoid and without scientific backing. Its dams are run-of-the-river, it says, aimed at generating hydroelectricity, or in the case of the Tulbul navigation project on the Jhelum, meeting other development needs like facilitating year-round trade. India's Indus Water Commissioner G. Aranganathan says that after India fills its reservoirs in the initial stages of each project, it only uses the water it needs to run its turbines and doesn't prevent any from flowing into Pakistan. "There is absolutely no question of interrupting or reducing Pakistan's water supply," he tells TIME.

The countries' early leaders anticipated this fierce rivalry over the waters that straddle their volatile border. Following protracted and painstaking negotiations, they signed an accord in 1960 called the Indus Waters Treaty that determined exactly how the region's rivers are to be divided. In the treaty, control over the three "eastern" rivers — the Beas, Ravi and Sutlej — was given to India and the three "western" rivers — the Indus, Chenab and Jhelum — to Pakistan. More controversial, however, were the provisions on how the waters were to be shared. Since Pakistan's rivers flow through India first, the treaty allowed India to use them for irrigation, transport and power generation, while laying down precise do's and don'ts for Indian building projects along the way.

The treaty has been widely hailed as a success, having survived three post-independence wars between the hostile nuclear neighbors. But its resilience is increasingly being tested by challenges thrown up by the 21st century. For one, Pakistan is on the brink of water scarcity. Its once-lush agricultural fields, which employ half of all Pakistanis and account for a quarter of its GDP, are now frequently parched. This predicament, experts say, is attributable in large part to the country's haphazard water management policies, unproductive agricultural practices, dilapidated infrastructure and grossly inadequate water storage facilities. Climate change, too, has begun to have an impact. A recent Dutch study found that by 2050, shrinking glaciers are predicted to reduce the flows of the Indus by 8%. But in Pakistan, which is deeply distrustful of its larger and more powerful neighbor, the country's crippling water shortage is seen as a direct result of India's upstream dams and water projects.

Indeed, India has ramped up its hydroelectricity projects in recent years to try to boost its woefully inadequate power supplies. The government has a total of 45 projects either already completed or in the proposal stage on the western rivers, some as large as 1000 megawatt and many as small as 2 and 3 megawatt. This expansion has irked Islamabad. "India is putting more and more restrictions and constrictions on Pakistan's waters," Kamal Majidulla, Pakistani Prime Minister Yousuf Raza Gillani's special assistant on water resources and agriculture, tells TIME.

A 2011 U.S. Senate Foreign Relations Committee report said that studies show no single dam will affect Pakistan's access to water, but the cumulative effect of multiple hydroelectric projects could give India the ability to store enough water to limit Pakistan's supply at crucial moments in the growing season. India has never abused its water supplies in this way, the report adds, and New Delhi rejects the theory as an unsubstantiated hypothesis. But the report's observations serve as a suitable analogy for India and Pakistan's water conflicts overall. While no single legal or diplomatic tussle will rupture the fragile relations between the countries, the cumulative effect of a series of standoffs could cause tensions to boil over.

The countries have already been embroiled in two high-profile legal fights over water. In 2005, Pakistan challenged India's 450-megawatt Baglihar dam before a World Bank-appointed neutral expert and lost. And last year, the countries went head to head at the International Court of Arbitration over India's 330-megawatt Kishanganga project in Jammu and Kashmir. The court has ordered India to temporarily stop some constructions on the dam while assessments are being made. Pakistan is also considering arbitration to iron out differences over another dam — the Nimoo Bazgo — on the Indus.

"Unfortunately, we are going towards conflict and not conflict resolution," says Majidulla, who heads a body called the Pakistan Trans-border Water Organization, formed in September to monitor what he calls "increased activity" on the Indian side of the border. The countries' antagonistic political relationship has certainly not helped to ease their differences over water. "Given the mutual hostility between the two countries, it is not surprising that there is a tendency in Pakistan to believe that the scarcity it is experiencing or fearing is partly attributable to upper riparian actions," Ramaswamy Iyer, India's former secretary for water resources, wrote in an op-ed in the *Hindu* newspaper. At times, the rhetoric has even reached a fevered pitch, such as when Hafiz Saeed, head of the Pakistani militant group Jamaat-u-Dawa and alleged mastermind of the 2008 Mumbai attacks, whipped up public sentiment against India's so-called "water terrorism" in 2010 by using slogans like "water flows or blood." Few believe India and Pakistan will actually go to war over the disputes, but one thing is for certain: water is making it harder for the long-time rivals to put their enmity behind them.

WATER CONSERVATION BY DAMS AND THEIR UTILIZATION

Dams as means of storing large quantities of water have been constructed for the past m ore than a century in different parts of the worked. During the 20th century, a very large number of dams were built in the USA, China, Russia, India, Europe and other parts of the world. Many of these were multi-purpose projects providing irrigation, hydropower, flood control and other benefits to the society. The vast network of irrigation canals in India provided a security against severe water shortages and famines of the past.

Coupled with the adaptation of modem farming practices with high yielding varieties of seeds, fertilizers etc., a sort of Green Revolution took place in the irrigated areas of the country and sustained food production with the population growth. Hydropower provided a significant part of power requirements in Europe, USA and India. Drinking water requirements for several large cities and parts of rural areas were also met by these newly created storages.

Large dam projects like the Bhakra, Nagarjunasagar, Tungabhadra, Hirakud, Beas. Ramganga, Sharavathi and hundreds of other medium irrigation projects provided the immediate requirements of water and power in the early decades of the country's independence. The Bhakra and the Nagarjunasagar have performed specially well and supported the increase in agricultural production over a vast area. In south India, the dams built on the Cauvery River in the early part of this century have sustained agricultural production (specially rice) for more than half a century and these structures (Krishnarajasagar and Mettur Dams) are revered by the farmers and the people of this area. In south India, hydropower from storage dams has been the main stay of the power requirements of the states of Karnataka and Kerala for the last several decades.

Cost Aspects

The large dam projects constructed prior to 1975 in India and many of the developing countries were cost-effective to some extent. After the world oil crisis in the mid 70s, with the increase in fuel costs for operating construction machinery and in the manufacturing costs of cement and steel (which are energy intensive), the costs of construction of large dam projects with their canal systems etc. also increased significantly. The costs of land acquisition for these projects (both submerged and canal lands) also rose sharply. The costs per hectare of irrigation, which was about Rs. 8,000 prior to 1975. Rose to about Rs. 80.000 in the 1990s. The result of these as well as other factors like delays in construction, brought down the cost-effectiveness of new projects to near unacceptable levels. Indirect social benefits and support to food production (though at higher costs) necessitated the continuation of execution of these projects towards their completion.

Due to faulty planning, some of the mega-projects which could give benefits on stage-wise completion were not executed with such a thinking in mind. Huge public investments were tied up without the people getting any benefit for unduly long periods. The environmental and displacement aspects had to be addressed in a proper and satisfactory manner for which the machinery available with the executing agencies was inadequate. The stage-wise benefits which could be given to the people were not given effect to despite precedents of getting such benefits elsewhere.

Policies Needed for the Future

All mega-dam projects should be thoroughly examined for cost benefits by independent authorities and feasibility of satisfactory rehabilitation of those affected and feasibility of mitigation of environmental impacts. If after all the studies the project appears to be feasible, it should be split up into several stages so that the benefits to the community start accruing with a minimum of investment. If during the stage-wise execution of the project, any of the environmental or rehabilitation aspects cannot be resolved satisfactorily to all concerned, the project needs to be reviewed before proceeding further. It is also necessary that those getting affected by the project should be made stakeholders not only in the execution of the project but also in their | management all through the operational life of the project Part of the benefits from the project should accrue to the affected people on a continuous basis throughout the life of the project.

Community Participation

As stated above, it is imperative that the community getting displaced from any dam project should form a partner in the dam venture, not only during construction but also throughout the life of the dam and its operation. They should have a share of the benefits from the project in terms of land or other permanent assets in the project area as well as annual financial returns from the project (revenue from power, water etc.). The execution and management of these projects should not be done by government departments but by a corporation with representatives of various disciplines like jam builders, environment specialists, representatives of the displaced and the beneficiaries. Such a setup should be made before starting the project and agreement reached with the displaced by assuring them financial incentives as stated above. This will be somewhat similar to any marketable venture in me private sector. The government can plan, regulate the taking up of such dam ventures and monitor their operation subsequently. Such dam ventures for hydroelectric projects seem attractive since they have good returns over their long life.

Where large scale transfer of water over long distances to water-scarece areas are involved, such ventures may not profitable, and public investment may become necessary in the national interest. The Peninsular Rivers Linking Scheme in India contemplates long-distance large-scale water transfers from surplus areas to water-scarce areas, and falls in this category.

Other Solutions

Major dams are not required in many cases for meeting the water requirements of communities. Small or medium dams/barrages can meet the drinking water needs of towns and urban areas. These should be encouraged 'wherever "needed and feasible. However, the catchment areas of these medium dam projects should be declared protected areas and should be so maintained by catchment area treatment, watershed management and treatment of industrial effluents. The management should be in the hands of a multi-disciplinary empowered Authority consisting of representatives of the municipal, forest and water supply agencies, along with reputed NGOs/ experts. Adequate funds should be made available to the authority to fulfil its obligations effectively.

Recent Trends

For augmenting the increasing water requirements of cities and rural areas, Rain Water Harvesting using rooftops of large buildings and open premises appear feasible for many cities. A start is being made in a number of cities in India and it appears that a significant requirement of the cities' needs can be met during the rainy season at very economical costs. In Chennai, the scheme is already in operation with some success. Other cities like Bangalore, Hyderabad, New Delhi etc. are also planning to take up this scheme in a similar way. Large consumers of water can meet a good percentage of their requirements through this clean means. In areas, where recharging of ground water is needed, the harvesting or rainwater for this purpose appears a dire necessity. In parts of western India, water harvesting has been tried for rural areas along with watershed management and has had appreciable success unlike mega-dam projects which take a long time to give benefits; rainwater harvesting fulfills immediate augmentation of water. This is specially needed for urban and industrial users. It is also cost-effective.

Tank Irrigation

Tanks are small reservoirs built across the slopes of valleys to collect natural flows during the rainy season. In southern India, thousands of tanks dot the landscape. These tanks have been the sources of water for centuries, but most of them have lost their storage capacities due to silting and other causes. Even so, these tanks irrigate well over two million hectares in the states of Tamil Nadu and Kamataka. The renovation of these tanks to their original or higher capacity can provide much needed water for the village communities and also recharge the wells in their areas. Large-scale community participation can be generated in their renovation and maintenance by suitable funding and rewards. In this region, these tanks can supplement the existing dams for meeting the water requirements to a considerable extent. Schemes for renovation of these thousands of tanks need to be taken up in a phased manner. An institutional setup like a Tank Development Board backed with adequate finance can initiate this program with the active participation of the village— communities. Piece-meal attempts made by the existing government departments at renovation of a few tanks here and there in recent years have not had any large-scale impact. A well-drawn out program to renovate and maintain such large number of tanks in a period of a few years is needed.

Fish Production

Although large dams impede migration of certain varieties of fish, the lakes formed by the dams increase fish production enormously and provide livelihood to thousands of fishermen. In general, high production of fish has been observed in reservoirs where commercial fishing has been encouraged. The water quality in reservoirs is adequate for survival and growth of fish. The vast areas and volumes of water in the reservoirs provide additional habitats for aquatic life. In Indonesia, fishery development in two reservoirs provided livelihood to 7,500 families and produced 10,000 tonnes of fish during the year 1992. Revenues exceeded those of rice harvest from farmlands submerged. Further, it is said that 21,000 additional jobs were created for fish production, marketing etc. by extending the scheme to several reservoirs in the country.

In the Gobind Sagar Lake of Bhakra Dam in India, 1,500 families get their livelihood from fisheries in the reservoir. Many other dam reservoirs in India provide jobs for thousands of fishermen. Properly designed fish passages can help migration of fishes affected by construction of dams. This will be discussed later while describing requirements for new dams.

Future Requirements

Irrigation currently accounts for 70 of all water withdrawals in the world and is likely to be still the major consumer over the next 2-3 decades. Irrigation grew very fast between 1950 and 1975 (from 95 to 220 million hectare), but subsequently the growth has been much slower due to a variety of reasons including the utilisation all easily available sources and the higher costs of new irrigation projects. Future trends indicate that the increase in irrigated area will come through better management of water to some extent and by new projects.

Urban Water Requirements

Urbanisation is taking place rapidly in the developing countries of the world. In 1998, 39 of the world's population was urban and it is expected that the figure will reach 57% by 2020 and 70 % by the year 2050. In southern and western India, urbanisation is occurring rapidly and the demand for water for domestic and industrial use is increasing sharply. The requirements of more dams of medium and small storage will be mainly for meeting the municipal and industrial uses. It is estimated that well over 500 medium dams or barrages on small streams and rivers will be required to meet the water supplies for urban centres in the country. Fortunately, these dams barrages do not submerge areas more than those occurring during floods as they need small storages to meet the dry season water supply requirements.

Industrial requirements may be met to some extent by recycled water. There is already a water-saving trend in various water-intensive industries all over the world. Cooling water for thermal power plants is a substantial requirement and is being met through recycled water in many cases.

Rural Water Supplies for Drinking and Sanitation

International agencies have proposed 55 litres per person per day as the basic human requirement for drinking, sanitation, bathing etc. In the year 1990, based on this figure, over a billion people were below this line, mainly in development countries. Rural water supply requirements in developing countries are mostly met by ground water pumping through borewells etc. Ground water is also being used extensively for irrigation and may reach shortage levels in many parts of the world in the next couple of decades.

In developing countries, rural sanitation programmes are being taken up on a large scale and the requirements of water for this sector will also be considerable. The rural requirements for drinking and sanitation may in due course encroach into the irrigation supplies, thus resulting in requirements of additional storage. Recharging of ground water on a large scale has to be taken up in the same way as other development projects.

Small Hydroelectric Schemes

There is need to take up these schemes in large numbers as in China. Rural communities can meet their power requirements for water pumping from these schemes, as captive power plants for their own use. These schemes can be taken up wherever irrigation canals or small streams flow nearby the villages. Similarly, greater use of solar energy for meeting the water pumping requirements of rural areas is called for.

Changes Needed in Dam Projects and Water Management

Since quite a number of new dam projects are likely to be taken up in developing countries, certain changes need to be incorporated in the light of experience gained with existing dams. There is need for changes in dam designs:

1. Dam projects involving large-scale submergence of forests with bio-diversity (which cannot be replaced) may not be taken up. There are

instances of abandonment of execution of such projects after the project plans were prepared (Bodhghat in Madhya Pradesh and Silent Valley in Kerala-both in India).

2. In some of the ongoing dam projects, there is need to review and plan them into stages which can be completed early to give benefits to the people. These are lingering on and are having difficulty in carrying out rehabilitation measures. Some of them do not have the financial resources to complete them in a reasonable time so that they are economical and cost-effective and such projects may have to be truncated ones or modified into run-off-the-river schemes etc.
3. Fish passages should be properly designed based on recent experiences and research in this field.
4. Devices for passage of silt should be incorporated in the designs. A number of recent dams built in the Himalayan regions in India have incorporated silt trapping and flushing tunnels in addition to under-sluices for silt removal.
5. Desilting of existing dams at a rate at which river conditions are not adversely affected should be taken up. Such measures have been tried successfully for many dams in China.
6. Pumped storage schemes should be considered near the existing dams for augmenting peak power requirements.

Integrated Land and Water Resources Management

This is needed with respect to land and water for sustainable development. The catchment areas of all dams (small or big) should be protected from environmental degradation by carrying out measures to prevent soil erosion and sustained growth of vegetation. District level authorities consisting of representatives of local administration, forests, water supply, pollution control boards and NGOs should be set up to monitor and implement the various measures so that the water supply sources are well protected. In India, there are institutions called Water and Land Management Institutes (WALMIS) in each state, and these should also be associated with the catchment area maintenance. Pollution of surface and ground water resources by industrial effluents etc. should be prevented by enforcing the control measures.

INDIA AND PAKISTAN AT ODDS OVER SHRINKING INDUS RIVER

"Pakistan's entire economy is driven by the textile industry," said Michael Kugelman, a South Asia expert at the Woodrow Wilson International Center for Scholars. "The problem with Pakistan's economy is that most of the major industries use a ton of water—textiles, sugar, wheat—and there's a tremendous amount of water that's not only used, but wasted," he added.

The same is true for India

That impact is an important part of a complex water equation in countries already under strain from booming populations. More people means more demand for water to irrigate crops, cool machinery, and power cities. The Indus River, which begins in Indian-controlled Kashmir and flows through Pakistan on its way to the sea, is Pakistan's primary freshwater source—on which 90 percent of its agriculture depends—and a critical outlet of hydropower generation for both countries.

Downstream provinces are already feeling the strain, with some dried-out areas being abandoned by fishermen and farmers forced to move to cities. That increases competition between urban and rural communities for water. "In areas where you used to have raging rivers, you have, essentially, streams or even puddles and not much else," said Kugelman.

In years past, the coastal districts that lost their shares of the Indus' flows have become "economically orphaned," the poorest districts in the country, according to Pakistani water activist Mustafa Talpur. Because Pakistani civil society is weak, he says, corruption and deteriorating water distribution tend to go hand in hand.

In the port city of Karachi, which depends for its water on the Indus, water theft—in which public water is stolen from the pipes and sold from tankers in slums and around the city—may be a $500-million annual industry.

In the balance is the fate not only of people, but important aquatic species like the Indus River dolphin, which is now threatened to extinction by agricultural pollution and dams, among other pressures. Scientists estimate that fewer than 100 individuals remain.

Threat to Peace?

One of the potentially catastrophic consequences of the region's fragile water balance is the effect on political tensions.

In India, competition for water has a history of provoking conflict between communities. In Pakistan, water shortages have triggered food and energy crises that ignited riots and protests in some cities. Most troubling, Islamabad's diversions of water to upstream communities with ties to the government are inflaming sectarian loyalties and stoking unrest in the lower downstream region of Sindh.

But the issue also threatens the fragile peace that holds between the nations of India and Pakistan, two nuclear-armed rivals. Water has long been seen as a core strategic interest in the dispute over the Kashmir region, home to the Indus' headwaters. Since 1960, a delicate political accord called the Indus Waters Treaty has governed the sharing of the river's resources. But dwindling river flows will be harder to share as the populations in both countries grow and the per-capita water supply plummets.

Some growth models predict that by 2025, India's population will grow to triple what it was—and Pakistan's population to six times what it was—when the Indus treaty was signed. Lurking in the background are fears that climate change is speeding up the melting of the glaciers that feed the river.

Mountain glaciers in Kashmir play a central role in regulating the river's flows, acting as a natural water storage tank that freezes precipitation in winter and releases it as meltwater in the summer. The Indus is dependent on glacial melting for as much as half of its flow. So its fate is uniquely tied to the health of the Himalayas. In the short term, higher glacial melt is expected to bring more intense flooding, like last year's devastating deluge.

Both countries are also racing to complete large hydroelectric dams along their respective stretches of the Kashmir river system, elevating tensions. India's projects are of a size and scope that many Pakistanis fear could be used to disrupt their hydropower efforts, as well as the timing of the flows on which Pakistani crops rely.

"Many in Pakistan are worried that, being in control of upstream waters, India can easily run Pakistan dry either by diverting the flow of water by building storage dams or using up all the water through hydroelectric power schemes," said Pakistani security analyst Rifaat Hussain.

For years, Pakistani politicians have claimed India is responsible for Pakistan's water troubles. More recently, militant groups have picked up their rhetoric. Hafiz Saeed, the founder of the Pakistani militant group allegedly responsible for the 2008 terror attack in Mumbai, even accused India of "water terrorism."

Hope for the Future

In the past few months, however, the situation has improved, according to Kugelman. "We've been hearing nearly unprecedented statements from very high-level Pakistani officials who have essentially acknowledged that India is not stealing Pakistan's water, and that Pakistan's water problems are essentially a function of internal mismanagement issues," he said. Militants are still griping, he said, "but not as shrilly."

This may be because the two countries are cooperating on water and other issues better than before, and because militants are now focusing less on their archenemy in India and more on coalition forces in Afghanistan.

"But I imagine this is momentary," said Kugelman. "The facts on the ground—the water constraints in both India and Pakistan—have not abated. They're both still very serious and getting worse."

What's needed, he says, is more conservation and adaptation—a smarter way of doing business.

WATER WARRIORS OF INDIA - INITIATIVE TOWARDS PURE AND AMPLE WATER

No water or contaminated water is commonplace news in the national or regional dailies of India. Such incidents are termed by newspapers as mismanagement of the government, bureaucrats calls it unfortunate incidents and the governing authorities term it as accident. Whatever the term used its the shame to the whole mankind that even being in 21st century, with such high development of technology some of our fellow beings living in certain sections of the society has a threat to ill health and in some cases succumb their lives to shackles of death because of water which itself is the originator of life.

Rainwater harvesting is what India can choose, and the youth consortium which will bring paradigm shift in this process will be Water Warriors of India Its an irony that India being surrounded by water bodies on three sides, house of 13 major rivers, largest river island (Majuli), highest rainfall (Mausingram) and many other facts which reflects Indias dominance in water resources, yet we face shortages every year.

Consider this the per capita water availability in India was 3450 cu m in 1952. It stands at 1800 cu m now and by estimates by 2025 it will fall to 1200 1500 cu m per person. Even though the rate of urbanization in India is among the lowest in the world, the nation has more than 250 million city-dwellers. Experts predict that this number will rise even further, and by 2020, about 50 per cent of India's population will be living in cities. This is going to put further pressure on the already strained centralized water supply systems of urban areas.

The urban water supply and sanitation sector in the country is suffering from inadequate levels of service, an increasing demand-supply gap, poor sanitary conditions and deteriorating financial and technical performance. Supply of water is highly erratic and unreliable.

Transmission and distribution networks are old and poorly maintained, and generally of a poor quality. Consequently physical losses are typically high, ranging from 25 to over 50 per cent. Low pressures and intermittent supplies allow back siphoning, which results in contamination of water in the distribution network. Water is typically available for only 2-8 hours a day in most Indian cities. The situation is even worse in summer when water is available only for a few minutes, sometimes not at all.

Looking at the condition at metro cities of India: Mumbais demand for water is expected to rise to 7,970 MLD (million litres daily) by 2011, current supply is 3100 MLD which already constitutes a substantial shortfall as the city receives only 2,500 MLD, the balance lost on account of leakages and pilferage. In the capital itself Delhi the supply of water is around 650 million gallons of water per day against the demand of 750 million. According to a World Bank study, of the 27 Asian cities with populations of over 1,000,000, Chennai and Delhi are ranked as the worst performing metropolitan cities in terms of hours of water availability per day, while Mumbai is ranked as second worst performer and Calcutta fourth worst

All these was regarding the shortage of water but the analysis remains incomplete if we dont emphasize on the quality of water available for drinking. Whether the water is potable? The fact is that it is deteriorating fast. As early as in 1982 it was reported that 70 per cent of all available water in India was polluted. The situation is much worse today. There are daily news reports on prime dailies showing the pictures of the contaminated water available in various localities of the city for drinking. The colour of the contaminated water supplied to these areas is worse to urine. Over extraction of ground water has led to salt water intrusion into coastal aquifers. It has also resulted in problems of excessive fluoride, iron, arsenic and salinity in water affecting about 44 million people in India. Ground water is facing an equally serious threat from contamination by industrial effluent as well as pesticides and fertilizer from farm run-offs.

Sanitation and water management should be looked at simultaneously. Too often attention is focused on drinking water supply, leaving sanitation and wastewater treatment for later. However, for every 100 litres of water going into a house about 90 litres will have to leave the plot again. Unless priority is given quickly to creating an infrastructure to assure availability of water, there may be no water to meet the agricultural, domestic and industrial needs of a population that has tripled in 50 years to more than a billion.

Water management in terms of availability and most importantly quality is therefore major challenge not only for town planners, state and central governments but being citizen of the worlds largest democracy its our supreme duty to overcome the hurdles regarding the water management and water warriors will take initiative in gratifying this duty. Water supply is an institutional process and an institutional framework for effective water supply and sanitation has to comply with the functions of policy, regulation and sector organization, management of quality, infrastructure and on-site sanitation. So we discuss about the major issues and their solution concerning institutional options in water problem and sanitation in Indian community, analysis can be further extended to other developing countries: First issue: Water supply should treat to all sections of society, but poor people are neglected

Institutions in developing countries dealing with water and sanitation issues have rarely been designed to cater for large numbers of poor people. At the level of operations, public utilities are often constrained by bureaucratic requirements. For instance there is often considerable inflexibility in the management of human resources within public utilities. Given the complexity of the problem in many countries there are a number of separate agencies responsible for wastewater and sanitation, particular in the case of public sector provision. For this, the role of Non-governmental organizations (NGOs) such as ours, particularly in low cost sanitation, community participation and creating public awareness has to be very positive. In cities, community toilets has to be constructed and managed mainly by NGOs or private firms, based on the user pays principle or as a charity. We will be active in raising awareness concerning health, hygiene, slum development, solid waste collection and disposal issue and equitable distribution of facilities. The challenge remains to increase the impact of these initiatives by multiplying them on a larger scale or mainstreaming the approach in the leading institutions for water and sanitation in India.

Second issue: Should privatization of water be done and confusion regarding the delegation of roles between public and private sector? An important issue according to this is the division of responsibilities between the government and the private sector. Ideally the government would set the framework, but there is often market failure. Then governments get involved and find it difficult to pull out. Also the type and scale of technology is important and has consequences for the management and financing. The larger the scale, the bigger the financial implications. In that case governments will also be more inclined to involve the private sector.

But majority of the public opinion favors water as a common resource while showing reservation about policy that seeks to make water a commodity of the state. Water policies adopted by states like Maharashtra and Rajasthan are being opposed by several groups including the environmentalists. A largely felt perception held by the people is that governments in India are buckling under pressure from the World Bank. These policies, it is felt, help declare water as a state property, which later facilitates its conversion into private property. But is the privatization of water the only viably efficient solution to our shoddy management of water resources?

The division between the public and private sector requires answering the question which tasks each one is fulfilling? To ensure effective provision of sanitation services it is imperative to have a good understanding of the roles and responsibilities of every entity (be it public or private) and the technologies used to perform its task. The emergence of the private sector and the users themselves as alternative providers leads to a formulation of a large number of institutional modes for the provision of services with private sector involvement. These modes vary from simple service contract to complete divestiture to the private sector, and a large variety of models for user involvement as owners or in the management.

On the other hand we as participants of the youth movement in water through our ways of harvesting water along with water activists, environmentalist and policy makers will work to provide alternatives to water policies so that the government and people are made aware that there are ways other than privatization to manage the countrys water resources.

Third issue: Willingness to pay or to contribute for water supply and sanitation is minimal. Effective demand for water and sanitation is often weak if measured by the willingness to pay or contribute to for example the installation of sanitary services. Public demand in context of making payments for water supply and sanitation services systems is low in spite of the high social cost assigned to the polluted sites. The public sector has also become increasingly aware of the high political risk of a significant raise in basic rates for providing these services. Key constituting elements of such systems are appropriate policies, laws and regulations, institutions, technologies and cost recovery systems. There is a need to look for appropriate technological solutions and to involve the people at the preparation and implementation stage.

In general the public is interested in getting sanitation facilities, but not very much concerned about the treatment of wastewater or the necessary off plot sanitation facilities. This usually means a limited willingness to pay and a negative attitude towards involving private parties. Water warriors in its programme will organize campaign stressing on bringing water democracy by ensuring that every drop is conserved, harvested and shared by the people.

Fourth issue: water supply and waste water management should be looked in an integrated way It is desirable to think of water supply, sanitation and wastewater in an integrated way. This implies that the cost of an integrated solution will be much lower than a solution at a later stage by a separate institution based on different cost recovery system. In big cities dealing with wastewater and offsite sanitation is often integrated. However, in the Indian case we also learn that this tends to be limited to the area of the Municipal Commission, leaving the rest of the city to the development authorities or even district authorities, who tend to have less money and no money raising responsibilities.

As a result we at our movement will make government and people aware to manage useable water and waste water with same assiduousness.

Fifth issue: there is a need for regulation in the system. The need for well-defined roles and responsibilities is clear. It is also necessary to make the institutional arrangements between the municipality and the private sector explicit. There needs to be a regulatory framework and the authorities need to take their responsibility. As public utilities are not usually subject to the disciplines of the market, they have fewer incentives to minimize costs (and maximize tariff collection rates). Regulatory arrangements can stimulate them to look at their cost, for example through a system of benchmarking.

The design of an effective institutional framework is a challenge in large metropolitan areas. If not done well, the existence of multiple institutions with primary or secondary responsibilities in sanitation can become a hindrance to effective development and management of sanitation services. A case in point is Bangalore where mandates not only overlap, but have also been defined at different levels, and for different technologies. Here, effective co-ordination is absent, as a result of which the services cannot be run effectively. So, if each section of the society is made aware of its role, such commotion wont arise at all, this is also an area where water warriors will emphasize.

Sixth issue: Finances cannot be ignored. Financing is crucial. What is the financial basis for supplying water and sanitation services? Some of the cost recovery mechanisms currently used includes infrastructure charges, connection fees, environmental user fees and local taxes. Raising sufficient revenue to cover for the cost is difficult. As already emphasized, the costs of these services are high and at the same time, the demand is usually little developed and the willingness to pay is low, and lower than that for other services.

In addition, enforcement of payment for sanitation and waste water services is difficult, as one cannot simply disconnect as is done with other utilities such power and telecoms. Yet, any sustainable water management initiative must address the key issues of financing and cost recovery.

In this context, raising the awareness of the need to have adequate wastewater and sanitation services, of the range of technologies, and of the cost of such services and of the inevitability of cost recovery in return for good service quality is a precondition for effectiveness. User participation is yet another key to success in wastewater services: several urban case studies have shown that willingness to pay is above expected levels in cases where the users have been given a chance to consciously participate in the selection and establishment of the sanitation system. Various cost recovery mechanisms or economic instruments can be applied to recover (at least) the operational cost of urban sanitation and the treatment of wastewater. These include user charges, effluent charges and taxation. There should be provision of 'polluter pays' in which the costs of wastewater management charged to a customer are calculated in function of wastewater quantity and pollution load.

Household charges may be uniform and based on an assumed pollution equivalent, or a volumetric rate based on recorded water consumption.

High charges may encourage pre-treatment and even process-redesign by industries in an effort to optimize water and wastewater costs. (Too) high charges may also have undesired effects such as illegal discharges inside or outside the wastewater system. So water warriors through advocating such policies will ensure maximizing of utility under the constraints of minimizing cost.

The youth consortium of water warriors will cater specifically to all the above concerned issues. Having discussed the current scenario, reasons and the issues and their specific solution regarding the water management in India, now we shift our emphasis on the ways in which an individual or a locality can take measures to solve its own major water problem

Urban centres in India are facing an ironical situation today. On one hand there is the acute water scarcity and on the other, the streets are often flooded during the monsoons. This has led to serious problems with quality and quantity of groundwater.

This is despite the fact that all these cities receive good rainfall. However, this rainfall occurs during short spells of high intensity. (Most of the rain falls in just 100 hours out of 8,760 hours in a year). Because of such short duration of heavy rain, most of the rain falling on the surface tends to flow away rapidly leaving very little for recharge of groundwater. As water shortage increases, alternative sources of water supply are gaining importance. These include sewage recycle, rainwater harvesting, generating water form humidity in the atmosphere etc.

Water recycle through rain water harvesting is a simple, effective and economical solution to conserve water so that more fresh water is available for essential uses drinking, bathing, cooking and laundry. Population, industrialization and pollution are putting pressure on our limited fresh water resource. There is limit to increasing water supply because we are running out of sources and cost of additional facilities is prohibitive. The best way to solve water problem therefore is by conserving water and recycling it wherever possible. Recycling must be made mandatory far all new projects- industrial or domestic and even should be promoted to existing buildings also.

One of the solutions to the urban water crisis and the best way to recycle water is *Rainwater Harvesting - capturing the runoff*. Rain harvesting will be really efficient in areas where there is inadequate groundwater supply or surface resources are either lacking or insufficient, it drastically reduces urban flooding from which our two major cities Mumbai and Chennai suffered drastically last year

Rain water harvesting is an ancient concept, the implementation of it does not requires any major technology and the cost is even low, as compared to the benefits cost should not even be considered. At this juncture its worth mentioning the ways in which an individual of the society can take part in such a process.

Rainwater harvesting can be harvested from the following surfaces:

Rooftops: If buildings with impervious roofs are already in place, the catchment area is effectively available free of charge and they provide a supply at the point of consumption.

Paved and unpaved areas i.e., landscapes, open fields, parks, storm water drains, roads and pavements and other open areas can be effectively used to harvest the runoff. The main advantage in using ground as collecting surface is that water can be collected from a larger area. This is part of the community project to be undertaken

Water bodies: The potential of lakes, tanks and ponds to store rainwater is immense. The harvested rainwater can not only be used to meet water requirements of the city, it also recharges groundwater aquifers.

Storm water drains: Most of the residential colonies have proper network of storm water drains. If maintained neatly, these offer a simple and cost effective means for harvesting rainwater.

Rain water though stored will only serve the purpose if properly filtered to meet the major drinking water needs. For this effect major invention in the field has been made which provides proper rain water purification mechanisms. These purification system works on the normal treatment method involving screening, flocculation sedimentation and filtration.

These purification systems are also available for micro scale projects to serve the need of a household. Such purification systems are simple in installing and easy to operate. The most important feature is that they dont require electricity.

Many entrepreneurs of industries tend to forget the fact that they are part of the living society and in turn they tend to foster the production of negative externality. It should be made mandatory for each industry to install water management solutions to recycle its waste water for reuse. Major step in this front is through the development of Industrial effluent recycle solution which integrates physiochemical, biological and membrane separation processes for optimum water recovery. They achieve water management through water recycle and source reduction, and waste management through product recovery and waste minimization. They are cost effective as they recover valuable products for reuse while recycling which gives industries a good return on their investment while protecting the environment and even the common people as it reduces the water usage of industries and transmittance of waste to water bodies.

After emphasizing the ways of tackling the problem through rain water harvesting and other recycling options, the following paragraphs paves the way to the essence of the whole discussion; it illuminates the role of the youth in curbing the problem of such a magnitude which can pose a threat to the very existence of the mankind in this world.

Any amount of government expenditure cannot solve this problem unless and until the community as a whole in its full might rise to the occasion and work for it.

In India the role of youth cannot be under estimated as India in its demography cycle has a position of Young India with more than half of Indias population below the age of 35 years. The youth of the nation has to take part in mass movement of awareness; they have to be the Water warriors of India

In this approach the youth will be enlightened to serve their locality and curb the water problem. Each locality in city will have its own group of members named as the water warriors whose primary work will be to impart awareness among the residents regarding rain water harvesting. Charity begins at home, so in the first step the members have to set up rain water harvesting system in their respective houses, so that they can put forward examples and other people can replicate these. Water warriors of respective localities will provide assistance in setting up of the system of rain water harvesting. In certain cases possible community projects can be taken as a whole where large tanks are to be constructed to store rain water. Major foray of water warriors will be in water harvesting but it will also simultaneously ensure that water is being properly utilized.

The promotion techniques will include the most believable of all- word-of-mouth, apart from other conventional means of imparting awareness such as newspapers, hoarding etc., as water warriors will be a youth forum, the awareness and membership will be imparted through the largest network of World Wide Web.

The major question which remained unanswered is that why will any youth join this consortium of water warrior? The answer to this question can be traced from last year experience of major cities of west and south India, which were struck by floods, the irony was that there was water everywhere but there was no water to drink, no water to cook food, no water to survive life. This incident in major way has brought into notice the major problem of water management in our country, and its the younger generations who have to foray into the scene, join the consortium and solve the problem simply because of the reason that we are the people who have to destine the future of ours as well as coming generation. It was first time that major important cities of India had confronted such a problem which made youth aware of the reality, and steps has to be taken to overcome the harsh realities of water mismanagement.

Among the factors that constrain performance of water management in India are: poor levels of service particularly for sanitation, inadequate pricing policies (poor cost recovery), undue political interference with service provision, highly centralized character of the sector, lack of accountability, lack of continuation in policies and programmes, low levels of productivity and efficiency and inadequate training or management and sector staff. These factors are exacerbated by external factors such as of population growth, urbanization, and economic development that jointly drive a growth in demand that providers fail to cope with. Successful approaches that has to be considered at macro level for policies should be effective decentralization, integration of hygiene and sanitation activities, demand-driven approaches, cost recovery and good governance, and focus on poverty alleviation, equitable distribution of health services, and gender-sensitive approaches.

It is heartening to note that in India, the water supply sector is at last moving away from an infrastructure- creation approach to a consolidation approach. But India still needs to make substantial infrastructure is that its growth has not been accompanied by an improvement in the quality of governance of water services in the country and that the water sector suffered from a policy of build- neglect and rebuild. Therefore, government and its agencies should not merely concern them with fixing pipes but also fixing institutions that fix pipes

These were the approaches at macro level but for effective utilization of these policies the work has to start from micro level, from each and every household itself. We as youth through our voice need to create awareness about the importance of water in the community so that mindset, attitudes, and habits change proactively rather than wait for legislation and regulation. Together we must work to see that waste of this precious resource is minimizes and we are able to conserve fresh water for future generations.

There is need to grab the water problem by the scruff of its neck. Enough has been written, discussed about the problem, hardly anybody takes a look at the solution. Residents of the locality blame it on the government; government on the other hand overlooks it as a seasonal or short term problem. Therefore, there is a need of a paradigm shift from problems to the solution, from despair to problem solving, form now to future. This is what the youth movement of water warriors will be about.

The water warrior campaigns, ultimate goal will be to see a world as an agglomeration of ecological - water harvesting - democracies.

KASHMIR'S RAGING RIVERS

A resolution of the Kashmir conflict seems as elusive today as it did in 1951. Since 1989, armed Kashmiri separatists, some with Pakistani support, have waged a low-grade, off-and-on insurgency against Indian security forces. (Protests last summer against India's heavy-handed rule in the Kashmir Valley roiled the region for several weeks, leading to the deaths of at least 110 Kashmiris, many of them teenage boys.) * Still, without the IWT, Kashmir might have been the source of even wider conflict.

Lilienthal recognized a truth that remains little discussed but as relevant as ever: The struggle for Kashmir was motivated in large part by Pakistan's desperation to control the rivers that flowed through the region. "The starting point should be ... to set to rest Pakistan's fears of deprivation and a return to desert," he wrote. The treaty would defuse these tensions at a critical point in the young nations' relations, by clearly spelling out how much water each was entitled to use from the rivers that crossed the western border.

India and Pakistan signed the IWT in 1960, after protracted negotiations facilitated by the World Bank. Before the partition of British India in 1947, each province had jurisdiction to build dams and other infrastructure for electricity and irrigation on the portions of the rivers that flowed through their land; after partition, a series of patchwork agreements left several key issues, such as whether and how much Pakistan should pay India for water and canal maintenance costs, unresolved. The IWT gave "unrestricted use" of the basin's three western rivers (the Indus, the Jhelum, and the Chenab) to Pakistan and the three eastern rivers (the Ravi, the Beas, and the Sutlej) to India. Today, the treaty governs the use of roughly 55 trillion gallons of water per year, which sustains more than 210 million people in the basin.

The IWT has since solidly weathered three Indo-Pakistani wars (including two over Kashmir) and countless flare-ups between the now nuclear-armed neighbors. The Indian and Pakistani members of the treaty-stipulated Indus Waters Commission have met at least once every year, conducting amicable discussions and sharing important hydrological data even when their nations' diplomatic relations have been severed.

Yet the treaty shows signs of strain. In 2005, Pakistan invoked the arbitration provisions of the treaty—for the first time in its history—in response to India's construction of a large hydropower project on the Chenab River. Pakistan has since raised objections to several other power projects on IWT-governed rivers, spurred by its ancient fears that India's storage of water in those dams could threaten its agricultural production. While the treaty's existing provisions have largely been able to contain these disputes, two emerging trends—climate change and Kashmiris' desire for greater control over their water resources—threaten to undermine the very foundations of the treaty as a tool for averting conflict.

The Indus receives at least 30 percent of its flow from the region's shrinking glaciers—more than any other Asian river. As global warming plods on, experts expect increased flows and possibly flooding in the near term as the glacial "water towers" melt. But this spike will be followed by a long, painful tail of perennial scarcity as the glaciers' role in providing water during the dry season becomes greatly diminished.

The Indus basin's overwhelming dependence on snow and ice melt has led Shakil Romshoo, a professor of geophysics and geology at the University of Kashmir in Srinagar, to conclude that global warming will destabilize the IWT within the next few decades. In Kashmir, "the surface runoff ... is decreasing," he says. "And on this surface water depends the entire economy of Pakistan."

About 80 percent of Pakistan's cultivated lands are irrigated by water from the Indus system, the lion's share being governed by the IWT. Of the IWT water, more than 70 percent of flows from the Indian state of Jammu and Kashmir. The math gets worse for Pakistan: The country's population is projected to increase by 82 percent, from 184 million in 2010 to 335 million in 2050; per capita water availability was nearly 80 percent lower in 2005 than 1947, plunging from 5,600 cubic meters to 1,200 cubic meters, dangerously close to the 1,000-cubic-meter-per-person-per-year "water scarcity" threshold defined by the widely used Falkenmark index. A growing alarm in Pakistan over this hydrological straitjacket has in recent years spurred jihadi leaders based there to frame their attacks against India as a struggle to secure the rivers that form Pakistan's "lifeline."

The stakes are high for Kashmiris as well. A recent study in the journal *Science* concluded that the eventual reduced flow of meltwater from glaciers and snowfields threatens the food security of close to 30 million people living in the Indus basin. Many Kashmiri farmers have switched from grain production to less-thirsty horticulture in recent years due to the increasingly uncertain availability of water at critical times in the growing season.

Rising local resentment is the second factor jeopardizing the IWT. Kashmiri perspectives have never had a prominent voice in IWT-related discussions. Their frustration stems in part from the way the treaty limits the construction of new irrigation works and storage facilities for hydropower on the Indian side of the three western rivers (the ones granted to Pakistan for unrestricted use). But Kashmiris are also unhappy with the Indian government's decision to retain control over most of the existing hydro plants in their state, thus depriving the local government and economy of a critical source of revenue.

Any wider effort to industrialize Jammu and Kashmir's economy will depend on greater exploitation of the state's hydropower potential. The state potentially has up to 15,000 megawatts of exploitable hydropower, less than 10 percent of which has been tapped. But India hasn't allowed the state to access international financing to develop and operate more power plants on its rivers. It "is non-negotiable for us that ... Kashmir will have to have control of its power resources," says Arjimand Hussain Talib, a Kashmiri newspaper columnist working on a book about Kashmir's water politics.

The state government recently hired an international consultant to do a thorough study of the economic losses incurred by Jammu and Kashmir due to restrictions on hydropower and agricultural development imposed by the treaty. Past speculative estimates have put the number around $1.5 billion per year. More detailed and credible numbers could give Kashmiris more leverage to wrest financial compensation from New Delhi.

Talib predicts that ongoing talks between India and Pakistan will ultimately result in "a kind of joint collaborative approach to the basin's management." This might take the form of a new successor agreement to the IWT, as some analysts call for. A more likely scenario than total renegotiation, according to Talib, would be India and Pakistan signing an "extension agreement." In this event, the countries would extend the IWT in a separate, complementary treaty to include joint planning and oversight in the early stages of infrastructure projects on the six rivers—even across Kashmir's militarized Line of Control.

This vision echoes a proposal Lilienthal floated sixty years ago. "The whole Indus system must be ... designed, built and operated as a unit," Lilienthal argued, to benefit both India and Pakistan optimally. This objective, he insisted, "cannot be achieved by the countries working separately; the river pays no attention to partition."

INDIA AND PAKISTAN FEUD OVER INDUS WATERS

The countries have harmoniously shared the waters of the Indus River for decades. A 50-year-old treaty regulating access to water from the river and its tributaries has been viewed as a bright spot for India and Pakistan, which have gone to war three times since 1947. Now, the Pakistanis complain that India is hogging water upstream, which is hurting Pakistani farmers downstream. Pakistani officials say they will soon begin formal arbitration over a proposed Indian dam. At a meeting that started Sunday, Pakistan raised objections to new Indian dam projects on the Indus River and asked for satellite monitoring of river flows.

"Water I see emerging as a very serious source of tension between Pakistan and India," said Shah Mehmood Qureshi, Pakistan's foreign minister, in an interview Friday. He said he has raised the issue with Indian Prime Minister Manmohan Singh.

A senior Indian government official denied India is violating the treaty. He blamed Pakistan's water shortage on changing weather patterns and the country's poor water management. He called the strident rhetoric from Pakistani officials a "political gimmick...designed to place yet one more agenda item in our already complex relationship." Indian officials declined comment on the record.

The latest dispute revolves around India's plans to build a 330-megawatt hydroelectric power project on the Kishenganga River, a tributary of the Indus. India says it is well within its rights to build the dam. The project has been on the drawing board since the late 1980s and is expected to cost about $800 million.

Water Woes

Pakistan says New Delhi's plans to divert the course of the river will reduce its flow by a third in the winter. That would make it unfeasible for Pakistan to move ahead with its own plans for a hydroelectric dam downstream.

Pakistan wants to put the Kishenganga project before an arbitration panel—the first time that mechanism of the treaty will have been used. If India agrees, a seven-person court of arbitration would include two members appointed by each country, and three outsiders. India hasn't yet responded formally to the proposal, according to the Pakistan delegation to the meeting.

"We're already a water-stressed country," Jamaat Ali Shah, Pakistan's Indus waters commissioner, said ahead of this week's meeting. India's construction of new dams is "aggravating the stresses."

The water dispute comes as the relationship between the nuclear-armed neighbors is at an inflection point. India last month invited Pakistan to discuss the resumption of regular peace talks, and the two countries' foreign secretaries met in Delhi Feb. 25. A water squabble could upset those peace efforts.

That would deal a major blow to Indian Prime Minister Singh, who views engagement with Pakistan as the best way to contain terrorism. Mr. Singh wants Pakistan's aid in bringing to justice Pakistan-based militants that New Delhi believes carried out the November 2008 attacks in Mumbai, a bloody siege that killed 166 people.

Further deterioration of relations between New Delhi and Islamabad would also be a setback for Washington's efforts to stabilize the region. Pakistan has told the U.S. that tensions with India on its eastern border over the disputed territory of Kashmir have prevented it from cracking down more aggressively on Taliban and al Qaeda leaders directing the insurgency in Afghanistan.

Islamist groups in Pakistan have taken up the water issue as a new focus. "If our government doesn't act to resolve this issue then the people will take it in to their own hands. If water doesn't flow in to these rivers, then blood will," said Hafiz Khalid Waleed, the political affairs chief of Jamaat-ud-Dawah, an Islamic charity. India and others call the charity a front for Lashkar-e-Taiba, the militant group it says orchestrated the Mumbai terrorist attacks in Nov. 2008. Mr. Waleed denies any link to terrorism, calling it "American propaganda."

Water scarcity is a growing political issue across the globe, from the Middle East to the U.S. West. South Asia's water politics date back to Britain's partition of the Indian subcontinent in 1947, when newly created nations India and Pakistan wrangled over how to divide resources.

The Indus River, whose waters Britain had harnessed through a vast system of irrigation canals, was a crucial lifeline to farmers in the Punjab region stretching across both countries. But India and Pakistan were fighting over control of Kashmir, where several Indus tributaries begin.

After years of tense negotiations, India and Pakistan signed the Indus Waters Treaty in 1960 with the help of the World Bank. As part of the treaty—which is widely viewed by water experts as a model of how water conflicts can be managed—each side got unrestricted use of three rivers and rights to use the others for nonconsumptive purposes such as flood control, navigation and bathing. India was granted limited agricultural usage of Pakistan's rivers, plus the right to build hydroelectric projects, as long as they don't store or divert large amounts of water.

The treaty provides for bureaucrats appointed by both governments to meet regularly, exchange data, and resolve disputes. Commissioners have held more than 200 site inspections and meetings since 1960, even during times of war.

Yet Pakistan's rows with India have intensified as its water situation has worsened over the years. Water availability in Pakistan has fallen 70% since the early 1950s to 1,500 cubic meters per capita. It is expected to reach the

1,000-cubic-meter level considered officially "scarce" by international standards in 25 years, according to a report last year by the Woodrow Wilson International Center for Scholars.

Pakistani officials acknowledge their water woes aren't caused by India's damming of rivers alone. Major reservoirs are filling with sediment picked up by the rivers on their routes to the sea. Canals are aging and breaking down. The World Bank says soil erosion and poor irrigation are sapping roughly 1% from Pakistan's Gross Domestic Product growth.

Skeptics in India say Pakistan is simply looking for a scapegoat as it struggles to manage its internal water politics.

The especially arid province of Sindh, for example, blames the powerful upstream province of Punjab for consuming too much.

"Their water management is in terrible shape, and it's convenient to put the onus on India," said G. Parthasarathy, a former Indian envoy to Pakistan.

But Pakistani officials say New Delhi's actions are exacerbating a precarious situation.

This year the Pakistan province of Punjab—the political heartland of the nation and a major producer of wheat, rice, maize and sugar cane—is facing unprecedented water shortages. At harvest time in Mandi Bahauddin, an area in the north of Punjab province of relatively prosperous farmland, the wheat still grows waist-high.

But farmers here complain that yields and incomes have dropped by a third in the past five years because of water shortages. In the past, canals used to supply water for irrigation year-round. They are now empty for about four months each year. That forces villagers to pump groundwater, which is fast turning brackish and causing diseases like hepatitis, said Tariq Mehmood Allowana, a local farmer and member of the provincial assembly. In the past, the area's only problem was regular flooding. India's dams stopped this, causing a dearth of water instead, says Mr. Allowana, who owns 25 acres of wheat fields. The farmer represents the Pakistan Peoples Party of the late former Prime Minister Benazir Bhutto. Farmers say they have stopped cultivating rice—a water-intensive crop—except for personal use. Nearby, more than half of the Chenab river bed has become a dusty plain where children play with the flow reduced to a trickle.

"India is engaged in an economic warfare against Pakistan. If the problem persists for another five years the whole area will become barren," said Mr. Allowana, as a group of farmers nearby filled irrigation channels from groundwater supplies using a diesel-fueled pump.

Over the years, tensions have built as Pakistan has objected to the size and technical design of various Indian projects. India says it has 33 Indus-related hydrological projects at various stages of implementation, and all have been contested in one way or another by Pakistan. India also says it has yet to make use of its limited rights to store water on Pakistan's rivers or use it for limited irrigation.

"We've found there's a pattern in Pakistan of raising technical issues ad nauseam to stall a project or delay a project indefinitely," the senior Indian official said Friday.

In 2005 Pakistan raised issues with the Baglihar dam, an Indian power project on the Chenab river—one of those allotted to Pakistan—saying it would store too much water upstream and reduce downstream flow to Pakistan. The countries agreed in 2007 to let the World Bank appoint an independent expert, who ruled that India had to make minor modifications to the dam, such as lowering its height. Pakistan now contends the dam, which began operations in 2008, is reducing the flow of the Chenab below levels stipulated in the treaty. India denies this.

Pakistan wants Washington to play a mediating role with India—in the water dispute and wider issues like the Kashmir conflict. The U.S. is pushing for tighter relations with Pakistan as it steps up pressure on the Taliban in Afghanistan but has to balance this with its close ties to India. For now, the U.S. is treading carefully, offering Pakistan stepped-up economic aid and military hardware supplies.

Pakistan raised the water issue in Washington during an official visit last week. Secretary of State Hillary Clinton has signaled that Washington isn't interested in mediating on water issues.

A State Department spokesperson pointed to an interview Mrs. Clinton recently did with a Pakistani news channel in which she said it would be "sensible" to stick to the Indus Waters Treaty for resolving disputes.

The Indian projects that Pakistan says are draining its water resources are primarily on Indus tributaries in Kashmir. Some experts say the water issue is a back door way for Islamic militants to push their political agenda regarding Kashmir.

"They're saying, 'We must liberate Kashmir to save our water,'" said B.G. Verghese, a veteran journalist who has studied water issues closely and is a visiting professor at the Center for Policy Research, a New Delhi think tank.

THE INDUS WATER TREATY IS A SUCCESSFUL INSTANCE OF CONFLICT-RESOLUTION

After the Partition of India and Pakistan in 1947, an understanding on the sharing of water of Indus River between the two countries became necessary to facilitate the development of water resources of this basin. After prolonged talks between the two Governments, the Indus Water Treaty was signed in September According to this Treaty, waters of the three western rivers (the Jhelum, the Chenab, and the Indus itself) were allocated to Pakistan, and those of the three eastern rivers (the Ravi, the Beas and the Sutlej) were allocated to India. Certain restrictions about water utilization were placed on India which is the upper riparian country. The highlights of the Treaty are:

- India has not been allowed to build storages on the rivers where water has been allocated to Pakistan.
- Restrictions have also been imposed on the extension of irrigation development in India. Less significant restrictions have been placed on Pakistan, being the lower riparian.
- The Treaty contains provisions regarding the exchange of data on project operation, extent of irrigated agriculture, etc.
- The Treaty provides for certain institutional arrangements. A permanent Indus Commission consisting of a Commissioner each for India and for Pakistan has been set up and there are periodical meetings and exchanges of visits between the two sides.
- Detailed guidelines were included in the Treaty for conflict-resolution. The Indus Commission is the first step for conflict resolution. If an agreement cannot be reached at the Commission level, the dispute is to be referred to the two governments. If the governments too fail to reach an agreement, the Treaty provides an arbitration mechanism.

The Indus Water Treaty is a successful instance of conflict-resolution. It has been working reasonably well despite the strained political relationship between India and Pakistan. Importantly, it continued to be honoured even during wars between the two countries. Undoubtedly differences do arise from time to time, but these usually get resolved within the framework of the Treaty. Minor differences are settled within the Commission, and major disputes go to the two Governments.

6

Asia's Water Challenges

In the face of rising populations, rapid growth of the middle class, expanding irrigation and water-intensive industries, and spiralling household consumption, per capita water availability in Asia is actually declining by 1.6% per year. The decline is greater across central, southern, southwestern and western Asia as well as in semi-arid northern China. In areas where water availability has traditionally been very low, such as the Near East and the Arabian Peninsula, even small declines or annual variation in precipitation can exacerbate the vulnerabilities of entire communities by creating drought-like conditions. The spreading water stress in Asia has direct consequences for economic and human development as well as environmental protection.

With aquifers being drained to dangerously low levels, a number of cities in Asia that rely on groundwater, such as Yemen's capital Sana'a and Quetta in Pakistan, face the spectre of running out. Beijing increasingly depends on water brought in from elsewhere. In an ever-deeper search for water, millions of pump-operated wells threaten to suck Asia's subterranean reserves dry, even as the continent confronts river depletion. Asian economies can import fossils fuels, mineral ores and timber from distant lands, but they must make do with their own water resources.

Pressure on national water resources is said to be high when water withdrawal exceeds 25% of total renewable water resources. This ratio is 34% for India and 26% for South Korea. China's 18.57% may be relatively decent, but the country remains chronically unable to meet its water needs in the north, where almost half its population lives and where rivers are dying. In contrast, Japan, at 21.26% is doing a better job than China in managing its water resources by maintaining water quality. The United Nations Economic and Social Commission for Asia and the Pacific (UNESCAP) captured the

Asian crisis through its 2009 Index of Water Available for Development, a measure of per capita water availability for human, economic and ecological uses per year on the basis of each country's internal renewable water resources minus total water used. This index reveals that there have been steep declines in water availability for development since the baseline year of 1980 in a number of Asian nations, including the two giants, China and India, that make up nearly two-fifths of the global population. The water situation in India looks particularly ominous. The report warned that 'water shortfalls on this scale heighten competition for a precious resource and frequently lead to conflicts, which are emerging as new threats to social stability'.

Although Asia's overall population growth has slowed, an important factor driving the water crisis is growth in consumption due to rising prosperity. This is best illustrated by changes in diet, especially a greater intake of meat, whose production is notoriously water intensive. In China, for example, meat consumption rose fourfold between 1980 and 2010, with its beef sector growing from almost nothing to become the third largest in the world. By 2030, Chinese meat consumption is projected to double further. This shift from traditional rice and noodles to a meatier diet has already fuelled a doubling of China's water footprint for food production since 1985: it takes ten times more water to raise a kilo of beef than grow a kilo of rice or wheat.

Once plagued by serious food shortages and recurrent famines, Asia opened the door to its dramatic economic rise by emerging as a net food exporter on the back of an unparalleled expansion of irrigation: total irrigated cropland in Asia doubled between 1960 and 2000. It is notable that few advanced industrial countries depend on other countries to feed their populations; many of them, on the contrary, are important food exporters.

This may explain why Asian nations have attached great strategic importance to food security, often equating that goal, rather imprudently, with food sovereignty. Yet the extension of agriculture to semi-arid and arid areas in Asia has necessitated intensive irrigation, which, in turn, has created serious waterlogging and soil-salinity problems and undercut crop-yield growth. Even in Asia's fertile valleys drained by major river systems, irrigation is usually necessary in the dry season; much of the continent's rainfall is concentrated in a three- or four-month monsoon period. By contrast, Europe, with its temperate climate and long rainy periods, is able to produce most of its food through rain-fed crops. In fact, such is the widespread prevalence of rain-fed agriculture among rich nations that industry, not agriculture, is their leading water consumer, except in Australia and New Zealand.

Asia now boasts the lion's share, about 70%, of the world's irrigated land. Three sub-regions — South Asia, China and Southeast Asia — by themselves account for about 50% of the global total. It is thus hardly a surprise that Asia leads the world in the total volume of freshwater withdrawn for agriculture. Indeed, almost 74% of the total global freshwater withdrawals for agriculture by volume are made in Asia. As a proportion of its own renewable water resources, Asia's yearly agricultural water withdrawals aggregate to 81%, or at least 10 percentage points higher than the global average. By contrast, that figure is just 29% in Europe and 38% in North America. Water withdrawals for industrial purposes account for a mere 11.4% in Asia; and for household needs the figure is 7.3%.

Yet the growth of rice and wheat output in Asia, after the dramatic increases of the previous quarter century, has slowed since the late 1990s, raising concerns that Asian countries such as China and India that are largely self-sufficient in food will become major food importers, disturbing the international market, which is not large enough to meet such demands. With population, consumption and developmental pressures growing and increases in yield gains flattening, Asia needs a second green revolution, for which water will be the single biggest constraint.

The fastest increase in water demand in Asia, however, is coming not from agriculture but from the industrial sector and urban households. The United Nations projects that industrial water withdrawals in the world will double between 2000 and 2025, with much of the increase likely to occur in the Asia-Pacific region, 'given its rapidly rising status as a global industrial production centre and the fast growth in subsectors with high water consumption, such as the production of transportation equipment, beverages and textiles'.

The fastest rise is projected for India, whose economy is currently led by the services sector but where industrial water use is expected to almost quadruple by 2050 as manufacturing rapidly expands. But water shortages are already impeding this rapid industrial expansion in Asia; water scarcity is, for example, causing billions of dollars' worth of annual losses in industrial output in China.

A final factor underlying water stress in Asia is the long-term environmental impact of large-scale sequestration of water resources through dams, barrages, reservoirs and other structures. Dams do bring important benefits: if appropriately designed and scaled, they aid economic and social development by regulating water supply, controlling floods, facilitating irrigation, generating hydroelectricity and bringing drinking water to cities. But they can affect water quality and quantity downstream, alter fluvial ecosystems, damage biodiversity and promote coastal erosion and saltwater intrusion.

Large dams have caused sedimentation, inundation, habitat damage, destruction of fish species, and other environmental and public-health problems in Asia. Equally significant is the fact that heavy damming upsets a river's natural tropical flooding cycle, which is critical to fisheries and the re-fertilization of soil. The Aral Sea in Central Asia has shrunk by more than half owing to the over-damming of its sources, the Amu Darya and Syr Darya rivers, and the heavy extraction of their waters for irrigation.

The vast majority of dams in the world have been built since the 1950s. The construction of large dams has, by and large, petered out in the West but continues in full swing in Asia, where a host of countries from Japan to Turkey are involved in major dam-building activities. Over the next decade, the number of dams in developed countries is likely to remain about the same, while much of the dam building in the developing world (in terms of aggregate storage-capacity build-up) will be concentrated in China, which already has slightly more than half of the approximately 50,000 large dams on the planet. But most of the best dam sites in Asia are already in use.

New dam construction to boost water supply may no longer be a viable option other than in underdeveloped countries such as Laos, Myanmar and Nepal that have not adequately exploited their water resources or in autocracies that can effectively stifle grassroots opposition. Yet the numerous new projects in Asia show that the damming of rivers is still an important priority for national and provincial decision-makers.

This focus on dam building has intensified water disputes and tensions in Asia, with implications for regional security and stability. These disputes are bound to worsen, given China's new focus on erecting mega-dams on international rivers, exemplified by its latest addition on the Mekong River (the 4,200MW Xiaowan Dam, which dwarfs Paris's Eiffel Tower in height) and a 38,000MW dam planned on the Brahmaputra at Metog, close to the disputed border with India.

The Metog Dam will be twice as large as the 18,300MW Three Gorges Dam, currently the world's largest, construction of which officially uprooted at least 1.7 million Chinese. Turkey, too, is building big dams on the Tigris and Euphrates rivers.

The countries likely to bear the brunt of such massive diversion of waters are those located farthest downstream on rivers such as the Brahmaputra, Mekong and Tigris–Euphrates: Bangladesh, whose very future is threatened by climate and environmental change; Vietnam, a rice bowl of Asia; and Iraq, still internally torn. China's water appropriations from the Illy River threaten to turn Kazakhstan's Lake Balkhash into another Aral Sea. Continued dam building in a number of Asian nations is also creating new intra-state tensions and challenges. Degraded watersheds constitute one of the most serious problems for sustainable development in Asia. Dams are also having other impacts, including changing river hydrology, sediment load, riparian vegetation, patterns of stream-bank erosion, migration of fish, and water temperature.

CONTAINING THE RISKS

To underpin strategic stability, protect continued economic growth, promote environmental sustainability and prevent the struggle for water resources from tipping into overt conflict, Asian states must invest more in institutionalized cooperation on transboundary basin resources. Water has emerged as a test case of Asia's ability to build cooperation rather than competition over a critical resource.

National dependency on waters from transnational rivers or aquifers is widespread across Asia. China is an exception: with less than 1% of its water resources dependent on cross-border inflow (one of the lowest rates in the world) it is happily placed. There are at least 57 transnational river basins in Asia, and most lack any kind of cooperative institution. The exact number of transnational groundwater basins is unknown as no scientific assessment has been undertaken.

Yet some of the shared aquifer systems have already become targets of rival appropriation plans and political tensions, for example al-Disi, which straddles the Saudi Arabian–Jordanian border. The existence of inter-country water agreements can be deceptive: most such accords in Asia relate to more mundane issues than sharing waters or sustainably managing transboundary basin resources. Commercial contracts, joint research or flood-control projects, use of river islands, hydropower development, and non-binding memoranda of understanding masquerade as water agreements.

In fact, only four of the transnational river basins in Asia are subject to treaties covering water sharing or other institutionalized cooperation. These are the Mekong (where the non-participation of China, the dominant upper riparian nation, has stunted development of a genuine basin community), the Ganges (between Bangladesh and India), the Indus (between India and Pakistan, with the greatest guaranteed cross-border flows of any treaty regime in the world) and the Jordan (a four-nation basin whose resources are the subject of a treaty arrangement restricted to Israel and Jordan).

The only treaties that incorporate a sharing formula on cross-border river flows are those covering the Indus and Ganges. But even these are far from perfect and often rife with dispute, especially in the Indus basin. They nevertheless serve useful purposes. In fact, all four Asian treaties demonstrate that inter-country basin arrangements can be concluded even among rival states and that such arrangements can survive political tensions and conflicts.

One imperative is to build Asian norms over shared transnational basin resources, using as a guide the codification of the principles of customary water law by the United Nations Convention on the Non-Navigational Uses of International Watercourses, even though this 1997 convention's entry into force still seems distant.

The only real way to avert or manage water disputes in Asia is to build basin arrangements involving all riparian neighbours. If a dominant riparian state refuses to join, such institutional arrangements will be ineffective.

The arrangements must be centred on transparency, information sharing, equitable distribution of benefits, dispute settlement, pollution control, joint projects and a mutual commitment to refrain from any projects that would materially diminish transboundary flows.

Water institutions, by facilitating constructive dialogue and structured cooperation, help stem the risk that disputes over water sharing or water quality could escalate to open conflict.

Building such regimes is never easy, given the complex physical, geopolitical and economic factors at play, including mismatched levels of economic development and the unilateral harnessing of shared waters by one or more coriparian states. Their legal, institutional and consultative mechanisms are designed not only to forestall interstate competition and conflict, but also to ensure that national water policies serve as a catalyst for social progress and economic growth through a stake in the integrated management of basin resources. Such cooperative arrangements can actually help improve water quality and availability.

Asia has little choice but to improve its water efficiency and productivity levels. Improvements in efficiency of water use in agriculture, energy and industry have stagnated at 1% or less per year for two decades. Greater investment is also needed to upgrade and maintain the water-supply infrastructure; losses from leaks amount to up to 29 billion m^3 of treated water a year, valued conservatively at $9 billion.

Asia's water crisis is opening opportunities for investment and technological innovation in two main areas. One is securing higher water efficiency and productivity gains, including through micro-irrigation systems and industrial water-use efficiency.

The other area is clean-water technologies, including wastewater treatment and recycling, desalination, and cleaning up contaminated or brackish water. These technologies hold the key to containing Asia's mounting water challenges.

Given Asia's exceptionally high water withdrawals for farming, savings will need to come primarily from water conservation and efficiency in agriculture so that more waters can be channelled to industries and cities.

Asian states have little choice but to upgrade their old irrigation systems and promote drip-feed irrigation, which is yet to be widely adopted.

This technology, which directs water flow straight to the root zone of plants, can help slash agricultural water consumption by 50–70% compared to gravity irrigation, and by 10–20% compared to sprinkler irrigation. Agricultural water productivity can also be increased through development of new grain varieties that are more tolerant of drought and flooding.

The Asian experience shows that the more populous a sub-region, a nation, or an area within a country, the greater are its water challenges, with water stress often being accompanied by a fall in water quality. But when water quality is maintained, the scarcity of water can be better managed. For example, Japan and South Korea have low per capita availability of freshwater compared with the global average, yet their good water quality overall better positions them to meet their national needs.

In cases where water quality and productivity have both appreciably increased, conditions of water stress tend to perceptibly lessen. South Korea's per capita water availability is close to Pakistan's, but it has done a much better job of building water quality and improving productivity.

As a result, South Korea, while prone to the ravages of drought, does not face the serious crisis situation haunting Pakistan. There is, in fact, much scope to increase water quality and productivity in many Asian countries, including those with already high efficiency and quality standards, such as South Korea, Japan and Singapore.

Even if energy- and cost-efficient clean-water technologies become available, the cost of water is set to rise sharply in Asia, especially for businesses.

Solar-powered desalination and wastewater recycling will help improve the situation, but the cost of supply is still bound to escalate because of additional infrastructure and maintenance needs. Desalination and wastewater-treatment technologies remain expensive as well as energy- and greenhouse-gas intensive.

MULTIDIMENSIONAL NATURE OF CENTRAL ASIA'S WATER DISPUTES

Water disputes contribute to the broader complex of problems across the region, including border disputes, Islamic extremism, high population growth, ethnic tensions, clan competition, human rights and political instability. The desiccation of the Aral Sea has been the important factor to the worsening socio-economic conditions in the area, fuelling nationalist ideas among the population of Karakalpakstan, the Uzbek autonomous republic adjacent to the disaster zone, and aggravating water situation in the region. Lack of public participation, particularly in authoritarian Turkmenistan and Uzbekistan, and attempts of those governments to find military decisions in already difficult relationships between those countries and upstream states makes the whole situation white-hot.

Ethnic dimension is extremely important for ethnically diverse Kyrgyzstan and Uzbekistan. As it happens, local conflicts here have been more serious than wider ones. Disputes over land and water resources provoking wider ethnic conflict have led to hundreds of victims in Kyrgyzstan in 1990. Poverty, rising costs and crumbling water infrastructure are adding to strains in local water system. Water affects the poor who end up paying the large proportion of their income for the resource.

Especially vulnerable to violent eruptions over water and ethnicity is the Ferghana Valley shared by Tajikistan, Kyrgyzstan and Uzbekistan which has already seen the outbreaks of violence, like it was in 1990, when bloody clashes between inhabitants of the Kyrgyz town of Osh claimed over 300 lives, or earlier, in 1989, when hundreds of the Meskhetian Turks, who had been deported to Central Asia by Stalin in the 1940s, were killed in the Uzbek town of Ferghana in what was called one of the most dramatic episodes of inter-ethnic relations in the Soviet Union.

The roots of any future ethnic strife in Central Asia lie in the unresolved social and economic problems, competition for scarce water and grazing resources and contentions over discriminatory land allocations (Elhance, 1997). Potentially explosive ethnic cleavages tear apart many countries in the region. Kyrgyzstan is divided between northern and southern part, with the latter gravitating towards Uzbekistan and inhabited by large proportion of ethnic Uzbeks who have repeatedly demanded to give the area more autonomy. Uzbekistan's headache is the large Tajik population living in Samarkand and Bukhara. Over the last years, Uzbekistan's policy was to suppress Tajik ethnic identity by not allowing schools to learn in Tajik language and forcing many Tajiks to call themselves ethnic Uzbeks in their Uzbek passports. The same situation is in Tajikistan where a lot of ethnic Uzbeks live. In the late 1990s, after the relations between Uzbekistan and Tajikistan have worsened, the Tajik government expelled many Uzbeks to neighbouring Kyrgyzstan and Afghanistan in an attempt to get rid of "extremist elements. Ethnic minorities have often been viewed by authoritarian governments as potential provocateurs, separatists and extremists (ICG, 2002a). Historic competition between peoples of Central Asia is fuelled by the fact that their leaders do not seem to like one another. There is a great personal competition between the three former Communist leaders, Uzbekistan's Islam Karimov, Kazakhstan's Nursultan Nazarbaev and Turkmenistan's Saparmurad Niyazov. Each wants to show that his country is the region's most powerful and he therefore should be viewed as the most prominent political figure in Central Asia. As a consequence, the leaders of the region does not see their countries to be the part of a functioning regional subsystem and are rather isolationist in their policies. For all this, they regularly meet to discuss their common problems (Olcott, 2001).

Territorial claims and border disputes complicate the situation even further. Given complex ethnic mosaic in Central Asia, Soviet planners did not build administrative units along ethnic lines and took great care not to construct republics with strong ethnic identity which would allow them to eventually secede from the Soviet Union. As a result, thorny disputes as to whose territory was initially whose have occurred, burdened by the territorial exchanges. For example, Karakalpakstan began life in 1924 as part of Kazakhstan but in 1938 had been given away to Uzbekistan. Moreover, Uzbekistan, Kyrgyzstan and Tajikistan all have small enclaves on each other's territory which are nominally a part of their country but are geographically isolated. Only Kyrgyzstan has two Tajik enclaves, with population of some 30,000 people, and five Uzbek ones, with population of about 50,000 people. Issues related to them are highly divisive, and solving this problem appeared to be very difficult (ICG, 2002a). However, the process of delimitation of the borders has already begun. In 2000-2003, Kazakhstan, Kyrgyzstan, Tajikistan and Uzbekistan signed a number of border delimitation agreements and started works on delimiting the borders. By 2001, Kazakhstan and Uzbekistan have finally settled the border problems and exchanged disputed territories. Yet many issues, like the problem of the Uzbek enclaves in Kyrgyzstan, still remain unresolved.

In this context, the growing need to take into account all factors surrounding water disputes is apparent.

MEASURING WATER CONFLICT POTENTIAL

Water is the most politicised of all natural resources and it is more likely to become a source of armed conflict. It is no wonder therefore that such possibility has been widely discussed. Despite the growing literature on water and conflict, little work has been done to provide arguments for the common thesis that "growing conflict over water looms ahead (Samson and Charrier, 1997). Generally, the Jordan and Nile basins are cited to give an example of international conflict prone basins. On the other hand, Wolf (1998) gave a historic evidence of co-operation between riparians and stated that the only recorded war over water was fought 4500 years ago between two Mesopotamian states, Lagash and Umma, in what is now southern Iraq. The same author pointed out at the "loose definitions in the terminology of the literature about water and conflict where "terms such as conflict, dispute, tensions, and war are regularly used interchangeably.

Nevertheless, in order to provide indication of potential water conflict, combinations of variables, or indicators, have to be developed. Undoubtedly, the practice of establishing various sets of indicators, including those for sustainable development, over the past decade has greatly influenced this idea. However, unlike indicators of sustainable development designed to communicate with the public at large to provide clear picture of a country's progress towards sustainable development, indicators of water conflict proneness are meant to serve as a 'yardstick' for decision makers who are involved in negotiations regarding specific river basin management.

Yet such 'limited' value does not impede the indicators of being used by international scientific and political community able to translate them into a pressure on the governments of the riparians involved in a dispute well before this would turn into a violent conflict. The use of Geographic Information System (GIS) makes such analysis even more effective by bringing together spatial and non-spatial variables, thus facilitating identification and interpretation of potential indicators.

One of the frequently cited instruments which could serve as a model for developing a set of water conflict indicators is the Index of Human Insecurity (IHI) developed to facilitate identification of vulnerable or insecure regions.

It is considered an "aggregate measure of human welfare that integrates social, economic, and political exposures to and capacity to cope with a range of potentially harmful perturbations (Lonergan, Gustavson and Carter, 1999).

The IHI identifies four key system components – the environment, the economy, society, and institutions. Within each of these four indicator categories are four variables, each of which measure either a key structural relationship (e.g., linkages, defining characteristics) or a key functional relationship (e.g., processes, flows) of the system.

Where data in a time series are missing, IHI developers utilize statistical techniques to establish a complete time series for all indicators and all countries, where there is sufficient initial data. However, the index for each year is specific to that year, making it difficult to compare changes in a country's IHI from across years (Yoffe and Ward, 1999).

Another water-specific indicator is water stress measured by Falkenmark's (1992) Water Stress Index (WSI) which divides the volume of a country's available water resources by its population. This measure, however, does not account for a country's ability to adapt to water stress, such as with more efficient irrigation technology. Ohlsson (1999) has developed a Social Water Stress Index (SWSI) to incorporate a measure of a country's adaptability. The SWSI is a water stress index (freshwater availability per capita) divided by UNDP's Human Development Index and then divided by 2 (rounded to nearest wholes). Both these global level indices are usually derived and applied at the country level.

Several other potential indicators were also mentioned in the literature, including overall population growth rates within a country, population density within and outside a basin, relative power and riparian position of countries within a basin (Wolf, 1999), the degree of democratisation of countries sharing a river basin and so on.

TESTING INDICATORS OF WATER CONFLICT

The methodology for establishing indicators of international freshwater conflict and co-operation was developed under Basins At Risk (BAR) project at Oregon State University, USA (Wolf, Yoffe and Giordano, 2003). BAR which has spanned for 4 years effectively developed and created legal and spatial framework to further evaluate international river basins at potential risk for future water conflict. All 263 international river basins were delineated and a database documenting historical incidents of international water conflict and co-operation between 1948 and 1999 was set up. Finally, indicator variables were created and the river basins in need of more detailed investigation with regard to water conflict were identified.

Indicators have been selected in accordance with the following criteria: relevance to the selected framework; general availability of the data; existence of a theoretical or empirical link with security issue; and an adequacy of spatial and temporal coverage allowing for effective representation and modelling (Lonergan, Gustavson and Carter, 1999). Emphasis was made on the regional and basin scale indicators rather than on indicators of potential water conflict at global scale. Internationalisation of a basin was at special focus. Assuming that there is a causal link between the internationalisation of a basin and incidents of conflict among the states that now share that basin, the presence of ethnic minorities with nationalistic aspirations becomes a potential indicator (Wolf, 1999).

A key question regarding the above variables is whether they are relevant to indicating water conflict. Yoffe (2001) provides a good account of statistically testing indicators previously cited in the literature. As main statistical tool, linear regression was used to assess the relative strength of various independent variables in explaining the variability of the event data. Also, other statistical methods such as two-sample t-test were employed. Linear regression has been chosen because it offered a concise summary of the mean of the response variable as a function of an explanatory variable (Yoffe, 2001).

Sixteen indicators, including GDP per capita, population density, number of dams, water stress, HDI, hydropower have been tested using linear regression, three indicators such as freshwater treaties, adjacency and riverine contiguity have been analysed using two-sample t-test, and four indicators such as dam density, freshwater treaties, climate and precipitation had no statistical tests conducted on them due to structure of data.

Yoffe's most important finding was that most of the commonly cited water conflict indicators proved to be unsupported by the data. Neither government type, climate, IHI, water stress or number of dams, nor agricultural dependence on water resources and energy needs showed a significant relevance with water conflict. Based on the assessment, river basins are at potential risk of freshwater conflict if:

- population density exceeds 100 people per 1 km^2
- per capita GDP is less than $765
- overall unfriendly relations (<-1 at water event intensity scale)
- there are politically active minority groups that may lead to the internationalisation of a basin
- large dams or other water development projects are planned
- no or limited number of water treaties is available (Yoffe, 2001).

This study will employ these indicator variables as the research framework.

ROLE OF GIS

A number of the attribute data mentioned above can be effectively represented within a Geographic Information System (GIS), such as ESRI ArcView, designed to capture, store, manipulate, analyse and visualize disparate sets of geographically referenced data. Moreover, some spatial information such as runoff and slope would be extremely difficult to analyse without the use of a GIS.

However, GIS has its limitations inherent to the technology, including problems of multiple scales and data interpretation. The examination of indicators at an international, national and sub-national level introduces questions of scale that will need to be further addressed. There is also a lack of distinct frameworks to analyse the interaction of human and environmental systems (Yoffe and Ward, 1999). Linked to the problem of frameworks is the problem with interpreting non-spatial matters using spatial analysis. For instance, the degree of democratisation of a country might be difficult to represent if one assumes that different areas have different levels of democratisation. Special problem regarding Central Asia's GIS is the lack of data; several important databases located in Tashkent, Uzbekistan, contain a lot of vital information but this information is virtually closed for external use.

Attempts at Applying Water Conflict Indicators to Central Asia

Previous attempt to apply potential indicators of water conflict to Central Asia's water disputes has been made by Myers (1993) who created a water scarcity index using population and per capita water availability data. Assuming that water stress is to occur when more than 2,000 people share every unit of one million cubic meters of available water, the author calculated water indices for each of Central Asia's countries by comparing 1991 population data with all available water and the amount of water available solely from indigenous sources (i.e. that available from precipitation within the borders of a country). In 1993, all the countries appeared to have sufficient water resources per capita. Both downstream countries of Turkmenistan and Uzbekistan relied on water flowing in from outside and indigenous water resources stress was high (2,180 people per one million m^3 of indigenous water in Uzbekistan and 3,287 people per one million m^3 of indigenous water in Turkmenistan).

Klötzli (1994) used a number of indicators for vulnerability to water scarcity developed by Gleick (1993), including the ratio of water demand to supply, the per capita availability of water, the dependence on imported surface water and the importance of hydroelectric production. Having calculated these, the author came to a somewhat obvious conclusion that "these indicators show a distinct difference between the water-rich republics of Kyrgyzstan and Tajikistan, and the republics not controlling the sources of water courses like Uzbekistan and Turkmenistan The vulnerability indices not only express different access and pollution control opportunities, but also different, often contradictory modes of water utilisation (hydropower vs. agriculture) (Klötzli, 1994). Similar method based on Gleick's findings was used by Smith (1995) to determine the relative degree of dependence of particular regions on water resources and to identify those regions that may become potential focal points for future intra- and interstate conflicts. It is argued that high population growth can be more damaging to the environment than high population density and southern Uzbekistani provinces as Surkhandarya and Kashakdarya and several regions in the Ferghana Valley that experienced some of the highest population growth rates in the region between 1981 and 1991 are most likely to become a scene of a resource-related conflict. The author points out that the areas combining high population growth and no indigenous water supplies (Andijan and Ferghana in eastern Uzbekistan, Karakalpakstan in the west) are of prime concern. As Turkmenistan's Dashhovuz region and Uzbekistan's Karakalpakstan share the water of the lower Amu Darya, future water-induced conflicts may occur in this region. Each region was ranked according to the basic characteristics believed to affect the water conflict potential (population growth rate/density, per capita water availability from total and indigenous sources, share of water derived from external sources, minority population share of total population). Eight of ten regions having the highest rankings for water-resource vulnerability are located in Uzbekistan, with top of the top four located in the Ferghana Valley. Thus, the regions constituting the Ferghana Valley and those occupying the lower Amu Darya appear to be the most sensitive to potential water-induced conflicts.

Carney and Moran (2000) examined the interstate affect in Central Asia toward Russia, i.e. "the current discernable feeling of a government toward another government which is expressed "...in all behaviour whether it takes the form of word or deeds, and developed "scale of affectivity ranging arbitrarily from -2 to +2. Although different in goals, this study employed the similar technique in scoring and coding news reports from Foreign Broadcast Information Service (FBIS).

Also mentioning the Aral Sea Basin's famous conflict potential, Yoffe (2001) and Wolf, Yoffe and Giordano (2003) argue that the basin countries tend to negotiate current conflicts. However, none of the treaties signed recently include all the basin riparians, and therefore potential for continued disputes, at least in the nearest future, is likely.

Given global scale of BAR project, considering and spatially interpreting all physical, social, economic and political variables for Central Asia becomes even more vital and can provide solutions based on a more holistic approach to natural resources, while recognising the historical, geopolitical and natural characteristics of the region.

WATER EVENT INTENSITY SCALE

Wolf, Yoffe and Giordano (2003) recount of compiling a systematic database for water conflict/co-operation worldwide, in an attempt to gather every reported interaction between two or more nations, where water was the driver of the event. Using various international news databases, like FBIS and its online version, World News Connection (WNC), the authors developed 'a friendship-hostility scale' – a ratio of all co-operative to conflictive events between nations over water, having modified a scale created by Conflict and Peace Databank (COPDAB) project directed by Professor Edward E. Azar.

COPDAB's scale ranges from level 1, representing the most co-operative events, to level 15, representing the most conflictive events, with level 8 representing neutral events. To make it water-specific, the authors inverted it so that neutral events were centred on zero, to make it ranging from -7 to +7, with -7 denoting the most conflictive events, 0 denoting neutral events, and +7 denoting the most cooperative events. The new scale also included the addition of water terms, and a new category, "formal declaration of war." To accommodate this category, which is not part of the original COPDAB Scale, category 13 (Small scale military acts) and 14 (Limited war acts) were merged into one category, number 13. Category 14 was given the heading and description of category 15 (Extensive war acts causing deaths, dislocation or high strategic costs), and Category 15 was changed to indicate a formal declaration of war (Yoffe, 2001).

For the purposes of this study, BAR global Water Event Intensity Scale is adapted to the Amu Darya basin countries in Central Asia to determine overall relations and identify focal points for the future conflicts while concurrently applying GIS-based variables of water conflict.

Aggregating Data for the Amu Darya Basin

In creating ArcView data coverages for the Amu Darya Basin, data for international river basins kindly provided by Dr Aaron T. Wolf was used which was then matched to the US Geological Service Hydro1k (USGS, 2000) dataset, a global coverage of streams and drainage basins derived from digital elevation data. The data collected fell into roughly two categories: biophysical (e.g. runoff, population, dams) attributes suitable for the spatial analysis and economic/political (e.g. GDP per capita, overall relations, ethnic minorities) attributes. Although some of the variables used are quantitative and can be measured, the indicators comprising political category are qualitative in nature (internationalisation of a basin, future water infrastructure, water treaties).

Population

In pulling various water-related attributes together in order to draw a picture of a basin's specific conflict proneness, population growth is among key factors for assessing water scarcity. The relation of water access to population distribution should therefore be assessed. As a river basin rarely follows political borders, per basin population density instead of per region population density was evaluated. In doing so, the Landscan gridded population of the world (Landscan, 2001) was used to approximate population distribution. Building on the Landscan data proved very effective as the Landscan team used remotely sensed slope, land cover, road proximity and night time lights to refine the GIS-based gridded population cell values, providing the best accurate dataset. Gridcell values for the Aral Sea Basin were summed to combine this table with the Amu Darya Basin, thus calculating a population density for that area, as described by Yoffe (2001).

Runoff

Runoff is considered the total amount of surface flow in a given area. Any assessment of a water resource related issue would be incomplete without some approximation of water availability within the study area (Yoffe, 2001). Data for the Amu Darya runoff were obtained through a spatial resolution grid of composite runoff fields based on observed river discharge and simulated water balances (Fekete, Vörsmarty and Grabs, 2000). The project was the outcome of a joint effort of the Complex Systems Research Centre at the University of New Hampshire and the Global Runoff Data Centre in Koblenz, Germany. The project combined "...two sources of information (observed discharge and simulated runoff) to estimate continental runoff which was "the most reliable assessment at present (Fekete, Vörsmarty and Grabs, 2000). To estimate the composite runoff for the Amu Darya, runoff data for the eight gauging stations located in the Amu Darya basin were used. The cell values in mm/yr were multiplied by the area of the associated grid cell in sq. km to produce a runoff volume grid (mm*km^2/yr).

Dams

The third key factor in assessing water scarcity is the number and density of dams in a study area. According to Yoffe (2001) and Wolf, Yoffe and Giordano (2003), when statistically testing potential water conflict indicators, dams themselves did not appear to be a potential indicator for water conflict, yet in basins without water treaties lower dam density basins tended to exhibit slightly less conflict. With negative overall relations between countries and absence of a transboundary institution, unilaterally setting a large dam or diversion project can provide a context for the conflict over water, while positive relations and presence of a transboundary institution can mitigate the situation. To determine the number of dams and dam density for the Amu Darya Basin, global dataset provided by Wolf was used, based on the Digital Chart of the World data and International Commission on Large Dams (ICOLD) World Register of Dams. More importantly, large proposed water infrastructure projects that proved to have significant influence on the whole water situation in the basin were identified (e.g. the Rogun Dam in Tajikistan, etc.).

Minority Groups

Internationalising a basin provides an important setting for future water conflict (Wolf, Yoffe and Giordano, 2003). Those basins whose management institutions were developed under a single jurisdiction and then became divided among two or more nations when that jurisdiction suddenly collapsed, showed much higher levels of conflict (Yoffe, 2001).

In order to check for the active nationalist movements who might cause future internationalisation of the Amu Darya Basin, data from two major sources have been analysed: Minorities At Risk Project, at the University of Maryland's Centre for International Development and Conflict Management (Gurr, 2000) and Unrepresented Nations and Peoples Organisation (UNPO, 2002).

GDP

Low per capita GDP (< $765/person according to the World Bank lowest income country definition) was identified to be one of the indicators of conflict over water (Yoffe, 2001).

As Wolf, Yoffe and Giordano (2003) put it, the higher the per capita GDP, or the lower population density, the greater the co-operation – barely. To establish macro-economic data for the Amu Darya Basin countries, the World Bank data for 2000 were used.

Overall Relations

It is pointed out (Yoffe, 2001) that countries that co-operate in general also co-operate over water, and countries with overall unfriendly relations are also unfriendly over water issues.

To construct a 'friendship-hostility scale' as appeared in Wolf, Yoffe and Giordano (2003), a rough water event intensity scale was built employing the technique.

In gathering country-to-country events and interactions, two major sources were used: the WNC and Transboundary Freshwater Dispute Database.

Both build on the reports about Central Asia by the two leading Russian news agencies – ITAR-TASS and Interfax, as well as on the news coverages by Eurasianet and the Mashhad Voice of the Islamic Republic of Iran (Tajikistan news). Notably, the water event data are based on public reports and therefore lack reports on non-public co-operation ("picnic table talks, non-official visits, etc.)

Freshwater Treaties

Generally, freshwater treaties mitigate conflict, and no or limited freshwater treaties for a basin increase the likeliness of conflict over water. To analyse existing freshwater treaties for the Amu Darya Basin, the International Freshwater Treaties Database at Oregon State University (TFDD, 2002), containing a full text of over 400 international freshwater related agreements, was used.

WATER CONFLICT POTENTIAL IN THE AMU DARYA BASIN

Population Density/runoff

The Amu Darya's population is extremely unevenly distributed. Only in Uzbekistan which has the region's highest population density (average >50 people per km^2, with total population of about 25 million in 2002), 80 percent of land is desert. In 1990, the rural population occupied a total of 4.5 million hectares of arable land, or about 16 percent of all available agricultural land in the country, and thus the effective density of rural population was 2.7 people per hectare of arable land. Given the rate of natural population growth in Uzbekistan being one of the highest among the former Soviet republics, rural population steadily increased from 1984 to 1994 to 61 percent, while the arable land and cultivated area remained practically unchanged (Lerman, Garcia-Garcia and Wichelns, 1996).

Population distribution in the Amu Darya Basin varies accordingly, from 20-30 people per km^2 in the downstream sections of the river (except for the river stretch just before flowing into the Aral Sea that runs across the Uzbek territory and where population density is about 40-50 people/km^2) to 25-40 people/km^2 in the middle course and to 20-35 people/km^2 in the upstream sections of the Amu Darya.

The population pattern in Central Asia has remained the same over thousands of years. People tend to inhabit fertile oases and valleys rich in water. Many human habitats can be found located along the rivers, and almost all of them date from the pre-Islamic times. In terms of runoff, the Amu Darya can be divided into three sections: an upstream section, a middle course section, and a downstream section. The upstream section extends from the point of confluence of the Vakhsh and Pyandj rivers up to the town of Kerki, the middle course is between Kerki and the Tyuyamuyun Gorge, and the downstream section is confined to the mouth of the river. In the upstream section, the flow of the Amu Darya steadily increases due to the Kunduz, Kafirnigan, Surkhandarya, and Sherabad tributaries.

The reverse situation can be observed in the middle course and in the downstream section: the flow gradually declines due to natural losses of runoff and huge water diversions for agricultural needs. It is quite difficult to evaluate those natural and anthropogenic losses as the data from many gauging stations for the last two decades are not available. Average annual runoff at the town of Kerki (upstream section) between 1957-1987 was 1903 m^3/s, together with water diverted to Karakum and Karshi canals, 1351 m^3/s in the Tyuyamuyun Gorge (middle course) in the same period and 656 m^3/s in the downstream section (Ivanov and Izmaiylov, 1995).

Planned Water Infrastructure

Unilateral decisions to embark on new water projects are not uncommon in Central Asia. While providing for national solutions, such decisions and further actions are among key drivers of potential water conflict. Trying to find a way out of the existing situation, some Central Asian governments were forced to develop plans for building more infrastructure to get control over water resources. Two projects which are the legacy of the Soviet-style gigantic undertakings and which caused extremely negative reaction among neighbours.

The Rogun Dam

Started in 1976, the Rogun Dam, on the Vakhsh river, was projected to be 335 metres high – the highest in the world - with the capacity to produce 3,600 MW of energy. The dam was expected to begin operation in 1993. However, in 1990 the construction was halted due to the escalating political situation which turned into a 5-year civil war in Tajikistan. In 1993, a massive flood destroyed most of what has been already built. By that time, $802 million was invested into the project, with the total cost of $2.3 billion.

Tajikistan already controls 40 percent of the flow of the Amu Darya through the Nurek reservoir. The Rogun would put it firmly in control of the river, allowing to control the flow into Uzbekistan's Surkhandarya and Kashkadarya Provinces that already experience sharp water shortages. Knowing Uzbekistan's opposition to the project, Tajikistan continues to press with the completion of the Rogun Dam that would need $700 million to $1 billion to complete.

Most international finance institutions are reluctant to put any money into the project, claiming that it would cost more than any benefit it might offer. They are also aware that the project would seriously strain relations between Tajikistan and Uzbekistan. However, getting Tajik government concentrate on more feasible, realistic and low-cost project yielded no fruits. On 29 October 2002, the Baltic Construction Company, one of the biggest Russian investment/construction groups, became a contractor and investor for completion of the Rogun Dam project (Dyuzheva, 2002; ICG, 2002b).

Golden Century Lake

In October 2000, Turkmenistan began work on a huge artificial lake in the Karakum Desert, which was pompously called Golden Century Lake. The lake is being built in the Karashor natural depression in the north-western part of the Karakum desert. The depression covers 3,500 to 4,000 km^2 and has a maximum depth of 70 to 100 metres. Once completed, the lake would contain some 132 to 150 km^3 of water. Drainage water is to be diverted to the lake from the five provinces through two major collector-canals. The project cost is up to $6 billion, and it will be financed from state budget. The first stage is to be completed in 2004 and the entire project covers 10 years. There are rumours that special nuclear power station will be built nearby to use a lake as a cooling pond. The government holds that only drainage water will be used to supply the lake.

The project raised immediate concerns in neighbouring Uzbekistan that the lake cannot be sustained by drainage water alone and about 10 cubic kilometres of water from the Amu Darya will be needed to maintain its level. Uzbekistan argues that drainage water has a high salt content and will gradually evaporate in the terrible heat of the Karakum desert creating a new Aral. By increasing the water use from the Amu Darya, Turkmenistan would leave the southern Uzbek provinces without any water. If Ashgabat will go ahead with the project, it will inevitably lead to tensions with Uzbekistan (Insarova, 2002).

Just like the Toktogul reservoir on the Syr Darya, this ambitious and costly undertaking risks becoming a source of conflict with Uzbekistan. Turkmenistan also threatens to resettle about one million ethnic Uzbeks from the southern province of Dashhovuz to the Karakum desert once the lake is completed (ICG, 2002b).

FURTHER INTERNATIONALISATION POTENTIAL

Possible Secession of Karakalpakstan

The Autonomous Republic of Karakalpakstan is one of the 13 provinces, or oblasts, in Uzbekistan. Its history began in 1925, when the Karakalpaks (a Turkic-language Muslim group whose name literally means "black hat") were given their own territory, declared the Autonomous Oblast, within the Kazakh Soviet Socialist Republic (SSR). In 1930, the Karakalpak AO was transferred to the jurisdiction of the Russian Soviet Federative Socialist Republic, where it remained until 1936, when it was joined to the Uzbek SSR and elevated to the status of the Autonomous SSR (Hanks, 2000). After Uzbekistan's independence, Karakalpakstan received autonomous republic status within Uzbekistan. Since that time, the central government in Tashkent has maintained pressure and tight economic ties that have kept the republic from exerting full independence.

Today, the population of Karakalpakstan is about 1.3 million people who live on a territory of about 168,000 km^2. Located in the fertile lower reaches of the Amu Darya where the river empties into the Aral Sea, Karakalpakstan has a long history of irrigation agriculture. However, because it is a tail end of the Amu Darya, Karakalpakstan received all the pollution the river has accumulated along its course. The health statistics (morbidity and mortality data) collectively reflect the poor and deteriorating health of the people downstream. My personal experience of work for the Eye Cancer Register Project at the Institute of Oncology and Radiology in Tashkent showed that while eye cancer incidence in Karakalpakstan was relatively low, mortality rate was the highest in Uzbekistan (2.2 people per 100,000 people, compared to 0.2 to 0.3/100,000 in other provinces of Uzbekistan) (Mouratova, 1992). More generally, the Karakalpaks showed one of the highest rates of cancer, comparable only to Kazakhs living in Muynak area of Karakalpakstan.

Even in the Soviet times, nationalist sentiment and identity among the Karakalpaks were stronger than scholars believed and Uzbekistan's independence marked by the rise of Uzbek nationalism has seen the Karakalpak national movement too. However, this group known as the Khalk Mapi was quickly suppressed and driven underground. Although the Karakalpaks never demonstrated publicly for the formal independence and the republic is not a member of UNPO, the Uzbek authorities view a possible nationalist tendency in Karakalpakstan as seriously threatening Uzbekistan's integrity.

In the meanwhile, little study has been undertaken to go deep into the question of a possible disintegration of Uzbekistan. Various researchers have briefly pointed out that Karakalpakstan has the potential to claim its independence from Uzbekistan (Kltzli, 1994; Baechler, 1998; Lietzman and Vest, 1999). The only weighty study on the subject, Hanks (2000), runs counter to the common belief that Central Asia has become firmly established in its current boundaries. Hanks supports that there are four factors that may contribute to the Karakalpak nationalism, notably: (1) a separate cultural identity; (2) a history of territorial identity and autonomy; (3) economic underdevelopment; and (4) severe environmental damage, resulting in drastic decline in human conditions.

Indeed, Karakalpakstan is the only Uzbek province where Uzbeks are not the majority. Unlike Tajiks in Samarkand and Bukhara, the Karakalpaks are allowed to learn in their native language in schools and 2.6% of the school-age population are enrolled in Karakalpak schools which means that most Karakalpaks are insistent that their children be educated in their mother tongue. And the Karakalpak language is quite different from the Uzbek one being linguistically closer to the Kazakh language just as the whole Karakalpak culture is. Historically and ethnically, Karakalpaks, with their nomadic culture, would show best in Kazakhstan where such culture is persistent and where Karakalpaks are still considered *oralman*, i.e. members of the Kazakh community living abroad. During the past 12 years, as much as 270,000 Karakalpaks, or 20% of the population, left Uzbekistan for Kazakhstan and Russia, largely due to the unbearable human and environmental conditions in the Aral Sea area (Glantz, 2002). Small, van der Meer and Upshur (2001) quote the study showing that 48.8% of respondents wanted to leave their homes because of the environment, and one half of those wanted to move out of the Aral Sea area.

In economic terms, Karakalpakstan represents a remote geographical hinterland, absent from global economy, with virtually no industrial development and soaring unemployment rates. Agricultural sector is on the verge of collapse and fisheries, once a profitable sector, disappeared along with the whole Aral Sea. Due to the fact that most imported goods are shipped to Tashkent, 1000 kilometres away from Nukus, capital of Karakalpakstan, fewer goods are offered there, adding to the general quality of life being the lowest in the country.

Officially, 100,000 people were unemployed in 2002 as a result of the multi-year drought that began in 1999 and by 2001 reduced cotton production in Karakalpakstan by 75% of the norm. Rice production was only 0.25% of the norm (Glantz, 2002). The situation aggravated so much that people are slaughtering livestock because animals started dying of thirst. In a region where cattle have implications for the future, killing cows means losing a major asset (Kohn, 2001).

All this resulted in the fact that most Karakalpaks began viewing themselves as the environmental victims and hostages of the central power, first in Moscow, then in Tashkent. Why don't Karakalpaks revolt? – ponders Bissell (2002). So far, only what can be called "a foot vote, i.e. the exodus of the Karakalpak population to neighbouring Kazakhstan, has happened. ICG (2002b) quotes one Uzbek official as saying that people of Karakalpakstan "...are patient and put their hope in God and the President.

Indeed, an independent Karakalpakstan may be unlikely in the future. Poor state of economy and environmental degradation undermined the region's development so much that an independent Karakalpakstan would have a little chance for survival.

But this in no way lessens the potential for the region to destabilise Uzbekistan and eventually the whole Central Asia (Hanks, 2000). Possible is also the Indonesian scenario – when the central regime grows weak, nationalist claims in the provinces become stronger and may eventually lead to a secession.

Role of Afghanistan

Northern Afghanistan belongs to the Amu Darya Basin. Until recently, before the US-led campaign against the Taliban and Al-Qaeda, this area was de facto independent from the rest of the country, remaining firmly under control of the Uzbek and Tajik warlords opposing the regime in Kabul.

Today, when the central government of Hamid Karzai is trying to spread its authority on the rest of the country, the question of separate northern provinces is less important in light of the emerging Afghanistan integrity. Before 2001, Afghanistan was itself the factor of risk for the Basin.

It is still unclear what share would Afghanistan's agricultural sector require from the Amu Darya water and when. It is clear though that Afghanistan will demand its share and that it is entitled to that share under the international agreements signed between the USSR and Afghanistan in 1946 (*Frontier Agreement between Afghanistan and the USSR*, 13 June 1946) and 1958 (*Treaty concerning the regime to the Soviet-Afghan frontier*, 18 January 1958, and *Protocol between the USSR and Afghanistan concerning the joint execution of works for the integrated utilisation of the water resources in the frontier section of the Amu Darya*, 25 June 1958). The 1946 Agreement subjects all matters associated with the water use to specific agreements between the two countries and provides for the establishment of a joint commission. Under it, Afghanistan is entitled to use up to 9 km^3 of water from the Pyandj river. Under the Treaty of 18 January 1958, the two countries commit themselves to take joint measures to prevent changes in the course of frontier rivers, streams or canals and to correct the effects of such changes and share the costs equally.

Furthermore, they commit themselves to prevent water pollution, to exchange regular information on the level and volume of water and meteorological data and to adopt a flood warning system. Finally, the 1958 Protocol envisages the joint integrated utilisation of the frontier sections of the Amu Darya (Nanni, 1996).

Since "localisable international agreements (i.e. those relating to identifiable parts of the territory of states) are subject to state succession under international law, these agreements remain in force for the newly independent Central Asian states (Nanni, 1996; Vinogradov and Langford, 2001).

Until now, Afghanistan has used only about 2 km^3 of the 9 km^3 of water it is entitled to use under the treaties. Meanwhile, the Pyandj river has the annual flow of 19 km^3, and Afghanistan's fresh involvement into the process of water use would radically change the Amu Darya flow if the new Afghan government decides to develop agriculture in the North. Plans of Afghanistan to increase its water share caused the respective reaction in neighbouring countries. ICG (2002b) quotes one Uzbek official quotes as saying, God forbid that we should give water also to Afghanistan. What will then become of us?

Given that the rehabilitation of Afghanistan is impossible without increasing its intake from the Amu Darya and that water resources are vital for Afghan people to feed themselves, the potential for water conflict in the Basin increases proportionally. Afghanistan's demands will have to be taken into account when negotiating the water situation in the Basin (Fuchinoue, Tsukatani and Toderich, 2002).

GDP

All Amu Darya Basin countries are considered low-income countries, i.e. those where GDP is less than $750, according to the World Bank classification. Below is per capita GDP in US$ for the four Amu Darya riparians:

Table : GDP per capita in the Amu Darya Basin countries

Country	*GDP per capita*
Afghanistan	not available
Tajikistan	170
Turkmenistan	765
Uzbekistan	449

Source: World Bank, 2000

Aggregate average GDP per capita for the Amu Darya Basin is $461.3. Given the extreme poverty people of Afghanistan still live in, this indicator may actually be even less.

Overall Relations/Water Events

In political science, overall relations indicate an interstate affect which in turn highly influences regional co-operation over water. By scoring an affective content of each of 100 events occurred in the relations between the Amu Darya riparians in 1995-2003, of which only 24 events concerned the region's water resources, it was possible to draw a rough picture of how the Amu Darya Basin countries feel toward each other.

For the purposes of this study, an event is defined as the instance of regional conflict and co-operation that occur within an international river basin, and water event as the instance of regional conflict and co-operation over water resources of that specific basin (Yoffe, 2001). Every event of interaction between two or more riparians mentioned in a database was grouped and included into either representing overall relations in the Amu Darya Basin or representing water-related events in the basin. Each table contains the following information:

- the date of the incident;
- riparians involved;
- the intensity of the event, based on the Water Event Intensity Scale;
- a summary describing the event;
- main issue area (economic co-operation, water quality, etc.);
- the source of information.

Three Amu Darya riparian countries – Tajikistan, Turkmenistan and Uzbekistan - have been considered. Afghanistan was excluded from the analysis as until 2001 this country itself manifested a serious threat for the region's security and by the time of preparing this study the central authority in Kabul was still in the beginning of the process of integrating the country. At the same time, northern Afghanistan was far from pacified and heavy fights between local warlords have been reported.

It is apparent that overall unfriendly attitude prevails in the relations between the riparians and despite friendship agreements signed and close economic ties the situation has repeatedly sharpened when Uzbekistan having the region's biggest military potential was not long in using force against its neighbours not even trying to enter into negotiation.

This dangerous trend may as well extend on the water relations, and according to informal sources it already has (situation around the Tyuyamuyun and the Toktogul).

Quite frequently, the relations between the three have become seriously strained and for several occasions the countries were on the verge of an open conflict.

Once it was an open conflict when on 16 August 1999 the Uzbek planes bombed Tajik and Kyrgyz territory targeting a group of Islamic militants. Uzbekistan's leadership never hesitated to use force and have always been insistent on establishing the way in which events should develop.

The country has also followed this course in its relations with Turkmenistan whose self-glorifying regime has much in common with the Uzbek one. But especially worrisome are Uzbekistan's relations with Tajikistan whose militant opposition has been steadily supported by Tashkent throughout the whole long civil war.

Claiming support for the Tajik government, Uzbekistan continued to feed ethnic Uzbek guerrillas on the Tajik territory and opened its borders for them when they were escaping from the Tajik troops.

Neither there was a shortage of assurances in eternal friendship and fraternal love, against a chilly history of land mines Uzbekistan used to plant along the entire length of Tajik border to build a ludicrous protection against Islamic terrorists and cutting off the pipes near the Tyuyamuyun reservoir in Turkmenistan. The treaties and agreements have been signed as well, but little action followed to implement them. Instead, the countries continued with hostile policies.

All in all, 4 incidents of "small scale military acts, 7 "political-military hostile actions, 8 "diplomatic-economic hostile actions and 7 "strong verbal expressions displaying hostility in interaction have been registered. In addition, the countries constantly displayed "discord in interaction (18 incidents), versus a much smaller number of events considered potentially positive (signing agreements, establishing common policy, visit of head of state, etc.)

While the picture of overall relations is definitely skewed to the left and tends to manifest rather conflict than co-operation, the history of relations over water looks at the first glance more co-operative.

Dozens of agreements have been entered into between the riparians. Some of these agreements had a status of an international water treaty designed to ease tensions between the basin countries. Meanwhile, the situation remains the same because the leaders prefer to do things informally rather than on the basis of an open agreement. However, when it comes to addressing conferences and summits, the presidents are always ready to mouth the rhetoric of regional co-operation while never lingering to use force against their "friendly neighbours (ICG, 2002b).

7

India-China: A Water Conflict over the Brahmaputra

WATER CONFLICT

Discourses over the waters of the Brahmaputra River have been doing the rounds ever since China's announcement about the construction of three dams on the river last year. Despite diplomatic talks, China is keen to divert the waters from the Brahmaputra. In the past, China did not have a strong raison d'être to divert the flow of the river. China's Vice Minister of Water Resources, Jiao Yong, stated in 2011 that the Chinese government was not planning to conduct any diversion projects along the Brahmaputra River given that there wasn't a pressing need.

However, at present, China's per capita water reserve is approximately 2300 cubic metres – one-fourth of the world's average. China is, therefore, considered as the 13th most 'water-poor' country in the world with 80 per cent of its cities severely water stressed. More so, China's northern region possesses only 14.5 per cent of the entire country's water resources. As water supplies tighten, the water quality is degrading, ecology is suffering, and lands are becoming barren. This threatens the country's economic growth. Thus, the ever-increasing gap in the demand and supply chain in China's northern region has now pushed the country to move forward with its many dam projects.

China is keen to divert 150 billion cubic meters (BCM) of water and 'push' the waters to irrigate northern China. Of this, 50 BCM would be diverted from the Brahmaputra. In October 2013, India asserted the need for a water sharing treaty with China. This came about, following the paranoia generated after the announcement of the 510-MW Zangmu project along the course of the river. However, although Indian Prime Minister Manmohan Singh returned with an agreement on sharing water-related information during the monsoon months, there was no mention of the planned diversion of the Brahmaputra. So far, India has been incapable in convincing China into building bilateral cooperation over the Brahmaputra River. The previous government in New Delhi did not want to antagonise bilateral relations with Beijing, and it is possible that the new government will follow suit.

India recognises that it is not in a position to wage a war with China. However, despite tensions and disagreements over common rivers, India has maintained relatively peaceful hydrological relations with its neighbours – with the Indus, Teesta, and Ganga Rivers being cases in point. On no occasion, did India seek to wage war as a means to resolve its water woes. In this light, India may not enter into a conflict with China over the Brahmaputra, but tensions seem probable.

THE BRAHMAPUTRA: WATER HOTSPOT IN HIMALAYAN ASIA

Strategic analysts around the world increasingly have their eyes on the Brahmaputra River, a transboundary watercourse that has its headwaters in the Tibetan Plateau of the Himalayan mountain range. In both length and discharge one of the Earth's most formidable rivers, the Brahmaputra (the Yarlung Tsangpo in China) has a lengthy run eastward of about 1,700 kilometers (1,100 miles) through China's Tibetan Autonomous Region before winding south into India's northeast, thence into Bangladesh from where it empties into the Bay of Bengal.

The three riparian states sharing the Brahmaputra – China, India, and Bangladesh– are the world's first, second, and seventh most populous countries. All three face severe problems of water scarcity. All three also face steeply rising demand for increased power – including hydropower – generation. The possibility of serious resource conflict involving these demographic giants stems primarily from Chinese and Indian plans, some already being implemented, to put the river's thus-far relatively unexploited waters to greater use.

Hydropower generation is one such use. The combination of burgeoning populations, rapid economic growth, and intensified global competition for energy resources is driving China and India to put increasing emphasis on hydropower. India, already the world's sixth largest energy consumer, ranks seventh globally (2008) in current hydropower generation. Possessing an estimated 148,700 MW of installed capacity potential, it ranks sixth globally (2010) among nations in economically exploitable hydropower. However, only about 19.9 percent of India's hydropower potential has been developed thus far. Hence, India's river resources loom large today in Indian energy plans. With its untapped potential standing at 95 percent, the Brahmaputra looms largest of all. China also has immense energy requirements. In 2010, it consumed 20.3 percent of the world's primary energy supplies; and in that year it overtook the United States to become the world's largest energy consumer. Its power sector is largely dependent on fossil fuels, coal in particular; but with China's energy consumption bound to grow immensely in coming decades, the need to lower coal- dependence means a massive shift to alternative fuels, including hydropower.

China already has more hydroelectric dams (over 22,000) than any other country in the world. With its installed hydropower capacity reportedly having reached 213,000 MW by the end of 2010, it was by far the world's leading producer of hydroelectricity. It plans to lift the proportion of non-fossil fuel use in the country's energy sector to 15 percent by 2020; and half of that is expected to come from hydropower. That means that China aims to have 430,000 MW of hydropower capacity hardly a decade hence, a better than doubling of its existing capacity. That figure is over two- and-a-half times larger than India's entire power sector could boast for all fuels in 2010, and nearly twelve times larger than India's hydropower output in that year. To put it most graphically, China's hydropower quest is intended to add the equivalent of one new Three Gorges Dam, at 22,500 MW the world's largest, each year over the current decade. Given the overall vast leap in anticipated energy consumption, this converts to a truly major surge in hydroelectric dam building.

China is now predictably casting its eyes on the Brahmaputra's hydropower potential on China's side of the border. According to one close observer, Tibet researcher Tashi Tsering, China has already constructed 10 dams on tributaries of the upper Brahmaputra, with 3 more under construction, 7 more under consideration, and yet 8 more proposed – a grand total, if eventually built, of 28.1. Those dams already built are small in scale and, since none are on the Brahmaputra mainstream, have stirred little interest outside China. However, China's plans apparently include building 5 major dams directly on the Brahmaputra mainstream. Completion of construction on the first of them, the $1.18 billion 510 MW Zangmu hydropower project in the middle reaches of the river, is expected by 2014.

More worrying yet was the possibility that China's aggressive search for promising hydropower dam sites in Tibet might ultimately drive Beijing to focus on the so- called Great Bend in the Brahmaputra, the point in the Himalayas where the river curves south onto India's Assamese plain. It was reported in May 2010 that research had indeed been carried out for a massive project at the bend.2 Tsering, noting the Great Bend's reputation "for having the greatest hydropower potential of any site in the world", with a drop of nearly 2500 meters over the length of the bend, predicted that China was likely to construct a 38,000 MW hydropower station and large storage dam near Motuo.

Such a dam, if built, would dwarf even the massive Three Gorges Dam. Interviewed by *The Hindustan Times*, Tsering said: "If or when the Motuo project is built, China will gain significant capacity to control the Brahmaputra's flow.... Basically, India will become dependent on China for flow of what is now a free-flowing international river".

Diversion of the Brahmaputra's waters is another – and much more portentous – potential use. Planned diversion of this river's waters from India's water-surplus northeast to drought-stricken western and southern states, though at least temporarily on hold, is the key to India's long-delayed River Linking Project (RLP). China's diversion plans, on the other hand, are lodged in the mammoth and already underway South-North Water Diversion Project (SNWDP). Thus far, the SNWDP has been confined to entirely indigenous rivers. If currently discussed proposals to include the Brahmaputra in an extended version of the still pending Western Route of the SNWDP were implemented, the consequences for downstream India and, even more so Bangladesh, might be disastrous.

River diversion on the drawing board China's southern belt has historically been a water surplus region while its north and northwest have been increasingly water scarce. China's north, with 42 percent of the country's population in 2003, had only 14 percent of available fresh water supplies; while its south, with 58 percent of population, held 86 percent of fresh water supplies. While China ranks sixth in the world in total naturally available fresh water flows from all surface and underground sources, its per capita ranking is one of the lowest in the world for a populous country.

A similar (but geographically reversed) pattern of spatial variability in water supply also exists in India, whose north and northeast regions have been water surplus while large portions of its west and south are water scarce. About 61.6 percent (1,202 km^3) of annual fresh water availability in India is found in the river basins of India's north, which cover only about 33 percent of the country's geographical area, leaving about 67 percent of the country – mainly its west and south – with water availability of about 38 percent (742.14 km^3).

Driven by this disturbing irregularity in nature's design, Chinese and Indian hydrologists have naturally been giving attention to the prospects for water diversion – for transferring major quantities of river water from south to north in China, from north to south in India. China launched the massive SNWDP in 2001; India gave official sanction to its equally massive RLP in 2002.

It is of course where Indian water diversion plans meet up with China's that trans- boundary concerns emerge; and it is the distinct possibility that they may meet up on the Brahmaputra that is currently exercising the imaginations of the region's strategic analysts.

A convergence of divergence?

Unknown presently is whether India's RLP will ever get off the ground. Also unknown is whether the RLP, if fully implemented, will include the Brahmaputra in its Himalayan component. Clearly, however, India's future diversion of the Brahmaputra's waters remains a live possibility – even a probability should the more threatening projections of the country's coming water scarcity prove correct. Moreover, should China move towards the Brahmaputra in coming years with an eye not just on hydro-power but also on diversion, pressure on New Delhi to match Beijing's with an aggressive plan of its own would likely become irresistible.

As for Beijing's plans in this regard, we are confronted with towering uncertainty. Official denials of any Chinese plans to divert the Brahmaputra's waters are common. Of late, however, there have been a number of to China's arid northeast from the Brahmaputra's middle reaches. This alternative route would allegedly transport over 200 billion cubic meters of water extracted annually from the Brahmaputra River at a point just to the southeast of Lhasa along a route moving north/northeast towards the headwaters of the Yellow River.

It would be premature to declare that the Chinese are without fail going to undertake a mammoth water diversion project anywhere on the Brahmaputra. However, it seems fairly certain that the Chinese are currently weighing various diversion proposals in terms of engineering feasibility and costs, and the possibility cannot be dismissed that they may at some point give one of them the go-ahead.

Brahma Chellaney, one of India's foremost strategic thinkers, has argued that it is not a question of if but when China will go ahead with the proposed diversion of Brahmaputra waters to its parched north. And such a diversion, he warns, "would constitute the declaration of a water war on lower-riparian India and Bangladesh".

The relations between India and China are driven, of course, by much more than water; and even water cannot be confidently said to be driving things relentlessly and unalterably in the direction of violent conflict between them. Still, China's dire water circumstances, combined with its impressive economic strength, military power, and uniquely advantageous upper riparian position, give us little reason for optimism when it comes to the offer of generous river sharing agreements with lower riparian countries. There are today no formal agreements at all between China and India in regard to water sharing of the transboundary Brahmaputra; and if the reasoning of many observers in regard to China's plans on the Brahmaputra is accurate, one should not expect any grand cooperative interstate scheme to develop any time soon in regard to that river. On the contrary, mounting tensions and at least verbal skirmishing between China and India over the Brahmaputra's contested waters seem more likely. There will surely be water woes impacting their relationship, in other words, even if water wars never materialize.

IMPLICATIONS OF CHINA'S HYDRO PROJECTS

Building of mega dams on the Brahmaputra is opposed by certain political parties and organizations in the Northeast. Rising protests against building dams in Arunachal Pradesh could make the Indian government decide to stop construction of dams there. But what about the dams China is likely to build on the Yarlung Tsangpo in Tibet? Even if construction of dams in Arunachal Pradesh stops, the existence of similar dams would still be a threat and would nullify any security acquired from preventing mega dams in Arunachal Pradesh. In such a case, what would be the stand of the anti-dam protestors? China would surely not be bothered even if there are protests against it in India.

India's Lower Subansiri Dam is the biggest hydroelectric project undertaken in India so far and is a run- of-the- river scheme on the river Subansiri. The project is facing stiff protests from political parties like Asom Gana Parishad, Bhartiya Janata Party and organizations like the Krishak Mukti Sangram Samity (KMSS), All Assam Students Union (AASU) etc. arguing that the project would affect the downstream riverine environment and could have an devastating effect in case of a major earthquake in the region. The Lower Subansiri dam is at an altitude of about 150 metres, 116 metres high and where the river perhaps flows at a gradient of not more than 30 cm/km. In contrast, the Zangmu dam has been constructed at an altitude of 3,200m where the river flows over a much steeper gradient. As such, the Zangmu dam is far more vulnerable to a dam break caused by an earthquake. Even if the dam doesn't collapse in an earthquake, damages to the sluices through which the water flows and to the spillways used to get rid of excess water could create havoc downstream. The Indian government and political parties should look into the Zangmu Dam issue first before worrying over the Subansiri project.

Moreover, diversion of the Brahmaputra, the lifeline of India's Northeast, would wreak havoc in the region. With the water being diverted, the amount of water in the Brahmaputra will fall significantly, affecting the region. Environmental experts report that roughly 60 per cent of the total water flow will fall drastically if China is successful in diverting the Brahmaputra. India has raised concerns about the project on the grounds that it could pose a grave threat to the farmers and environment in northeast India. It will severely impact agriculture and fishing as the salinity of water will increase, as will silting in the downstream area. Moreover, India being a lower riparian state would be at the mercy of upper riparian China in matters of releasing pre-regulated water flows back into the river whenever needed.

The threat to Bangladesh is even greater as Bangladesh is the lowest riparian state of the Brahmaputra and the river is more vital to it than even India. Bangladesh is very much concerned over water diversion of the Brahmaputra by China as well as on the building of dams by China and India on the Brahmaputra. It fears the quantity of water reaching Bangladesh would reduce drastically leading to lowering in agricultural production and aggravate environmental problems.

China's dam projects on the Mekong have already caused tension with its neighbours- Vietnam, Laos, Cambodia and Thailand. China's Minister for Water Resources, Wang Shucheng, said that this project is "unnecessary, unfeasible and unscientific. But no matter what China's real plans may be, if Beijing goes ahead with its plans on the Yarlung Tsangpo without any sort if international agreement, it would affect not only China's nuclear neighbours, India and Pakistan, both facing water crisis, but could also lead to regional instability in an already volatile South Asia.

Solutions

Experts like Brahma Chellaney insists that, "*interstate conflict will surface only when an idea is translated into action to benefit one country at the expense of a neighbouring one.*" In this context, South Asia will not have a real water war unless China goes ahead with its proposed plans of diverting the Brahmaputra at the expense of its neighbours India and Bangladesh.

As such, international water sharing treaties will play a key role in addressing the threat of a water war. India is an upper riparian state with respect to Pakistan and Bangladesh and a lower riparian to China, Nepal and Bhutan. Therefore, India needs to recognise its geo-strategic location and aim to effectively pursue new trans- boundary riparian treaties while reworking on the existing treaties.

India has water treaties with Bangladesh and Pakistan (both downstream) and with Bhutan and Nepal (both upstream) but it doesn't have any water treaty with China. China has about 10 major rivers - Yangtze, Yarlung Tsangpo, Yellow, Heilongjiang, Songhuajiang, Zhujiang, Lancang, Nujiang, Hanjiang and Liaohe flowing out of its territory to 11 countries - India, Bangladesh, Vietnam, Russia, Kazakhstan, North Korea, Myanmar, Mongolia, Laos, Thailand and Cambodia and none flow in from outside. This puts it in the unique position of controlling international rivers and India urgently needs to pursue a regional water treaty with China. The Indus Water Treaty (1960) which demarcated the Indus river waters between India and Pakistan shows that despite historical conflicts, water sharing treaties could prove to be quite successful.

Also, even though China has leverage over rivers flowing out from its territories, the Berlin Rules on Water Resources, 2004 states that nations sharing water should make reasonable efforts not to cause harm to one another by the ways in which the water is used. The document states the requirement of transparency of information related to water resources and their usage to the international community, particularly in those cases where nations share a water resource. It asks for equitable and reasonable utilization of the water resources by the water sharing nations. China cannot unilaterally start massive hydro-engineering projects without formal river-basin arrangements with downstream states. It would have been wise on the part of India and China to have signed the UN convention on non-navigational uses of international water courses, 1997, which provides a mechanism to deal with trans-border waters. Only 17 nations signed this convention which doesn't include the major South Asian actors— India, Nepal, Bangladesh and China. Also, building up on the issue of transparency, China has always been opaque on its hydro- engineering plans, refusing to share information or permitting on- site visits. India should keep track of what China is doing with the Brahmaputra. Talks with China should be held at regular intervals so that India remains apprised of the situation.

The Brahmaputra River has not been properly utilized in India. Out of the total of 84,044 MW hydropower potential of the country, the Northeast carries a potential of 31,857 MW (37 per cent of the country), of which only 3 per cent has so far been tapped (Brahmaputra Board, 2005). Enough projects are needed on the Brahmaputra if India wants to have a stake on the river.

Retired Colonel P K Gautam, research fellow at the Institute for Defence Studies and Analyses, adds that *"if China builds a dam on the Brahmaputra now, and we complain about lesser water flows later, it could say that India doesn't have any projects in the northeast."*

The Brahmaputra was declared National Waterway No. 2 of India and though the river is navigable most time of the year, it has not been fully utilised. Water transport services are used for the transportation of passengers and goods alike across the state and to neighbouring West Bengal but the infrastructure is not good. Water transport service should be modernized on the Brahmaputra so that it can also become a major mode of transport for passengers and cargo. There is urgent need for utilising the water of the Brahmaputra in an effective way through multi-purpose big dams on the river, with provisions for irrigation and flood control besides generation of electricity. However, environmental norms should not be flouted for this.

In an interview with Tariq Ahmed Karim, Bangladesh's High Commissioner to India on this important issue, the need for better monitoring and regulating fresh water sources in South Asia was highlighted. He stated, "...In such a diminishing fresh-water world, water may have to be declared as a scare and fungible resource whose management and administration needs to be reposed with an authority that is larger than the present geo-political configurations of states-provinces and national governments. Citizenry of such a hard-pressed fresh-water world must adopt rules analogous to the rights of citizenry in today's nation-states, the fundamental underpinnings of which are two, namely: rights go hand in hand with responsibilities (to the state and fellow citizens): and no one citizen's rights can be at the expense of the rights of another fellow citizen..."

What Karim suggests is a South Asian water regulatory and monitoring body, something that is in India's interest like a Himalayan Rivers Commission to better manage water issues in the sub-region. He goes on: "... In this context, we in South Asia must, sooner rather than later, politically evolve to a regime of water governance, in which the member states will have, by mutual consensus and consent, set up a South Asian Water Resources Management Authority (which will have real authority and powers vested in it, as opposed to the present configuration of a 'South Asian Association for Regional Cooperation'). This supra- national authority will measure, monitor and keep track of all available water resources (whether ground or surface), set strict uses, conservation and management regulations, and oversee adherence to and enforcement of these regulations, to ensure the rights equally for all its denizens."

Another option that China and India could explore is constructing shared dams that would mutually benefit each other. The concept of having shared dams has worked out for Brazil and Paraguay with the Itaipu Dam, located on the border of Brazil and Paraguay. It is the world's largest operating hydroelectric project. The electricity generated from Itaipu Dam is estimated to be greater than the electricity generated by China's Three Gorges Dam. The dam supplies Paraguay with more than 90 per cent of its electrical needs.

The government should hold awareness camps, conduct seminars, prepare documentaries to make the general public aware about the requirement of building dams across the Brahmaputra so that people stop protesting over projects like the Subansiri Dam and instead focus on the broader picture.

WATER WARS: CHINA'S NEW 'POLITICAL WEAPON'

The wall of water raced through narrow Himalayan gorges in northeast India, gathering speed as it raked the banks of towering trees and boulders. When the torrent struck their island in the Brahmaputra river, the villagers remember, it took only moments to obliterate their houses, possessions and livestock.

No one knows exactly how the disaster happened, but everyone knows whom to blame: neighboring China.

"We don't trust the Chinese," says fisherman Akshay Sarkar at the resettlement site where he has lived since the 2000 flood. "They gave us no warning. They may do it again."

About 800 kilometers (500 miles) east, in northern Thailand, Chamlong Saengphet stands in the Mekong river, in water that comes only up to her shins. She is collecting edible river weeds from dwindling beds. A neighbor has hung up his fishing nets, his catches now too meager.

Using words bordering on curses, they point upstream, toward China. The blame game, voiced in vulnerable river towns and Asian capitals from Pakistan to Vietnam, is rooted in fear that China's accelerating program of damming every major river flowing from the Tibetan plateau will trigger natural disasters, degrade fragile ecologies, divert vital water supplies.

A few analysts and environmental advocates even speak of water as a future trigger for war or diplomatic strong-arming, though others strongly doubt it will come to that. Still, the remapping of the water flow in the world's most heavily populated and thirstiest region is happening on a gigantic scale, with potentially strategic implications.

On the eight great Tibetan rivers alone, almost 20 dams have been built or are under construction while some 40 more are planned or proposed.

China is hardly alone in disrupting the region's water flows. Others are doing it with potentially even worse consequences. But China's vast thirst for power and water, its control over the sources of the rivers and its ever-growing political clout make it a singular target of criticism and suspicion. "Whether China intends to use water as a political weapon or not, it is acquiring the capability to turn off the tap if it wants to – a leverage it can use to keep any riparian neighbours on good behavior," says Brahma Chellaney, an analyst at New Delhi's Center for Policy Research and author of the forthcoming "Water: Asia's New Battlefield."

Analyst Neil Padukone calls it "the biggest potential point of contention between the two Asian giants," China and India. But the stakes may be even higher since those eight Tibetan rivers serve a vast west-east arc of 1.8 billion people stretching from Pakistan to Vietnam's Mekong river delta.

Suspicions are heightened by Beijing's lack of transparency and refusal to share most hydrological and other data. Only China, along with Turkey, has refused to sign a key 1997 U.N. convention on transnational rivers. Beijing gave no notice when it began building three dams on the Mekong – the first completed in 1993 – or the $1.2 billion Zangmu dam, the first on the mainstream of the 2,880-kilometer (1,790-mile) Brahmaputra which was started last November and hailed in official media as "a landmark priority project."

The 2000 flood that hit Sarkar's village, is widely believed to have been caused by the burst of an earthen dam wall on a Brahmaputra tributary. But China has kept silent.

"Until today, the Indian government has no clue about what happened," says Ravindranath, who heads the Rural Volunteer Center. He uses only one name.

Tibet's spiritual leader, the Dalai Lama, has also warned of looming dangers stemming from the Tibetan plateau.

"It's something very, very essential. So, since millions of Indians use water coming from the Himalayan glaciers... I think you (India) should express more serious concern. This is nothing to do with politics, just everybody's interests, including Chinese people," he said in New Delhi last month.

Beijing normally counters such censure by pointing out that the bulk of water from the Tibetan rivers springs from downstream tributaries, with only 13-16 percent originating in China.

Officials also say that the dams can benefit their neighbours, easing droughts and floods by regulating flow, and that hydroelectric power reduces China's carbon footprint.

China "will fully consider impacts to downstream countries," Chinese Foreign Ministry spokeswoman Jiang Yu recently told The Associated Press. "We have clarified several times that the dam being built on the Brahmaputra River has a small storage capacity. It will not have large impact on water flow or the ecological environment of downstream."

For some of China's neighbours, the problem is that they too are building controversial dams and may look hypocritical if they criticize China too loudly.

The four-nation Mekong River Commission has expressed concerns not just about the Chinese dams but about a host of others built or planned in downstream countries. In northeast India, a broad-based movement is fighting central government plans to erect more than 160 dams in the region, and Laos and Cambodia have proposed plans for 11 Mekong dams, sparking environmental protest.

Indian and other governments play down any threats from the Asian colossus. "I was reassured that (the Zangmu dam) was not a project designed to divert water and affect the welfare and availability of water to countries in the lower reaches," India's Foreign Secretary Nirupama Rao said after talks with her Chinese counterpart late last year.

But at the grass roots, and among activists and even some government technocrats, criticism is expressed more readily. "Everyone knows what China is doing, but won't talk about it. China has real power now. If it says something, everyone follows," says Somkiat Khuengchiangsa, a Thai environmental advocate.

Neither the Indian nor Chinese government responded to specific questions from the AP about the dams, but Beijing is signaling that it will relaunch mega-projects after a break of several years in efforts to meet skyrocketing demands for energy and water, reduce dependence on coal and lift some 300 million people out of poverty.

Official media recently said China was poised to put up dams on the still pristine Nu River, known as the Salween downstream. Seven years ago as many as 13 dams were set to go up until Chinese Premier Wen Jiabao ordered a moratorium.

That ban is regarded as the first and perhaps biggest victory of China's nascent green movement. "An improper exploitation of water resources by countries on the upper reaches is going to bring about environmental, social and geological risks," Yu Xiaogang, director of the Yunnan Green Watershed, told The Associated Press. "Countries along the rivers have already formed their own way of using water resources. Water shortages could easily ignite extreme nationalist sentiment and escalate into a regional war."

But there is little chance the activists will prevail. "There is no alternative to dams in sight in China," says Ed Grumbine, an American author on Chinese dams. Grumbine, currently with the Chinese Academy of Sciences in Yunnan province, notes that under its last five-year state plan, China failed to meet its hydroelectric targets and is now playing catch-up in its 2011-2015 plan as it strives to derive 15 percent of energy needs from non-fossil sources, mainly hydroelectric and nuclear.

The arithmetic pointing to more dam-building is clear: China would need 140 gigawatts of extra hydroelectric power to meet its goal. Even if all the dams on the Nu go up, they would provide only 21 gigawatts.

The demand for water region-wide will also escalate, sparking perhaps that greatest anxieties – that China will divert large quantities from the Tibetan plateau for domestic use.

Noting that Himalayan glaciers which feed the rivers are melting due to global warming, India's Strategic Foresight Group last year estimated that in the coming 20 years India, China, Nepal and Bangladesh will face a depletion of almost 275 billion cubic meters (360 billion cubic yards) of annual renewable water.

Padukone expects China will have to divert water from Tibet to its dry eastern provinces. One plan for rerouting the Brahmaputra was outlined in an officially sanctioned 2005 book by a Chinese former army officer, Li Ling. Its title: "Tibet's Waters Will Save China," Analyst Chellaney believes "the issue is not whether China will reroute the Brahmaputra, but when." He cites Chinese researchers and officials as saying that after 2014 work will begin on tapping rivers flowing from the Tibetan plateau to neighboring countries Such a move, he says, would be tantamount to a declaration of war on India.

Others are skeptical. Tashi Tsering, a Tibetan environmentalist at the University of British Columbia who is otherwise critical of China's policies, calls a Brahmaputra diversion "a pipe dream of some Chinese planners."

Grumbine shares the skepticism. "The situation would have to be very dire for China to turn off the taps because the consequences would be huge," he said. "China would alienate every one of its neighbours and historically the Chinese have been very sensitive about maintaining secure borders."

Whatever else may happen, riverside inhabitants along the Mekong and Brahmaputra say the future shock is now. A fisherman from his youth, Boonrian Chinnarat says the Mekong giant catfish, the world's largest freshwater fish, has all but vanished from the vicinity of Thailand's Had Krai village, other once bountiful species have been depleted, and he and fellow fishermen have sold their nets. He blames the Chinese dams.

Phumee Boontom, headman of nearby Pak Ing village, warns that "If the Chinese keep the water and continue to build more dams, life along the Mekong will change forever." Already, he says, he has seen drastic variations in water levels following dam constructions, "like the tides of the ocean — low and high in one day."

Jeremy Bird, who heads the Mekong commission, an intergovernmental body of Laos, Cambodia, Thailand and Laos, sees a tendency to blame China for water-related troubles even when they are purely the result of nature. He says diplomacy is needed, and believes "engagement with China is improving." Grumbine agrees. "Given the enormous demand for water in China, India and Southeast Asia, if you maintain the attitude of sovereign state, we are lost," he says. "Scarcity in a zero sum situation can lead to conflict but it can also goad countries into more cooperative behavior. It's a bleak picture, but I'm not without hope."

INDIA AND SOUTH ASIA: FROM CONFLICT TO CO-OPERATION

This World Water Day comes in year which has been declared as the "International Year of Water Cooperation" by the United National General Assembly. In addition, the UN has proclaimed the decade 2005-2015 as the International Decade for Action, "Water for Life".

The UN declarations would be welcome if we are able to take credible and effective steps towards water cooperation at every level in an equitable, sustainable way and through local participation. This becomes increasingly relevant when demand for water is increasing due to rising population, urbanisation, industrialisation, increased per capita use and increased losses due to climate change. The available and utilisable supply of water is either stagnant or decreasing due to increased pollution, increased temperatures, changing rainfall pattern, melting of glaciers and over exploitation. Moves towards centralised and undemocratic governance and privatisation of resources are not helpful as they do not promote cooperation, but only further conflicts. The prevailing and emerging situation is a sure fire recipe for increasing conflicts, not cooperation.

At the same time, UN Declaration of July 2010, declaring water as a human right remains only on paper. UN and the governments will clearly need to go beyond mere words and pious declarations.

Water: Some key characteristics Water is not just a commodity for market or an economic good. It is an ecological entity embedded in larger ecology that includes the climate, land, forests, and biodiversity. This includes, but is not limited to: Glaciers, rivers, wetlands, lakes, aquifers, soil, snow and water vapour in the atmosphere. In fact our understanding of the interplay of water in the larger eco-system is still far from complete. When we use water from any source, we should be mindful of its impact in the larger ecosystem. The UN resolution for declaring the 2005-2015 decade was not called "water for life" for nothing. Life here includes not just life of every human being but life on the entire planet.

INDIA AND NEIGHBOURS

On this occasion, it would be useful to take a look at the situation in the region. India and China are locked in one-up man ship in Brahmaputra basin,

India and Pakistan are competing in destroying shared rivers, ecology and connected livelihoods through hydropower projects in the Indus river basin while India and Bangladesh are struggling to arrive at an agreement on sharing the Teesta waters. When it happens, this will be only the second water sharing treaty, among the 54 rivers shared by India and Bangladesh.

Considering that the countries in this region share the Himalayan watershed on which numerous big and small rivers and millions of people and biodiversity depend, there is an urgent need to have a Regional Policy for the common good of the people of the region.

Possible Chinese diversion The Chinese government officials have often talked about China's intention of diverting the Brahmaputra (basically Siang River, one of the main tributaries of the Brahmaputra) river to North China, just before the river enters India. China has officially declared its plans to build at least four hydropower projects on the river. The work on the water diversion project is yet to start and China has denied that the project is being taken up. However the Indian government is pushing more big hydro projects in Arunachal Pradesh, claiming that these will help establish India's prior use rights over the waters of these rivers when China does decide to take up its North South diversion project.

Such a push for big hydro in Arunachal Pradesh under the bogey of Chinese plans is only likely to worsen the situation for the people of Arunachal Pradesh and also for downstream areas in India and Bangladesh. This will only create new water conflicts. Moreover, there is no international mechanism that would help India claim its prior user right. The 1997 UN Convention on the Law of the Non-Navigational Uses of International Watercourses could have been of use, but India has yet to ratify the convention. The best course for India is to push China for a water sharing treaty.

In view of the crisis of climate change, this need has become even more acute. Today, there is no such policy and each country is developing multiple projects on its own, and many of the so-called development projects are actually accelerating climate change impacts and conflicts. Hundreds of hydropower projects are either constructed, are under construction or are being planned across the countries in the region. These projects, along with their paraphernalia of roads, townships, mining, tunnelling, blasting, muck dumping, diverting of rivers and dams are cumulatively having huge, though as yet unquantified impact on the glaciers, forests, aquatic and terrestrial biodiversity, communities, water availability and water supply,thereby impacting the climate as well.

Flood forecasting: One of the areas where information sharing is immediately required is in the area of sharing information about forecasts related to floods in the shared rivers. The governments in the region seem to have a number of agreements to share information in this regard, including Pakistan-India, Nepal-India, Bhutan-India, Bangladesh-India and China-India. Unfortunately, the shared information in this aspect is not in the public domain. Such shared information must be in public domain. What use is the flood forecasting related information if it is not shared among the people who are going to face the disastrous impacts of floods?

Transparency and Participation in governance in shared river basins There are elaborate, mostly bilateral inter-governmental mechanisms on governance of water and rivers in a number of cases in the South Asia region. These pertain to the bilateral arrangements of India with Pakistan, Bhutan, Bangladesh, Nepal and China. These arrangements include basin level commissions, minister level committees, officer level committees, project specific commissions and so on. Unfortunately, there is practically no transparency in the functioning of these mechanisms, nor is there any role for any concerned actors outside the government. In governance of rivers, waters and related projects, local people have the right to know what is going on in these committees and commissions.

The need for such public participation was acutely felt in the aftermath of the Kosi Disaster on the Indo-Nepal border in August 2008. During the initial period of this disaster, it was shown how the bilateral Kosi High Level committee had failed to achieve the proper maintenance of the embankment that breached with the flow of water in the river was less than 1.5 lakh cusecs (Cubic Feet per Second) even as the design capacity of the embankment was over 9 lakh cusecs. In the days that followed, it became clear that if there had been some non government people on the Indo Nepal Kosi committees and there was more transparency with representation from local communities and civil society in the committees, it would have helped ensure the maintenance of the embankment and that possibly would have saved it from breaching at least on that particular occasion.

Conditions for water cooperation We need to understand key conditions that would help achieve better cooperation in water sector. Some key conditions in this regard include: Clearly defined priorities for water use, rules of allocation of water to different users, water allocation mechanisms among various sectors, democratic rules of governance of such mechanisms, understanding the importance of ecosystem resources, Conservation of ecosystem resources including Wetlands, forests, rivers, lake, biodiversity; clearly defined and legally enforceable Right to Water and mechanisms to enforce the same. Good governance in this context would include clearly defined norms for key aspects like transparency, accountability and participation. There is need to have legal and institutional set up to achieve these goals.

The weaker sections (tribals, Dalits, women, marginal farmers, coastal and mountain populations) or weaker stakeholders (environment, rivers) have always been losing at the negotiating table. Centralising of authority and decision making being more and more away from local stakeholders creates possibility of more conflicts and conflict resolution becomes more difficult. Local water management can help reduce and also help address conflicts at the local level.

CHINESE DAM ON BRAHMAPUTRA MEANS TO INDIA

China's official Xinhua news agency said the first section of the $1.5 billion dam went into operation on Sunday afternoon. Five other sections will be completed next year. The dam will generate 2.5 billion kilowatt hours of electricity every year, reported the agency.

The implications of construction of the dam for India are on several fronts. It reduces water flow in the river. This is not so serious if the dams are RoR (run of river) hydro stations. But if reservoirs are built, or waters diverted, it could affect the river's ecosystem in the upper stretches.

Second, it gives China a stronger say in water sharing discussions because it has established claim of use of these waters. India will have to move quickly to establish its own user rights quickly.

Also, rapid development of infrastructure in the N-E could create social tensions with local tribes. That must be avoided to prevent China instigating Arunachal Pradesh locals to agitate against India.

The Zangmu dam construction began in 2010. It sparked off panic among China's southern neighbours, including India. The fear was that China may actually drain this river of water, just as it had done with the Mekong river.

The 4,350 km long Mekong is the 12th largest river in the world, the 7th largest in Asia. It originates from Tibet (China) and flows through Myanmar, Laos, Thailand, Cambodia and Vietnam. Today, all the downstream countries of the Mekong river accuse China of starving them of water.

Could this become the fate of India's North-East and Bangladesh as well? This is because out of the Brahmaputra's total length of 2,880km, 1,625km is in Tibet (or China), 918km in India, and 337km in Bangladesh.

But, on the other hand, the average annual rainfall is just 400mm in Tibet, but 3,000mm on the Indian side. This is in spite of the fact that (according to data provided by the Central Water Commission), of the total catchment area of 580,000 sq km, 50% lies in Tibet, 34% in India, and the balance in Bangladesh and Bhutan. Significantly, only 40% of the water comes from the Chinese catchment area.

Some policymakers in Delhi believe that the precipitation in China contributes only 7% to the flow. It is the Brahmaputra's tributaries in Arunachal Pradesh, along with the rains in India, that contribute to the rest of the river's water supply.

That could explain the absence of any shrill reaction from New Delhi. But there is tremendous cause for concern.

First, many experts believe that the 7% precipitation theory is all hogwash. You cannot compartmentalise any river, they say. Brahma Chellaney, a noted China and water expert, warns that any diversion of water from the upper reaches of the Brahmaputra could have devastating consequences for the way the river flows for downstream areas. He believes that all sorts of data is being fed to journalists, and that the only reliable data is from the United Nations.

According to the United Nations, the cross border annual aggregate flow of Brahmaputra river system is around 165.4 billion cubic metres (bcm). That, add experts, is greater than the combined trans-boundary flow of the three key Asian rivers—Mekong, Salween and Irrawady—that run from the Tibetian plateau to South East Asia.

Second, reservoirs along the river could staunch the flow of water into India. True, most of the hydro-projects China is building are of the run-of-the-river (RoR) type, generating electricity from the flow of the river and not trapping any of the water in dams. However, reservoirs are also being built, and it is only a matter of time that much of the water originating and collected in China could get trapped in reservoirs for diversion to the northern parts of China.

But, most critically, almost every policymaker in New Delhi is painfully aware that under international law, a country's right over natural resources it shares with other nations becomes stronger if is already putting these resources to use. China has already begun first use of the Brahmaputra waters.

If India does not move fast and establish its own claims over water use, it could lose out in subsequent water sharing discussions under international law.

That partly explains the Modi government's urgency in building projects and linking Arunachal Pradesh to the rest of India. It also throws light on why Indian strategists are suspicious of any moves by environmental groups protesting against the setting up of such projects along the Brahmaputra.

INDIA AND CHINA SHOULD LEAVE THE BRAHMAPUTRA ALONE

In October 2012, Indians learned that China had begun to construct a 700 megawatt (MW) capacity dam on the Brahmaputra river (Yarlung Tsangpo). The news aroused fears that China intended not only to generate power from the river but also divert some of its waters to the arid northern regions of the country.

This possibility was first mentioned at the international conference of the Global Infrastructure Fund in Anchorage, Alaska, in 1986. Although Chinese officials rubbished the idea as being impossibly expensive to implement, they did not rule out the possibility of constructing dams on the river to generate power. This ambivalence raised understandable alarm in Bangladesh and India, but Beijing sought to allay their fears by assuring them that it intends to build run-of-the-river dams that will redirect, but not stop, the flow of its waters into India and Bangladesh.

These reassurances have not, however, prevented China and India from entering into an undeclared race to capture the hydroelectric potential of the Brahmaputra river basin. Chinese writers began to air plans for harnessing the Brahmaputra in 2005, but it is possible that the Indian government had already begun to formulate its plans after the publication of a book by Li Ling in 2003 entitled *Tibet's waters will save China.*

As the downstream riparian, India is hoping to establish first user rights to stake its claim to an uninterrupted flow of the Brahmaptura's waters. In international law, first user rights start upon the completion of a project, so the number of projects that India has signalled it will take up in the Brahmaputra basin has risen rapidly – from 146 announced in a 10-year hydroelectricity plan unveiled by India's Central Electricity Authority in 2007, to about 200 today. What is more, a scramble has developed to start as many of these as soon as possible.

The pace of planning and implementation has also picked up in China. Citing the need to cut down carbon dioxide emissions, the 12th Five Year energy plan, shifted its emphasis back onto giant hydroelectric projects once more. One of its most important goals is to harness the hydropower potential of the Brahmaputra basin.

In all, China intends to build 40 dams on the river and its tributaries. Of these, 20 dams on the Brahmaputra will generate 60,000 MW of power, while 20 smaller dams upon its tributaries are expected to generate another 5,000 MW. Eleven of the 20 projects on the Brahmaputra will be located between its source and the Great Bend where the Brahmaputra turns northwards, executes a huge 'U' turn and falls from 3,500 metres on the Tibetan plateau to 700 metres in the undulating hills of Arunachal Pradesh in India. These will generate 20,000 MW of power, while the balance of 40,000 MW will be generated at the Great Bend itself.

The plan for doing this has been put forward by ex-premier Li Peng's family-dominated corporation, the Three Gorges Dam Company. It envisages building a vast tunnel under the ridge that separates the two arms of the Great Bend to divert 50 billion cubic metres of water a year from the northwestern flowing arm of the river to the southeastern arm over a succession of nine cascading hydropower dams that will generate 40,000 MW of power. India, for its part, plans to generate 22,000 MW from two large dams on the Brahmaputra in Arunachal Pradesh and 10,000 MW from dams on its tributaries. In all, therefore, the two countries plan to generate 97,000 MW of power from this tiny region of their respective countries.

Such ambitious but conflicting plans were bound to have political repercussions. The first was a statement by the Chinese ambassador in New Delhi that China considered the whole of the northeastern state of Arunachal Pradesh to be a part of Tibet. This was a reversal of its earlier position, developed in a succession of bilateral negotiations since 1994, that China was prepared to settle for a substantial modification of some parts of the existing temporary boundary, called the Line of Actual Control.

The announcement took the Indian government by surprise and was followed by three years of rising tension along the border. China began to refer to Arunachal as "South Tibet", and to its principal monastery at Tawang as Tibet's second most important monastery after Lhasa. It also began to deny visas to Indian officials who were serving in Arunachal Pradesh. The tension was not defused until there was a meeting between then premier Wen Jiabao and prime minister Manmohan Singh, at Hua Hin, Thailand, in October 2009, designed specifically to prevent its spilling over into military conflict.

CHINESE BIGGEST HYDRO-ELECTRIC PROJECT IN BRAHMAPUTRA RIVER AT TIBET

Chinese hydropower lobbyists are calling for construction of the world's biggest hydro-electric project on the upper reaches of the Brahmaputra river as part of a huge expansion of renewable power in the Himalayas. Zhang Boting, the deputy general secretary of the China Society for Hydropower Engineering, told the Guardian that a massive dam on the great bend of the Yarlung Tsangpo - the Tibetan name for the river - would benefit the world, despite the likely concerns of downstream nations, India and Bangladesh, which access water and power from the river.

Zhang said research had been carried out on the project, but no plan has been drawn up. But documents on the website of a government agency suggest a 38 gigawatt hydropower plant is under consideration that would be more than half as big again as the Three Gorges dam, with a capacity nearly half as large as the UK's national grid. "This dam could save 200m tonnes of carbon each year. We should not waste the opportunity of the biggest carbon emission reduction project. For the sake of the entire world, all the water resources than can be developed should be developed." That CO_2 saving would be over a third of the UK's entire emissions.

The mega-facility is among more than 28 dams on the river that are either planned, completed or under discussion by China, according to Tashi Tsering, a Tibetan scholar of environmental policy at the University of British Columbia. Tsering publishes a map today of all of the projects that have been reported by Chinese newspapers and hydro-engineering websites.

From this, he concludes that the Tsangpo-Brahmaputra – until recently considered the last great undammed river in Tibet – will be the next focus of government efforts to increase the nation's power supply. One of them is a map of planned dams showing a 38-gigawatt hydro-plant at Motuo on the website of Hydro China, an influential government enterprise responsible for dam construction. A separate State Grid map of future transmission lines indicates the remote area will soon be connected to the rest of China's power supply. Hydro China and State Grid declined requests for clarification.

The government has not confirmed the existence of the scheme, but Tsering cites several newspaper reports of survey teams exploring the area and provides links to other online documents that indicate preparations for large-scale hydro-development of the area.

Given the huge expense, technical difficulties and political sensitivities of the scheme, it is far from certain of final approval by the government. But several Chinese hydroengineers see it as the ultimate goal in an accelerating race with India to develop water resources in one of the planet's last remote regions.

Tapping the power of the river as it bends and plunges from the Himalayan roof of the world down towards the Indian and Bangladeshi flood plains has long been a dream of the world's hydro-engineers. Along with the Congo river at the Inga falls, this is considered one of the two greatest concentrations of river energy on earth, but it was long thought impossible to access because of the rugged, high-altitude terrain and the risk of water-related conflict with neighbouring countries.

But China has overcome many engineering obstacles with the construction of the railway to Tibet, and its growing energy demands are spurring exploration of ever more remote areas. "Tibet's resources will be converted into economic advantage," Yan Zhiyong, the general manager of China Hydropower Engineering Consulting Group, told ChinaEnergy News earlier this year. "The major technical constraints on damming the Yarlung Tsampo have been overcome." He declined the Guardian's request for an interview, saying the subject was too sensitive.

The exploitation of the Brahmaputra is already under way. China recently announced plans to build five dams further upstream, including a 500MW hydroplant at Zangmu, which is under construction by the power utility Huaneng. According to Tsering, the biggest of them will be a huge plant at the great bend – either at Metog, known as Motuo in Chinese, or at Daduqia. The former would involve the construction of a series of tunnels, pipes, reservoirs and turbines to exploit the spectacular 2,000-metre fall of the river as it curls down towards India.

Although there has been no official confirmation of plans for a dam, the discussion is far from secret. On a prominent Chinese science forum, Zhang said a dam on the great bend was the ultimate hope for water resource exploitation because it could generate energy equivalent to 100m tonnes of crude coal, or all the oil and gas in the South China sea. He warned that a delay would allow India to tap these resources and prompt "major conflict" in a region where the two nations have sporadically clashed over disputed territory.

"We should build a hydropower plant in Motuo... as soon as possible because it is a great policy to protect our territory from Indian invasion and to increase China's capacity for carbon reduction," he wrote last year Any step forward is likely to be controversial. Tibetans consider Metog a sacred region, and environmental activists warn against building such a huge project in a seismically active and ecologically fragile area.

"A large dam on the Tibetan plateau would amount to a major, irreversible experiment with geo-engineering," said Peter Bosshard of International Rivers. "Blocking the Yarlung Tsangpo could devastate the fragile ecosystem of the Tibetan plateau, and would withhold the river's sediments from the fertile floodplains of Assam in northeast India, and Bangladesh." China's construction of dams also raises the prospect of a race with India to develop hydropower along south Asia's most important river.

"India needs to be more aggressive in pushing ahead hydro projects (on the Brahmaputra)," Jairam Ramesh, the Indian environment minister, told the Guardian during a recent visit to Beijing. "That would put us in better negotiating position (with China). To minimise the risk of water-related conflict, the two nations have agreed to share information about hydro-plans on the Tsangpo-Brahmaputra.

Indian media have raised concerns that Beijing may ultimately embark on a gigantic diversion scheme that would channel water away from India to the dry northern plains of China, but such fears are dismissed by Tsering, who says the dam at Metog would be for hydropower, not water diversion. "The laws of physics will not allow water diversion from the Great Bend."

CHINA AS HYDRO- HEGEMON : THE ONSET OF WATER WARS

The Chinese civilization is characterized by its ability to do long term perspective thinking of an unusual order. As far back as 1952, Chairman Mao Ze dong had articulated that Water Stress in the Northern and Western parts of China would be a very major challenge that would emerge a half century or so later. In fact this strategic long term thinking seems to have originated much earlier than 1952 and seems to have been instrumental in China's decision to invade and conquer Tibet – the Water Tower of Asia – in 1950 itself.

The following facts are pertinent:-

- The region South of the Yangtze River in China has 36% of Chinese territory and 81% of its water resources.
- The Northern Areas of China (that include the major metropolises of Beijing and Tianjin) have 64% of the nation's territory but only 19% of its water resources. These plains also have 47% of China's total population.
- Due to rapid industrialization, increasing urbanization and massive population pressure, by 2030 China is expected to face a severe supply gap in its projected water demand of over 25%. In fact by 2050 China's water deficit will be a staggering 400 Billion cubic meters. Two thirds of China's cities are already experiencing serious insecurities about water supply. In fact out of 640 Chinese cities, 300 are currently facing water shortages and 100 are faced with severe scarcities.
- The problems of water stress are being exacerbated by environmental pollution, highly uneven distribution of water within its territory leading to disproportionate levels of water availability.
- China's agriculture in fact is a miracle of 22% of the world's total population being fed as just 7% of its land area.
- Over-pumping of water has caused the water table to fall at an alarming rate. Over- pumping has depleted shallow aquifers. Due to overuse of fertilizers and chemicals each year China looses 180,000 hectares of farm land to salinity and 200,000 hectares become desert.
- Hence water stress is not a theoretical issue in China. It is a civilisational nightmare for a nation that tends to look far ahead into the future and do perspective thinking of an order that systematically spans the decades. These cold statistics bear testimony to the grave seriousness of the problem and the decision pressure they are bound to put on the Chinese decision makers and leadership.

8

Water Conflict and India-Pakistan Relations

As far as India and Pakistan are concerned, no two countries in the world have so much in common as these. Both countries have similar cultural roots, linguistic similarities and shared economic system. However, since independence they have continuously been in a state of undeclared war with uncompromised issues, especially over water. The idea of sharing water is historically constructed, emotionally stimulating, and politically divisive. Though water is technically not a core issue between the two countries, differences over the use of water of the rivers is a core issue. In recent years, utilization of water has become an issue that is gaining prominence in the bilateral relationship between India and Pakistan.

In 1960, both governments agreed to sign the Indus Water Treaty, but public reaction to the treaty was very different. People in Pakistan criticised the loss of three eastern rivers to India, although Pakistan received a huge amount of financial aid in lieu of this loss even though this loss imposed heavy financial and ecological penalties upon Pakistan. In 1964, opposition parties of the countries attacked on President Ayub Khan, and used the termed as "selling" the historical rights of the country over the common rivers. While in India, the public often criticised the loss of its three western rivers to Pakistan and the treaty makes it impossible for India to utilise the full power potentialities on three western rivers.

Media, academicians, and different groups of society and agricultural communities from both sides opposed the Indus Water Treaty. Even for opposition members of both the governments, the Indus Water Treaty is suspicious and unfair. The water experts from the both countries are also not happy with the treaty. This has eventually led to the politicisation of the water issue within both countries, and thereby, creating an immense pressure on respective governments.

It is not difficult to understand the changing tone of political relations between the two countries vis-à-vis water. It can be understood by revision of recent projects being executed by India on western rivers, which are severely criticised by Pakistan. The treaty has survived various external and internal threats which were related to the two countries political relationships, but recent years have marked strained relations vis-à-vis water and therefore the Indus Water Treaty has come under the strains, mainly due to construction of hydroelectric projects, including the Salal, Baglihar, Wullar Barrage, (Tulbul Navigation) the Kishanganga, the Nemo-Bazgo. Not all of them are sans disputes and are deemed as controversial projects.

On the other hand, Indian experts have expressed frustration over long delays in approval of these projects due to Pakistani objections, and about 27 projects on the western rivers have been questioned by Pakistan. Indian analysts and media are of the view that the provision of neutral experts should be the last option and not the recourse for each and every project that India proposes. The reference does cost time, money and efforts, in terms of delaying the projects, thereby increasing the cost of not only construction but also related expenditures in not making use of the hydro potential.

Moreover, Pakistan argued that India's line of action on the riparian issue hardly warrants a high degree of trust in good neighbourliness. In addition, the political mobilization on dam construction on the western rivers has stimulated anti- Indian sentiments among farmer associations, military consortium, politicians, and fundamentalist groups in Pakistan. From a security point of view, some strategic analysts in Pakistan are of the view that the Indian intentions are directed towards flooding Pakistan during tensions and that flood waters could destroy Pakistani defenses. Pakistan has also certain economic and defensive apprehension on the construction of projects, especially on Jhelum and Chenab River.

In 2008, after filing of the Baglihar project and subsequent reduction of the water flow in Pakistan, the project has drawn serious concerns and gained critical currency among the countries' political circles. With regard to Wullar Barrage, it has also incurred political and strategic voices from Pakistan, as it fears that with the construction of the Wullar Barrage in Indian administrated Kashmir (IAK), India could close the gate of Wullar Barrage during a warlike situation, enhancing the ability of Indian troops to enter Pakistan. The project is also frequently criticized in farming communities.

The difficulties in interpretations of the treaty can be attributed to political motives rather than to differences over technical and engineering aspects of water management. Some non-state actors, especially radical extremist groups from two countries have their vested interests in the complex issue of water sharing and the treaty. Some are of the view that if the gap between water availability and requirements widens, terrorist operations and recruitment in the region will increase.

Given the present political atmosphere viz-a-viz water, it seems that water has gained a critical value within the two countries and none of the parties are ready to compromise. It seems that the temperament of the political systems, interests of non- state actors and the regional political atmosphere determine the state of affairs of India-Pakistan conflict over water. Indo-Pak water relations can be well understood taking into consideration the statement of President Asif Ali Zardari in the Washington post. According to Asif Ali Zardari, "The water crisis in Pakistan is directly linked to relations with India. Its relations with India could prevent an environmental upheaval in South Asian region, but failure to do so could fuel the fires of discontent that may lead to extremism and terrorism".

The Indus water dispute is overtly linked with Jammu and Kashmir, (a disputed territory) where the major rivers of disputed water originate. It is quite vividly expressed by the US Assistant Secretary of State, George McGhee, in his letter to David Lilienthal, in 1951. " A settlement of the canal waters question would signify those basic reversals of policy by the governments of both India and Pakistan without which there can be no political rapprochement. Thus, the canal waters question is not only a functional problem, but also a political one linked to the Kashmir dispute".

In 1960, it was hoped that the resolution of water dispute would pave the way for resolving the Kashmir dispute. At the time of signing of the treaty, Jawaharlal Nehru the Indian Prime Minister, before coming to Pakistan expressed in the Indian parliament that he was ready to resolve any issue including Kashmir. Similar views and hopes were also expressed by Pakistani President Ayub Khan. Hitherto, three wars has been fought between India and Pakistan over Kashmir, but the dispute still remains unresolved and problematic. Until and unless the Kashmir issue is settled, both countries will not be able to develop good relations in the future. If the countries came up with an agreement to settle the Kashmir dispute, nothing will prevent them from building good relationships.

INDUS WATER TREATY: NEED FOR REVIEW

Disputes between India and Pakistan over the Indus River basin began with partition in 1947. Between 1947 and 1960 the two sides addressed their differences through a number of short term agreements but the dispute could not be settled through bilateral negotiations, and international mediation had to be sought. In 1960, after nine years of negotiations, the two sides signed the Indus Water Treaty (IWT).

Under the Treaty, all the waters of the Eastern Rivers - Sutlej, Beas, and Ravi - were allocated to India for unrestricted use, except during the transition period of 1 April 1960 to 31 March 1970, during which water had to be supplied to Pakistan so that Pakistan might construct replacement works (two storage dams, eight inter-river link canals and six barrages) for water that was being received earlier from the Eastern Rivers. India agreed to make a fixed contribution of 62 million towards the cost of the replacement works. Pakistan received unrestricted use of the Western Rivers - Indus, Jhelum, and Chenab - which India is "under obligation to let flow" and "shall not permit any interference with these waters," except for irrigating existing areas and to develop a further 701,000 acres of irrigation from these rivers subject to certain specific conditions. Specific provisions were made for regular exchange of river and canal data between the two countries.

MODIFICATIONS' POTENTIAL BENEFITS TO INDIA

India has developed disputes with three of its neighbours i.e. Pakistan, Bangladesh and Nepal. She is accused for infringing on their water rights by usurping their resources with potential to ultimately drain their respective resources during hostilities through construction of various projects on rivers whose water is flowing downstream. (Ahmad) Siddharth Varadarajan of The Hindu says: "New Delhi needs to factor in a new reality: More than Kashmir, it is the accusation that India is stealing water that is rapidly becoming the 'core issue' in the Pakistani establishment's narrative about bilateral problems."

India in pursuit of the position of regional power and on that ground desires to get the status of permanent member in the UN Security Council. In order to get international support for her case India needs an image of a cooperative country in the region. The resolution of water issues with the neighbouring states will go a long way in this regard. In past IWT has won good repute for her and for Pakistan as issue resolving countries. The review of IWT will lessen the degree of conflict in South Asia, remove the doubts of South Asian countries against India and also enhance Indian image all over the world.

India is also not satisfied with the present state of affairs and it has to bear serious economic losses because of the delays in the mechanism of IWT which have arisen due to disputes which started to arise during last decade. Indian professionals have expressed frustrations over long delays in approval of projects due to Pakistani objections. India argues that the IWT limits its ability to exploit the Indus's hydroelectric potential, representing an opportunity cost. The waters of the Indus river system have a direct impact on the state of Jammu and Kashmir and are therefore crucial to its economic prospects. The Kashmir Valley, which is the main source of the dispute between India and Pakistan, has been affected by the IWT. In February 1951 Prime Minister Nehru invited David E. Lilienthal, virtual founder of IWT, in order to resolve the water issue since the core of the Kashmir problem stemmed from a "struggle over rivers, rivers with their headwaters in the Kashmir, flowing through Pakistan."

That is why even today the most important internal issue that strains the IWT is the view of the people in Jammu and Kashmir who see the Treaty as exploiting their rights by both India and Pakistan and they call for its annulment as an economic liability. People of the northern areas in Pakistan are also opposed to dam projects in Pakistan like the Mangla dam. Likewise Indian government is faced with the criticism over the IWT from the Kashmiris in Indian held Kashmir, who show concern over division of waters. Motions were moved in the state assembly on three different occasions by the legislators asking the Indian government to review the IWT and pay compensation to the state. (Feyyaz) According to Kashmiri Separatists, IWT has deprived state of Jammu and Kashmir to use its own water resources and became one of the reasons for the alienation of people and has severely affected the economic development in the state.

The revision of IWT and solution of water disputes can lead to the dissolution of the most important of the conflicts in the region. New ponderings on the water issue may include the concerns of the Kashmiri people an all dimensions of the water issue may be taken into consideration. This can provide India as well as Pakistan a fair chance towards longstanding solution of the Kashmir issue.

Indian government is not altogether opposed to the negotiations over the IWT. It is ready to change the IWT though under the mechanisms of the Treaty. Indian External Affairs Minister S. M. Krishna told Indian Parliament, that the Indian government "is in full compliance with the Treaty. All issues regarding implementation of the Treaty should be resolved through the existing mechanisms under the IWT" It means that India feels the need of some progress in the IWT in the wake of new realities which have appeared during last decades.

WATER AND POWER NEXUS

Hydroelectricity is the prevalent most economic source of white energy. There is little chance of inventing a genius innovatory energy source anytime soon that will not engage nations to water conflicts to produce electric power. Hydroelectricity is derived from gravitational force (potential energy) of the flowing or falling waters. A hydropower house may take the form of a run-of-river (flowing) or dam (falling). Hydroelectric power plants use water turbines instead of water wheel. The Water turbine has a swirling component for force to pass on kinetic energy to spinning rotor.

French engineer, Bernard Forest de Belidor, conceived the idea of water power in the 1770s. Different types of turbines such as Francis (1849), Pelton (1879) and Kaplan (1913) are considered suitable for10-350, 50-1300 and 2-40m heads whereas waterwheels are used for 0.2-4m falls. Typical capacities of pico, micro, small, medium and large dams are <5 kW, 5 to 100 kW, 100 to 10 MW, 10 to 10,000 MW and >10 GW. There only three large dams worldwide namely Three Gorges Dam (22.5 GW), Itaipu Dam (14 GW) and Guri Dam (10.2 GW). Global small scale hydropower capacity is 85 GW out of which 65 GW in China, 3.5 GW in Japan, 3 GW in USA and 2 GW in India. Norway, Brazil, Venezuela, Canada, and Sweden produce 98.25, 85.56, 67.17, 61.12 and 44.34% of their national power demands by hydro power plants. Hydropower is considered the cleanest white energy.

The World's first DC hydropower house, Cragside in Northumberland, was operated in England (UK) in 1878. Thomas Edison invented the first long life incandescent lamp in 1879 before which carbon filament based short lived lamps were available. The first US Niagara hydropower station started delivering DC electricity in 1881.

Nicolas Tesla invented the first three phase AC generator used in the Niagara Falls hydro station. Most European countries got hydropower stations from 1880 to 1890 simultaneously. The British brought this technology to India in the early 1900s. The Water and Power Development Authority (WAPDA) was established in Pakistan in 1959.

The British government had already developed large barrages and canals systems for irrigation. WAPDA engineers constructed 1000 MW Mangla dam in 1867, 3500 MW Tarbella dam in 1976 and 2000 run-of-river Chashma power house in 2004. World's largest hydropower producers are China, Canada, USA, Brazil, Russia, India, Norway and Japan which have total installed capacities of 196.79, 88.974, 79.511, 69.08, 45.00, 33.60, 27.528 and 27.229GW. Famous Chinese three gorges dam since 1994 produces 22,500 MW electricity and proposed Congo Grand Inga dam will produce 39,000 MW by 2014.

A 50,000 MW dam is under proposal on the Red Sea. China's installed hydropower capacity is more than the total combined hydropower capacities of USA, Canada and Japan. Chinese hydropower generation capacity is about six times more than that of India and 33 times more than Pakistan's hydropower generation. India's hydropower generation capacity is about 5-6 times more than Pakistan's, yet it is building dozens of dams on rivers which were given to Pakistan under the Indus Water Treaty in 1960. India had 300 dams in 1947. This number increased to 4000 by 2000. About 70% of new dams were built during the 1971-1989 period.

TRANSBOUNDARY RIVERS CONFLICTS

In view of widespread water scarcity, due to climate change, it is time to fine tune the clauses of international rivers sharing laws. The United Nations adopted existing European and US agreements in light of Helsinki rules in 1997 as an international water law which has failed to protect downstream "riparian rights" (Pakistan) when the "upstream riparian" country (India) started building multiple dams on the Indus, Jhelum and Chenab without permission.

World Bank Vice president, Ismail Serageldin, said in 1995 that the next century wars would be fought over water and not over oil.

If there has not been any exclusive war on waters in past that does not mean it can not be in future. European countries share 4 river basins under 175 treaties, 4-5 African countries share 12 river basins under 34 treaties, 4-5 Asian countries share 5 river basins under 31 treaties. There are 48 joint river commissions in Europe, 23 in the Americas, 10 in Africa and 9 in Asia. European and American states had disagreements over water quality in Rhine and Colorado rivers but African, Middle East and Asian countries have water quantity disputes on Zambezi, Mekong, Nile, Euphrates, Tigris, Indus and Ganges. We love or hate each other we have to share the water, air and sun. Oil and water do not mix but can entangle to develop water, watts and war trinity. Some social scientists are covertly producing amphoteric solutions of oil and water in blood geopolitically.

Upper riparian India has started diverting and holding off shared rivers waters under its innovatory dam policies which is starving lower riparian Pakistan.

India has embarked on diverting western rivers waters through connecting canals from Jehlum to Chenab through an 80km long tunnel, Chenab to Ravi through the Marhu tunnel, interconnection of Beas to Sutlej and Sutlej to the Ganges through a proposed express link canal which is in blatant violation of the Indus Water Teaty.

IPCC experts believe that global warming caused the August 2010 flash flood in Pakistan which affected 20-25 million people. Climate change experts speculate that under rapidly rising global warming, water distribution conflicts could potentially lead to armed conflicts among nations in future.

Transboundary river conflicts include water shortages as well as geopolitical issues.

Water conflict between Pakistan and India is building up due to the fast melting of the glaciers. Middle Eastern countries take water availability as a strategic weapon. Palestinians per capita water consumption is 60 liters per day in the West Bank whereas Israelis use 330 liters per day (5 times more).

Fair water distribution is one of the key issues in Israel-Palestinian agreement today. Arab-Israel conflict is getting aggravated by water conflicts. Israel is also trying to secure access to Nile, Euphrates and Ceyhan in Turkey. Global research observers blame Israel for stealing Arab waters. People have been occupying waters since antiquity but the water flows today and they have gone the same is going to happen with present and future generations.

Historic wrecks are often the source of conflict as well as consensus. Transboundary water conflicts cannot be resolved using game theory geopolitics bearing undercurrents. Fair rules must be developed by United Nations in the name of International Rivers Water Sharing Laws. Shared river waters conflicts are both of the inter and intra state types that require global laws to safeguard lower riparian. Without UN backed water laws, the long held agreements may break leading to political confrontations.

Water distribution experts have already proposed several models that facilitate the UN to formulate transboundary water sharing and conflict resolution laws. Mass migrations and water conflicts intensification has been noted in Tanzania since last one decade and Pakistan during August 2010 floods. The developed countries sustain dilemmas in developing countries that lead to talent migration causing serious blows to economies of developing countries.

The Water situation is getting worse in the USA and China. It is extremely critical in Brazil, and in India and Pakistan where the underground water table is falling at rate of 3-5cm per year.

India is building several dozen dams and diversion canals on shared rivers; Indian hydro tactics have caused droughts and flash floods horrors in Pakistan. India is constructing 24-25 dams on river Chenab that feeds to central Punjab housing 90-100 million people.

India relates it to her growing power needs but Pakistan takes it aqua bomb capable of causing droughts and flash floods. The Recent flash flood due to monsoons rains and timed injection of Indian dam waters has inflicted 25000 lives, 1-2 billion crops and 5-7 billion property losses.

The United Nations have no global law on transboundary water distribution. Due to natural scarcity of freshwaters, concerned experts have long been warning of water wars.

European and Americans water agreements under Helsinki Rules and the International Law Commission Convention on Law of the Non-Navigational Uses of International Water courses have been universalized for global water treaties which have no consensus across the board. Despite 2 dams on Beas, 4 on Sutlej, 6 on Ravi, 7 on Indus, 8 on Jhelum and 24 on Chenab India assumes full right on all six rivers falling down to Pakistan and blames colonial period water laws creating schism that locks the water sector into a developmental catharsis.

In response to a satellite research on ground water depletion in Punjab reporting underground water table declining rate of 3-5cm/yr, an Indian water expert tried to justify multiple dams policy on western Pakistani rivers as a sensible measure to mitigate their water depletion crisis. Pakistan, being downstream riparian, supports Radha's demand for international legislature on transboundary water sharing laws to avoid water conflicts but does not support Saumitra's innovatory policy to steal others waters to solve own problems. Pakistan proposes United Nations to frame laws governing distribution of international river waters including construction of dams in high hazards seismic areas. In view of multiple river basins shared by two or more countries it has become imperative to formulate global river water distribution laws acceptable to upper and lower riparian, déjà vu, water fracas and frays might escalate to dismal water wars in forthcoming decades. Several water experts have pointed out Indian ingenuity based maneuvers to hoodwink lower riparian.

WATER, POWER AND ENERGY CONFLUENCE

Population growth, industrial expansion and the consumer economy have increased electricity demand from 17PWh in 2000 to 20PWh in 2010. Demand is esitamted to increase to 24 PWH by 2020 and 30PWh by 2030.

About 2.5 billion people out of global 6.8 billion population lived with severe water conditions in 2005 which are likely to increase to 3.95 billions out of 8.5 billions population by 2030.

The IEEE believes trading water for watts is start of hard choices era. Hydroelectric, solar, nuclear and wind power plants consume 5.4, 2.5-2.8, 1.5 and 0 liters water per kWh but produce no carbon.

Coal and gas fired power plants consume 1.1-1.8 and 0.5-1.8 liters per kWh energy producing 0.43 to 0.96 kg/kWh carbon. P

hotovoltaic power generation uses 0.1 liter/kWh water producing 0.02 kg/kWh carbon. Wind power is the cleanest form energy which neither uses water nor produces carbon. Pakistan is among least coal burning countries but global warming is hitting hard on it since 1998. A recent temperature rise to 54°C in Mohenjo Daru followed by 1200,000 cusecs flash floods has affected over 2 to 2.5 million people across Pakistan. The climatologists say it makes no difference whether a single country increases or decreases greenhouse gases emissions at global scale. A country injecting thousands miles away can affect you through the common atmosphere. Recent industrialization in China and India has led to accumulation of green gases over Pakistan that has changed monsoon flow patterns from Bangladesh to India to Southern Punjab to northern mountains exacerbating glacier melting.

World power demand is 17 PWh whereas thousands of dams installed electric power capacity is 777 GWe that supplies just 2.9 PWh which is 18% of total demand. The remaining 82% demand is met with fossil fuels which are likely to be deplete after 2050.

NEEDS FOR MODIFICATIONS

Despite being a long lasting successful treaty there are some limitations within the IWT that require review. Michel T Klare opines that it does not allow for the joint development of the Indus basin; nor does it eliminate the grounds for conflict over water distribution between India and Pakistan since it is a plan for the separate development of the basin (Feyyaz). It is also unusual among international water-sharing agreements because allocation is based on tributary locations; water is neither allocated on a quantitative basis between the parties nor managed by an operating rule. It is specific about which nation uses which tributary, but it does not create mechanisms to address issues specified in the treaty per se, such as groundwater use, changes in flow due to climate change, changing domestic demand due to population increases or rainfall variability.

Daanish Mustafa (2010) observes that it, by performing an amputation surgery on the basin that was much the same as the political bifurcation of the subcontinent, made matters simple and allowed the two countries to pursue their nationalist agendas without much need for more sophisticated and involved cooperation in the water field. This lack of cooperative sharing of water has considerable negative consequences for the ecology and societies of the Indus basin.

Moreover environmental and ecological changes call for re-consideration of IWT. Projections of climate change on water resources have important implications for both water scarce and flood prone regions, as many indicate dry regions becoming drier and wet regions becoming wetter. Because of climate change, the Himalayan glaciers are melting at an alarming rate. For water resources, this means an increase in water initially due to flooding. Within the next 50 years, however, experts believe there will be a 30 to 40 percent drop in glacial melt because the glaciers will have receded. A strategy to create more storage capacity for water is the only option available.

In this regard the canal withdrawals in Indus Irrigation System, more or less stagnated in 1979 after construction of Tarbela Dam, have now declined to around 103 MAF, partly due to silting of the reservoirs. This aspect has not been considered at the political level or at least has not gained prominence while it demands a common water vision by India and Pakistan that will be based on realization of the importance of the shared rivers as being a natural resource that is integral to their survival.

Pollution control is another issue that needs consideration in the review of the IWT. Given the lack of pollution controls on industry and recent reports of hazardous industrial and chemical-rich water crossing the border into Pakistan it could be inferred that water quality is deteriorating in the Indus. There are no provisions in any treaty on water between Pakistan and India for the control of pollution. Through the review of IWT the issue of the pollution can also be addressed properly.

Pakistan's Federal Minister for Kashmir Affairs and Gilgit-Baltistan, Mian Manzoor Ahmad Wattoo, pointing towards another drawback of IWT, contended that the IWT was signed by a military dictator, General Ayub Khan. He observed "Since no consultations were held or a consensus evolved, the treaty has some inherent flaws and India has been misusing it at the cost of Pakistan's interests." Fresh review of the Treaty may be helpful in dissolving more differences and is, if it ever happens, likely to produce a consensus in modern times when democratic institutions are getting progress in both states of India and Pakistan.

Thus the IWT is a product of its time and could be fruitfully modified and renegotiated to bring it more in line with contemporary international watercourse law, the Helsinki rules, and emerging concerns with water quality, environmental sustainability, climate change, and principles of equitable sharing.

INDIAN PROJECTS

More problematic is the provision in IWT relating the use of the western rivers by India. The crux of IWT is that India was given full control of Eastern rivers and Pakistan was given full control of western rivers. But the provision of usage of western rivers to India for non irrigative use of western rivers has created problems afterwards. India by virtue of the upper riparian could always use and obstruct the waters of Indus Basin. IWT was signed to protect the interests of Pakistan and not of India. Pakistan gave off the right of 3 eastern rivers for the sake of complete and unhindered use of western rivers.

India got the benefit of the three eastern rivers in full but Pakistan's usage of the waters of three western rivers is yet on stake because India has started work on many projects on the cost of Pakistani concerns.

The challenge to the treaty came regarding the construction of the Wullar Barrage, as it is called by Pakistan, or Tulbul Navigation Project as termed by India. There is controversy on the explanations of the specific provisions of the IWT. The 330 MW hydroelectric Kishanganaga project that is located about 160 kilometers upstream of Muzaffarabad and involves diversion of Kishanganga or Neelum River to a tributary, Bunar Madumati Nullah of the River Jhelum through a 22-kilomtre tunnel, is another controversial water issue between the two countries which could not have been resolved under IWT.

Located on the River Chenab in Doda district, the Baglihar hydropower project is one of the nine major hydroelectric projects identified by India on the Chenab. Pakistan protested over the design of the dam in 1992 and demanded a halt to its construction.. Taking cue from the Bagliahr verdict of the Neutral Expert that reinterpreted the Treaty in the light of "new technical norms and new standards," "state of the art" and "best and latest practices in the field of construction and operation," the risks of increased floods associated with "climate change," it appears that the Treaty has to accommodate the new realities in the Indus basin, not only in terms of technical norms but also growing pressures on the health and viability of the Indus basin rivers.

The invocation of neutral expert clause has revealed another drawback in the IWT and has damaged an impression that satisfied the doubts of many Pakistanis that the World Bank was the guarantor of the IWT. It so happened that when Pakistan approached the World Bank for mediation it clearly noted that it was "not a guarantor of the treaty," (Haq, 4) The note of World Bank, though correct legally, has raised dissatisfaction in some circles of Pakistan who always remains suspicious for Indian deception and trust only on third party that may be a guarantor in the compromises of both countries.

During 2006 to 2011 Pakistan's concerns over another controversial project Nimoo Bazgo near village Alchi in the district Leh in Indian held Kashmir could not be highlighted due to alleged negligence of its Indus Water Commissioner Jamaat Ali Shah against whom a probe on his alleged secret compliance with India has started in Pakistan. However, during a recent inspection, the Pakistani team learnt that more than 80 per cent of the work on the dam had been completed and the expected date of its inauguration is July 2012.

Notwithstanding Indian concerns over delay in the execution of the projects, Pakistan's concerns for the projects are too much serious. Though

India as per the IWT is allowed to generate power from the waters of these rivers yet it did stop Chenab river flow on various occasions notable being from August 19 to September 5 wherein Pakistan was deprived of 1.2 million cusecs of water at one time alone.

Moreover through IWT Pakistan does not find immediate relief. She, through a lengthy process defined in IWT, has only option just to deliver complain to India or put the case in international tribunals that definitely requires huge amount of time and money. During the whole process, India loses nothing and Pakistan gradually gets loss. India often continues to start new projects day by day and Pakistan continues to complain over them. India has planned to make 62 more dams. Therefore, there is dire need to alter the clause that allows India to use the waters of western rivers.

Whenever India takes decision to construct a dam or reservoir and the matter enters the framework of the treaty, which only provides technical specifications for building such a dam or reservoir, Islamabad invokes the jurisdiction of a neutral expert or arbitration court.

During the time the case takes, the construction is completed and Pakistan in that sense 'loses' the cases. Some observers point out that Pakistan is feeling alienated from the IWT after repeated failures to get redress of its grievances and, hence, would like to replace it with a new treaty. But it is not easy to agree on a new pact. A pragmatic approach is required to amend and update the treaty to remove the lacuna it suffers from.

It looks altogether unjust that India can use all of the rivers without restrictions but Pakistan is bound to use only western rivers even with apprehension of Indian obstruction.

The question remains unsolved what to do of the projects which India has already installed. Second issue may be this why the waters of western rivers should not be used before entering into Pakistan. For the sake of prosperity to both nations joint projects can be initiated on the western rivers and benefits may be shared by both nations. Already initiated projects can also be shared on these grounds. But it is necessary that the clauses of the IWT must be altered in order to give Pakistan unrestricted control of the western rivers and it will be a great benefit to energy starved nation of Pakistan.

An array of upcoming Indian projects has unfolded many challenges to the functioning of the Permanent Indus Water Commission. The institution is unable to cope with the issues which were originally not within its purview as they did not exist at that time. All above mentioned controversial projects highlight the need of mediation as well as such new mechanism and consensus under which the issues which have risen during implementation of IWT can be resolved. For this an overall review and new negotiations on the water issue are the call of the hour.

There is no provision in IWT which allows India to construct a certain number of dams. Nor is there one that prohibits India from making dams beyond a certain number. Notwithstanding prescribing restrictions on the features and operations of Indian projects on the western rivers the Treaty does not lay down any limits on the total number of projects that can be built, the height of the dams, the total power-generation capacity, etc. Ramaswamy R. Iyer (2012) thinks that the point about 'cumulative impact' needs to be considered. He however proposes a joint study by experts of both countries for this purpose.

9

Water Conflicts and Hydroelectricity in South Asia

RIVERS WATER DISPUTE

The periodic scarcity of water in the Indus River System (IRS) gives rise to inter-provincial disputes especially between Punjab and Sindh which is the lower riparian of this system. Before proceeding further it is important to explain in common language certain technical terms used in case of flow, quantity and storage of water for irrigation and hydel power generation. The basic unit to measure the flow of water is 'cusec' which means a quantity of one cubic foot of water flowing in one second or commonly 6.24 gallons or 28 litres of clean water per second. The quantity of water is measured in terms of acre foot which equals the quantity of water needed to flood one acre of level ground to a depth of one Foot. This means 43560 cubic feet or 271,814 gallons or 1,223,165 litres of water. For very large quantities of water the term million acre feet (MAF) is used which equals a million or ten lakhs acre feet. In case of hydel-power, one cusec of water dropped from a height of 100 feet possesses gross potential energy to generate approximately 8.5 KW of electrical power and the amount of electricity produced is directly proportional to the height from which the same quantity of water is dropped. In the case of food production one acre foot of water applied to ordinarily levelled ground without any special inputs will produce 45 maunds of wheat. One cusec of water flowing continuously for 24 hours equals 1.98 acre foot of water.

These terms have been explained in order to enable ordinary readers to appreciate the potential that nature has hidden in the natural annual flow of water of a river both in terms of irrigation as well as hydel power. The flow of water in any river varies greatly from season to season and also from year to year. For this reason daily flows are recorded and tabled over a long period of time on weekly, monthly and annual basis. For the principle rivers of Indus River System, these records are available for seventy five years indicating maximum as well as minimum flows during different seasons. The rivers of this system are Indus itself and its tributaries Kabul, Jhelum, Chenab, Ravi, Bias and Sutlej. Since river Kabul merges with Indus at Attock ahead of classic Indus plains, therefore, the Indus River System is counted to comprise Indus below Attock and its tributaries the five rivers of Punjab.

There is one thing that must be very clearly understood. Allah Almighty holds into His exclusive discretion the quantity of water that flows into rivers at any time. Human ingenuity may make any device for storage and diversion of river flows but the sum total of the quantity shall always remain the same as Allah Almighty allows into the rivers. The construction of storage (dam) and diversion (barrage) schemes, therefore, solely depends on the total quantity of water that is available in a river during a year, particularly how these flows dovetail into the quantity of water needed during crop seasons.

This is the reason that has necessitated recording of river flows for long period of years. On the basis of over fifty years' record the mean flow in Indus River System (IRS) totalled 175 MAF on the eve of Partition of Punjab in 1947. This comprised 93 including 27 of Kabul for Indus, 23 for Jhelum, 26 for Chenab, 6 for Ravi, 13 for Bias and 14 for Sutlej in MAF annually. Out of this 175 MAF; 167 flowed into Pakistan at the time the boundaries of partitioned Punjab were fixed according to the Radcliffe Award. This means that the Indian East Punjab drew only 8 MAF of a total of 33 MAF of water that annually flowed in three eastern rivers Ravi, Bias and Sutlej before waters of these rivers entered West Punjab of Pakistan. Under the Internationally agreed rights of lower riparians and also Indian Independence Act 194, the balance 25 MAF waters of three eastern rivers were to be shared between India and Pakistan and India was also to guarantee non-interference in the existing supplies of canal waters flowing into Pakistan from Head Works (Madhopur and Ferozpur) in India. The sordid tale must first be told as to how this life blood of Pakistan's agriculture was sold out to India first through the criminal conduct of Punjab Government in 1947 and later the infamous Indus Waters Treaty of 1960 which deprived Pakistan nearly one-sixth of its total surface water resources. This sell out is indeed a bigger act of treason against Pakistan than the separation of East Pakistan connived by 'patriots'.

Under Independence Act a Punjab Partition Council was set up comprising equal members from both East and West Punjab governments. An Arbitral Tribunal, with life up to March 31, 1948, was also set up to finally decide upon any contentious issues between the two governments. Committee B of the

Partition Council was to decide upon the share of the three eastern rivers between the two governments and the canal waters. It was agreed between the representative of two governments that existing supplies of canal waters will not be disturbed and that the river waters shall be shared 'proportionally'. Under this formula the Rau Commission of 1941 had awarded East Punjab area of undivided Punjab construction of Bhakra Dam with a storage capacity of 4 MAF on river Sutlej. Both sides had, therefore, agreed to Pakistan's share of 21 MAF of three Eastern rivers and non-interference of supplies of waters of canals flowing into Pakistan from Madhopur and Ferozpur Head Works. The West Punjab government of Khan Mamdot with Daultana and Shaukat Hayat as key members, however, failed to draw out an agreement to this effect and register it with the Partition Council and relied only on the verbal assurances of their lingual brothers of East Punjab.

Consequently, as soon as the Arbitral Tribunal was abolished, India turned off the tap on canal waters on April 1, 1948 and on Pakistan's protest denied any agreement and claimed all waters of canals and eastern rivers to it. Chaudhri Muhammad Ali then Secretary General of Pakistan writes on the episode that on the part of East Punjab there was Machiavellian duplicity. On the part of West Punjab there was neglect of duty, complacency and lack of common prudence which had disastrous effects on Pakistan. In May 1948 a delegation led by Ghulam Muhammad with Daultana and Shaukat Hayat as members went to Delhi to sort out the issue. On May 4,1948 Ghulam Muhammad signed a statement which said that apart from the question of law involved, the governments were anxious to approach the problem in a practical spirit. The East Punjab government would progressively diminish its supplies to Central Bari Doab and Dipalpur canals in West Punjab to give it reasonable time to tap alternative sources. The legally agreed right of Pakistan to the waters of three Eastern rivers and the canals flowing into it from India, was thus abjectley surrendered by the delegation which went to discuss the problem with Indians.

When news of this reached Karachi, Liaquat Ali Khan in a telegram to Nehru immediately disowned the 'statement' as signed under duress and also informed UNO not to register it as an expression of government of Pakistan since the dying Jinnah was still alive. It should be remembered that the canal waters flowing into Pakistan from India irrigated less than ten percent of the total irrigated area in then West Punjab and contributed little to overall agricultural output. The Ghulam Muhammad Delegation, however, laid the basis for India to claim all the waters of Eastern rivers to which India stuck during all negotiations between the two countries. Pakistan persistently refused such claims until India finally assembled 90 percent of its army on West

Punjab borders to brow beat Pakistan into submission. It was at this time that Liaquat challenged India for a fight to finish although the first Pakistani Commander-In-Chief of Army advised against war. Unable to confront a nation aroused to fight to finish, India withdrew its army and the canal supplies continued to flow.

It was at this juncture that Chairman of Tennessee Valley Authority in United States described the canal water dispute as 'Punjab powder keg' and went on to say that with such 'inflammables' around there is no chance of peace in the sub-continent. This made World Bank President, Eugene Black, contact the two governments in September 1951 and made India agree to Liaquat's demand that until a just solution is found the existing arrangement of water supplies to Pakistan shall not be disturbed. However, no sooner the 'hurdle' of Liaquat was removed in October 1951, India started throttling the canal waters which the post Liaquat factional governments were not able to confront on 'principle', eventually ending in the anti-Pakistan Indus Waters Treaty of 1960. Indians, perhaps, waited for the assassination of Liaquat to squeeze Pakistan on canal waters much the same way as they waited till the death of Quaid-e-Azam to occupy Hyderabad in blatant disregard of its own Stand Still Agreement.

TRANSBOUNDARY WATER DISPUTES IN CENTRAL ASIA

Over the last decades, there has been a growing speculation about the likelihood of an acute conflict or even war over freshwater resources.

Scholars increasingly point out that the 21st century might see the battles fought due to water scarcity. Indeed, water is the only resource having no substitute, and the demand for it is constant and burning. All forms of the Earth's life, including humans, need water to survive. The fact that we inhabit the 'water planet' soothes little as only less than 3% of total water resources on the Earth are freshwater. Its distribution is obviously uneven, with some nations suffering severe droughts every year and the others blessed with water abundance.

It is no wonder then that through the whole history of human race, water allocation and quantity fuelled tensions between various states, with particular role played by transboundary river resources. And although history shows that full-scale wars over water, proving to be neither strategically rational nor hydrographically effective, have never been fought, water continues to be a source of intense disputes worldwide.

The problem grows harder when it comes to the relationships between two or more countries over river water as a result of the "internationalisation of a basin through political change. The number of international basins has grown from 214 in 1978 to 263 today. These international basins cover 45.3% of total land surface, affect about 40% of the world's population, and account for about 60% of global river flow.

Nineteen basins are shared by 5 or more riparian countries, with only the Danube being shared by 17 riparians, whereas five basins – the Congo, Niger, Nile, Rhine and Zambezi – are shared by between 9 and 11 countries.

In this situation, such long-negotiated instrument of international water law as the 1997 UN Convention on the Non-Navigational Uses of International Watercourses, is of little help as it provides for equally contradictory 'equitable use' and 'no significant harm' principles: while the former is favoured by upstream countries, downstream riparians insist on emphasising the latter because it protects their own rights.

It is also difficult to enforce the Convention in the absence of any international enforcing mechanisms. More importantly, the Convention hardly weighs out a variety of political, social, economic, demographic and environmental factors that encompass each shared river basin.

Negotiators whose task is to provide timely diplomatic intervention, or apply means of the so-called 'preventive diplomacy', in order to avoid the escalation of a dispute into open conflict need to be aware which basin is prone to water conflict well in advance.

To do that, they need to identify potential indicators of conflict that incorporate a wide range of physical, social, economic and environmental variables, including those which can be analysed within a Geographic Information System (GIS), and to develop a comprehensive model to explore specific linkages between them. In particular, this method can be applicable in those cases of internationally shared rivers where progress towards successful resolution of a dispute was slow or unachievable.

Considering all factors having influence on the river basin regime is becoming crucial to elaborate meaningful and workable framework to provide resolution to the growing water conflict.

Since the collapse of the Soviet Union, Central Asia has become a tangle of unresolved transboundary water disputes. Water is the most critical resource in Central Asia and it "has more often been the source of competition rather than the focus of conservation.

The absence of mechanisms to handle the water problems has already resulted in various accusations of improper water use. Consequently, the whole region becomes the site of potential conflict that requires a framework which should incorporate a great many variables to identify the proneness to water conflict and to allow for the possibility of preventive diplomacy.

Such method which has never been used towards the specific problem of Central Asian water disputes can provide solutions based on a more holistic approach to natural resources, while recognising the historical, geopolitical and natural characteristics of the region.

This study seeks to identify potential indicators of water conflict and analyse some of them within the Geographical Information System (GIS).

Unlike other studies that involve global level analysis, the thesis will focus on Central Asia's regional and basin specific information. An attempt to answer a question of what indicators better point to water conflict will be taken.

Hypothesis

The study aims at testing the working hypothesis that proneness of a specific river basin to water conflict can be identified through a variety of indicators representing physical, political, environmental and socio-economic processes occurring in this specific region, thus providing better chance for using preventive diplomatic actions.

Methodology

The study's methodology is based on the concept of international river basins offered by the Transboundary Freshwater Dispute Database (TFDD), Oregon State University. The database contains a large collection of water treaties and agreements and is a sound foundation for transboundary water conflict research. For the purposes of this study, the Amu Darya Basin is examined. Taking the basin as a unit of research, the proposed study offers a model of relationship between water resources and social, political, economic and environmental patterns in Central Asia. There is also chance to explore the use of GIS such as ESRI Arc View for social research. A parallel analysis of water conflict related variables focuses on finding combinations of indicators that provide an indication of potential water conflict.

KASHMIR AND THE POLITICS OF WATER

The Indus River originates in the Tibetan plateau, making its 3,200km journey southwards along the entire length of Pakistan, before emptying into the Arabian Sea. The river basin is divided between Pakistan, which has about 60 per cent of the catchment area, India with about 20 per cent, Afghanistan with 5 per cent and around 15 per cent in Tibet. The two major riparians, Pakistan and India have extensively dammed the Indus River to provide for irrigation and hydro-electricity.

The Indus has five main tributaries. The Jhelum, the largest of these, originates in the Valley of Kashmir. The Chenab, a second tributary, flows through the Jammu region of the state of Jammu and Kashmir before entering the Indian state of Punjab. The remaining three tributaries (Ravi, Sutlej and Beas) either originate or flow through India's state of Himachal before entering Indian Punjab.

As a result, if the Line of Control (LoC) between India and Pakistan in Kashmir, were to move from being a defacto to a recognised international border, India would permanently become the upper riparian and Pakistan the lower riparian of the Indus River and all of its tributaries.

The Indus is a river system that sustains communities in both India and Pakistan. In Pakistan, it is the only river system supporting the country, where more than 92 per cent of the land is arid or semi-arid. In India, it is one of two main river systems supporting the country's northwest: Punjab, Haryana and Rajasthan (generally considered to be water deficient areas).

Given that over half of Pakistan's population is employed in the agricultural sector and that Punjab produces more than 20 per cent of India's wheat and is known as the "bread basket" of the Republic of India, the importance of the Indus River to the well-being and economy of both countries cannot be overemphasised.

In arbitrating the border between India and Pakistan in 1947, Sir Cyril Radcliffe, the chairman of the bodies set up to demarcate the borders, was unable to decide what to do with the Indus River system, given that it was likely to be vital to both states.

The biggest problem, of course, lay with the partitioning of the state of Punjab, as it contained a complex irrigation system built by the British to be run under a single administration. The task was eventually delegated to the Chief Engineers of East Punjab (India) and West Punjab (Pakistan) who agreed to allow the existing water sharing systems to continue until the following year. This Standstill Agreement between India and Pakistan expired on March 31, 1948. On the following day Indian Punjab cut off water flow to Pakistan.

The conflict in Kashmir overlapped with the water disputes, and by January 1948 India had taken the Kashmir issue to the United Nations Security Council (UNSC). On April 21, 1948, a resolution calling for a ceasefire and withdrawal of all troops was passed.

The Kashmir dispute and disputes over the sharing of water resources are intertwined. From independence to the present day, they remain the two biggest challenges when it comes to normalising relations between the states of India and Pakistan.

Later in 1948, Eugene Black, then president of the World Bank, offered the services of his organisation to help negotiate a solution to the water-sharing dispute between the two countries. Although India was not eager to allow third-party involvement, both countries eventually agreed to this proposal.

Evidence and records from the time suggest that in 1948, when the Kashmir issue was taken to the UNSC and the canal dispute between East and West Punjab first arose (in April of that year), they were treated as distinctly separate political and economic issues.

In the early days of independence, the fact that India was able to shut off the Central Bari Doab Canals at the time of the sowing season, causing significant damage to Pakistan's crops, exposed a central weakness and vulnerability in the newly created state that was desperately trying to establish its independence.

As noted by one British general on a visit to the area in 1948, the dispute centres around the "water insecur[ity]" of Pakistan, as all of its rivers either originate in or pass through India.

Experts agreed, saying that resolving water disputes under the auspices of the World Bank was "one way to reduce hostility" over Kashmir.

Nevertheless, military and political clashes over Kashmir in the early years of independence appear to be more about ideology and sovereignity, rather than sharing water resources. A communique from the British High Commissioner's office in Karachi, then capital of Pakistan, from November 1951 seems to suggest otherwise, however:

"But one assumption they have refused to entertain: that India should have control over Kashmir. By having such control India could ruin Pakistan, simply by refusing to operate Mangla at the headworks. It is almost certain therefore that Pakistan would reject any solution of the Kashmir problem which would give these powers; she would rather embark on a war which she fully understood to be suicidal."

Indian ministers at the time were also issuing statements, saying that controlling the entire flow of the Indus river would be impossible, "even if India controlled Kashmir".

It would appear that somewhere along the ideological path, as negotiations on water were being held, politicians worked out that a resolution to the water dispute may well directly influence the Kashmir problem.

Indeed some experts have suggested that Pakistan thought that it could solve the Kashmir dispute through solving canal-related issues, but India completely denied this route of resolution.

Consequently, the Indus Water Treaty was signed by both countries in September 1960, giving exclusive rights over the three western rivers of the Indus river system (Jhelum, Chenab and Indus) to Pakistan, and over the three eastern rivers (Sutlej, Ravi and Beas) to India.

The signing of the treaty and the FINANCING of various water storage projects to benefit Pakistan and India meant that tensions were minimal and to a great degree much of Kashmir's water importance was forgotten for the next couple of decades.

As the populations of both countries increased exponentially, however, water resources came under increasing stress. With India preparing ambitious irrigation project plans, it was possible to see how, by the 1990s, Kashmir's hydrological importance had once again become a serious issue.

The fact that, unlike India, all of Pakistan is wholly dependent upon the Indus River system is a geographical reality. Another reality that compounds this one is the fact that, as the upstream riparian on all five of the main Indus tributaries that flow into Pakistan, India has the strategically advantageous position with regards to control and flow of water.

John Briscoe, a subcontinental water expert, former World Bank senior water expert and currently a professor at Harvard University, recognised Pakistan's unhappy position in the following words: "This is a very uneven playing field. The regional hegemon is the upper riparian and has all the cards in its hands." Pakistan is all too aware of its vulnerable position vis-a-vis water and the fact that more than half of independent Pakistan's time has been spent under military rule has not helped to de-escalate or 'de-securitise' the water discourse in the country.

Over the years, water has been raised as an issue directly linked to Kashmir. Pakistan's political leaders and military elites have emphasised that if they are forced to let go of their claim to Kashmir, that will mean letting go of the source of Jhelum and Chenab as well and being at the mercy of India for water. Though it is unrealistic to assume that India could readily and easily violate the terms of the Indus Water Treaty, Briscoe emphasises that Pakistan and India do not have "normal, trustful relations". The trust deficit along with the fact that India once blocked water flows to Pakistan has the military establishment convinced that they must hold on to their claim to Kashmir in an effort to maintain the country's water security.

Interestingly enough, another Pakistani organisation that has been vociferous in defending Pakistan's rights over Kashmir and criticising India's "aggression" against Pakistan through reduced water flows is the 'charity' Jammat-ud-Dawa (JuD). The JuD is widely believed to be a front group of the militant outfit Lashkar-e-Taiba (LeT) that has been linked to the Mumbai attacks of 2008.

Though there is widespread conjecture on the organisation's close association with Pakistan's intelligence agencies, officially, such a relationship has always been denied. It is worth noting that the JuD has publicly declared

India's "occupation" of Kashmir unacceptable and has also termed its policy of blocking water to Pakistan a justification to wage jihad. In most public statements, however, the JuD tends not to link water and Kashmir, in contrast to the Pakistani military's position on the argument.

India has consistently and emphatically maintained that it has never meddled with Pakistan's share of the Indus waters. Even as the Indus Water Treaty was being negotiated, with the Indian government assuring Pakistan and the World Bank that water was not being blocked, Chintamanrao Deshmukh, the then IndianFINANCE minister, stated in a 1953 parliamentary address that the serious food shortage in Pakistan was not a result of India blocking river flows.

"Even if it were assumed that some mistakes were made at some short period, which in any case did not exceed one or two weeks," he said.

Throughout the history of the dispute, India has rarely, if ever, acknowledged that it has tampered with the supply of water flowing into Pakistan. Since there is also a large amount of secrecy that surrounds the governance of the Indus waters and data is not readily shared, there is no definitive way to prove whether India has just got caught up in Pakistani sensationalism or whether the seeds of resentment and securitisation of water were sowed and are being maintained by the Indian side.

In negotiations and meetings with Pakistani counterparts on the wider Indo-Pak relationship, India does not deal with water and Kashmir as the same issue. In fact, it has often been suggested by analysts that a more consolidated agreement on water might perhaps be a more readily achievable goal in India-Pakistan composite dialogue as COMPARED to Kashmir.

Briscoe finds that the Indian press seems to have a uniform view on water issues, in relation to Pakistan. He says that it was explained to him as follows: "When it comes to Kashmir - and the Indus Treaty is considered an integral part of Kashmir" - the ministry of external affairs (India's foreign ministry) instructs the media about what they are allowed to say. In certain cases, India is happy to conflate the Kashmir and water issues, whereas in negotiations with Pakistan it would like to deal with them as distinct and separate.

Currently, India is in the process of building a number of dams on the Jhelum and Chenab Rivers (both of which originate in Kashmir), such as the Kishenganga, Dal Huste, Sawalkot etc. The Indus Water Treaty allows India to harness the hydropower potential of the Jhelum and Chenab Rivers, as long as it does not reduce or delay the supply to Pakistan. India therefore maintains that its projects are in compliance with the treaty and sees no conflict with Pakistan on these issues.

The region of Kashmir sees itself losing considerably from the Indus Water Treaty because it is not allowed to fully exploit the hydropower potential of its own rivers.

In June 2011, a Chinese news agency reported that the state government of Kashmir was looking for reputed multi-national consultancies to calculate the exact loss to Kashmir from the Indus Water Treaty so that the government will have a number it can take to the Indian federal government. Given that both Pakistan and India are dangerously energy and water starved and nowhere close to an agreement on Kashmir, teamed with the impact of climate change and population pressures, the prognosis on the Indo-Pak water problem involving Kashmir is anything but positive.

DAMS HAZARDS & DRAWBACKS

A large dam may fail during earthquake and flash flood. Dam failures may lead to serious consequences. It causes flash flood causing catastrophes. The Chinese Banqiao dam failure killed 26,000 by drowning in flood water and 145,000 people by subsequent epidemics in addition to billions dollars property losses.

Vajont Dam failure by geological reasons killed 2000 people in Italy in 1963.

Kelly Barnes Dam failed due to flash flood killing 27 people in 1957.

It is very dangerous to construct dams on geological fault lines.

Dam construction devastates lots of fertile land and causes the evacuation of rural populations. It is estimated that 50-80 million peoples have been displaced worldwide due to dam construction.

IMPLICATIONS OF THE INDUS WATER TREATY

The Indus Water Treaty has successfully ended a decade-long water dispute, which had been a major cause of tension between the two countries since partition. It was appreciated by the international community and considered as a good example of water conflict management. The immediate result of the treaty was that the Indus Basin became politically and economically viable for two countries. It has opened new ways for independent development of the water of the Indus Basin. Some are also of the view, had the Indus Treaty not been in place, water dispute would have remained a contentious issue in the political arena between the two countries and the subsequent development might have been wholly or partially withheld.

Development of Indus Basin in India

During partition, both India and Pakistan are agricultural economies, water formed an integral part of their economy. There was a dire need to develop good infrastructures to provide irrigation facilities to those agricultural areas which were uncultivated before partition. India, as an upper riparian country wanted to develop its irrigation facilities in these areas and Pakistan as the lower riparian also needed sufficient water supply for its own irrigation and agriculture.

In 1960, by the signing of the treaty, India has been able to expand her irrigation system. The Article III of the treaty facilitates India to unrestricted harness the water from eastern rivers for any purposes. Immediately after the treaty, a major step was taken by India to construct interlinking canal projects from the Ravi, Beas and Sutlej rivers through the diversion of the rivers. The interlinking canal system increased the irrigated command area, which brought a green revolution in the Indus Basin states and made the country self-sufficient in food production. India implemented various other new schemes, such as the Upper Bari Doab Canal, the Sirhind Canal and the Rajasthan Canal system and the gigantic Indra Gandhi Canal Project. The canal system is connected with the Bhakra Nangal, Pong and Harike barrage. The Bhakra and Nangal dams were constructed on the Sutlej River while the Harike barrage has been constructed at the confluence of Beas and Sutlej rivers to provide supply to Rajasthan and Ferozpur feeders.

The Bhakra Nangal project was designed to provide irrigation to some 1.46 million hectares in Punjab, Haryana, Chandigarh and Rajasthan. The construction of the project has enlarged India's irrigation efficiencies which led to the growth of agriculture in Punjab, Haryana and Chandigarh and Rajasthan. From 1960 onward, the project has added an irrigated area of 6.8 million hectares over 35 years. Moreover, the production of rice and wheat in the Bhakra command area in 1996-97 was eight times as much as 1960-61 figures. Moreover, after the treaty, entire Indian part of the Indus Basin, large and small projects, led to the growth of irrigated area that was estimated 22 million hectares in 1947 to 55 million hectares in 2000.26 Of late, a third major storage project—the Thein dam—was built on the Ravi River, which has a potential to provide eight million acre feet of water to Rajahstan and Thar Desert. This project has transformed desert with a swathe of greenery running north- south along the Pakistan border.

While as the treaty permits India to increase her power potentialities from the Ravi, Beas and Sutlej River, the development of hydropower potential in the Indus Basin has become a priority for the Indian Government over the past few decades. From 1960 onward, India has achieved steady growth in power potential on three eastern rivers. The total estimated power potential of the Indian side basin is measured as 19988 MW at 60 per cent load factor. Out of total 190 schemes in the Indus Basin, 35 schemes are in operation with installed capacity of 3715 MW and 14 schemes with 5626 MW potential is likely to be commissioned in the near future. Furthermore, 32 schemes that remain to be developed, account for nearly 28 per cent of the assessed potential of the basin.

Taking advantage of the various sections of the treaty India has earnestly initiated well designed futuristic planes for the Indus basin. India has developed many hydro-power projects in Jammu & Kashmir State like Salal, Dulhasti, Uri, Baglihar etc. India is also entitled to develop irrigation schemes in its territory to enhance the regional development in terms of agricultural areas through western rivers.

DEVELOPMENT OF INDUS BASIN IN PAKISTAN

The treaty granted independent share of water to Pakistan from western rivers and assured permanent water supply because its large canals used to get water from eastern rivers before 1947. In 1961, with the ratification of the treaty, the Indus Basin Development Fund (IBDF) became effective and Pakistan was able to develop world's largest hydraulic works in the country. In fact, the IBDF caused the green light in Pakistan.

After the treaty was signed, Pakistan secured her water supply through the diversion of three western rivers to meet requirements of irrigation canals that were dependent on eastern rivers before partition. Several immense link canals were built after the treaty. The biggest link canals are the Chashma-Jhelum link canal, the Haveli canal, and the Sindhani-Mailsi-Bahawalpur canals. The other link canals are the Rasul-Qadirabad link canal, the Qadirabad-Balloki canal, the Balloki-Sulemanki canal, Trimmu-Sindhani, Sindhani-Mailsi canal and the Taunsa-Panjnad canal.

Financial aid through World Bank helped Pakistan to build massive storage projects to ensure her electricity needs and water availability for irrigation during critical sowing seasons. The mega projects include Mangla dam on Jhelum River, Tarbela dam and Jinnah dam on Indus River along with various canals and tube wells.

These projects provide cheap and clean hydroelectricity to boost up the industrial and irrigation requirements for the country. In the post-treaty period, Pakistan has constructed other 19 barrages or head-works and 43 major canals with a total conveyance length of 57 000 km on western rivers. These various projects meet the irrigation requirements of 40 million acres irrigated land and provide the fresh water supply to the population of 172 million besides sharing aggregate energy at 33.07 percent. Over all, the irrigation system which is lies in the Indus Basin of Pakistan serve an area of 8.88 hectares, and it is continuously increasing with significant agriculture out puts.

In 1947, at the time of independence, the total installed power potential of the country was only 60 MW for its 31.5 million people, which in 1958, increased to 119 MW. Power infrastructure gained momentum immediately after the treaty. The 1000 MW Mangla and 3478 MW Tarbela dams were completed to meet the increasing demands of the growing population, and Pakistan's installed power potential is continuously increasing. Presently 35 major and medium hydropower projects are in operation in Punjab, Khyber-Pakhtunkhawa (KPK) and 84 small hydel projects are in operation with less than 2 MW installed capacity on the Indus River and its tributaries at Gilgit Baltistan.

In Pakistan, the massive development in water infrastructure subsequent to the treaty has resulted in economic growth and green revolution. Even the treaty has provided employment opportunities in different sectors. For instance, Water and Power Development Authority (WAPADA), which is the largest civilian employer, was set up as a direct consequence of the treaty with international financial and technical assistance. The foreign technical assistance proved helpful for introducing water management know-how, irrigation development and construction of dams to Pakistani engineers.

India and Pakistan are agro based countries; growth of irrigated areas in the Indus Basin provided a boost to the agricultural economies of the two countries. Though the political relations between the two countries are strained, the signing of the treaty has removed some basic related obstructions in the economic development in the countries concerned. They are now pursuing their own interests independently, which has made the Indus Basin a highly developed river basin of the regions serving the largest section of humanity. Development of gigantic projects across the Indus and its historical tributaries enabled both the countries to revolutionise their economies.

NEGATIVE IMPLICATIONS OF THE INDUS WATER TREATY

Despite being appreciated in different quarters, the treaty has drawn flaks from different sections of society as well. The common opinion shared in both the countries is that the distribution of water under the treaty is unfair. Most of the Indians are of the view that the allocation of 80 per cent of the Indus water to Pakistan and 20 percent to India is unjustifiable and unfair. There are also some opinions that the treaty imposed a heavy financial burden on the country, as it does not permit to utilise the full potentialities of the three western rivers to India. Number of Indian scholars such as S.K. Grag, K. Warikoo, B.R. Chauhan40 and M.S. Menon41 is of the view that on the basis of population, drainage area and cultivated lands, India should have been given a 42.8 percent share of the Indus Basin but the treaty was generous 80 percent in Pakistan and 20 percent in India. Hence, the treaty gives a false impression of the water distribution of the Indus Basin.

The Indus Water Treaty was neither envisaged nor implemented to help in equitable distribution of water. It was based on the de-facto possession of the rivers. India was immediately left with independent possession of so called eastern rivers—Beas, Ravi and Sutlej, while Pakistan though in sovereign position to exploit and manage amount of water (Jhelum, Chenab and Indus) flowing through its portion of land had share a meagre amount of water with India (in Kashmir) as it upper riparian right. It was compromise which India was itself campaigning for. Indus Water Treaty also ignores the water rights of a region on the basis of any historical usage of water it is, the absence of any plausible, possible and acceptable alternative a just and pragmatic solution. Furthermore, it needs be understood that Pakistan has to negotiate its position on the water given to it by the treaty (geography in fact) with two upper riparian countries, Afghanistan and China (Tibet). Had India to share its three eastern rivers with Pakistan it would have been deprived of the progress it has made in agriculture sector in Punjab.

In this particular case, neither the quality nor quantity of land under the usage of the waters, nor the number of people living in that region, and nor any consideration for any future demands on water was made basis for the division of the basin. Raising these questions now is to play to the psyche of certain sections of the society—who thrive on the hatred of the opposed country—; it is to play to respective vote bank.

On the other hand, large sections of the Pakistani society opined, the territories that went to India during partition were historically used less than 10 percent of the Indus waters, and the treaty was generous to India in giving it 20 per cent of the water of Indus Basin. Secondly, Pakistan's worry was that India's hold in Kashmir enables it to deprive of the water flow of the Jhelum and Chenab rivers which are the major sources of Pakistan's water supply. But the treaty in a major way gave some satisfaction and security to its water supply as long as India is in possession of Kashmir.

The treaty under study was not intended to solve and by its very formulation could not have had solved all the issues for all the times. It was an arrangement to bring two countries together, enter a compromise and work for better future and developmental avenues. Now the treaty has come under strain from various quarters for various reasons. While as demographic changes and decreasing water availability, demand more judicious approach to treaty. Some new parties (China, Jammu and Kashmir and Afghanistan) claiming their rights as upper riparian or mid riparian countries have entered into the space till now exclusively claimed by India and Pakistan.

Apart from Indian and Pakistani perspectives, one of the major issues attached to the treaty is that it has led to a regional disparity and discontent. In Jammu and Kashmir State, the treaty is perceived as discriminatory. Common view of Kashmiris about the treaty is that while signing the treaty both the countries overlooked the water rights of Kashmir. There are also a lot of current discussions on the treaty at political fronts in the state of J&K. Even on 2 March, 2003, the state legislature passed a resolution against the treaty and demanded an instant review of the treaty.

CONFRONTATION OVER THE USE OF INDUS RIVERS WATER

In 1960, the Indus Water Treaty was signed with the spirit of cooperation which ended a decade-long water dispute between the two countries. To resolve the dispute permanently, conflicting demands and claims was put aside, the rivers were divided, financial arrangements were made and technical assistances were provided. In fact, the division of the rivers provides substantial development to both the countries. The large scales of works in the Indus Basin have been taken place without any interference. But now, with the increasing rate population and accelerating demands for water in both the countries, the water dispute again occurring with new perspectives. The treaty which took a decade of intensive hard work to resolve the dispute is now in the clutch and controversies due to a different set of challenges.

Existing Disputes over the Share of Indus Basin after the Treaty

The Article III (2) (d) of the Indus Water Treaty allows India to utilise the water of western rivers for (i) domestic use, (ii) non-consumptive use, (iii) agriculture use (iv) generation of hydroelectric power from run-of-the river projects. On the hand it is also subjected in the treaty that such utilisation should not cause of damage for lower riparian Pakistan.

For the generation of hydroelectric power on western rivers of India, the treaty has different provisions. Any hydroelectric power project constructed on western rivers by India after the signing of the treaty shall be a run-of-the river project that develops power without live storage as an integral part of the plant except for pondage and surcharge storage. The maximum pondage in the operating pool is allowed to reach a level that is twice as much as the pondage required for firm power. To utilise the permitted water from western rivers, India has planned to construct some projects on the western rivers which are often opposed by Pakistan as the violation of the treaty. Pakistan feels that the Indian projects do not follow the technicalities laid down in the treaty, while India uses permissive clause of the treaty to justify its rights over projects.

The first controversy that aroused in the aftermath of the treaty was in 1970 over Salal Project on Chenab River. Pakistan objected to the design as well as the storage capacity of the project. The issue was formally taken up in 1975 when the two countries stated their negotiation over the project. In 1975, Pakistan's Minister for Foreign affairs visited India and discussed the issue with his counterpart. Therefore, India provided the required information to Pakistan that bridged the gap of many aspects related to the project, but certain fundamental issues remained unresolved.

When several subsequent meetings failed to produce any outcome, Pakistan moved to appoint the neutral expert to settle the issue. But India tried to settle the issue by mutual understanding rather than by third party involvement. Discussion again started at the political level between the two countries and after prolonged discussions by both the Commissioners, and later on at governmental level, the dispute was resolved with some alterations. Following an agreement was signed on 14 April 1978.

Salal Project dispute was not the last in the series. The other projects including the Tulbul Navigation Project (Wullar Barrage), Baglihar, Kishanganga Nemo-Bazgo, Chutak, Dumkhar and Bursar, are also under controversy mainly due to conflicting approaches from the both sides.

The Tulbul Navigation Project (Wullar Barrage) Dispute

The Wullar Project was proposed to be built at the mouth of Wullar Lake in Baramulla district of Kashmir Valley. The original Indian plan was to construct a barrage of 139 meters long and 12 meters wide with maximum storage capacity of 300,000 acre feet (AF). The basic objective of the project was to increase the flow of water in the Jhelum River during the lean season to make it navigable. The project was envisaged in 1980 and the work began in 1984, but Pakistan raised the objection on the ground objected that the project allegedly violates the provisions of the treaty.

Pakistani Perspective on Wullar Project: Pakistan objected that the project's storage capacity violates the Article I (15) [b] of the treaty, which barred both parties to create man-made obstruction that may cause changes in the daily flow of the rivers. Further, Pakistan claimed that the Article III (4)50 of the treaty specifically prohibits India from creating any storage or constructing any storage works on western rivers. Indus Water Treaty, India is entitled to construct an 'incidental storage work' on western rivers on its side, but storage capacity should not exceed more than 10,000 acre feet. Tulbul project's storage is more than 300,000 acre feet, which is more than thirty times as the permitted capacity. 52 Some more apprehensions of Pakistan over the project are:

- The project would adversely affect the triple canal project, Upper Chenab Canal, Upper Jhelum Canal and Lower Bari Doab Canal;

- Construction of the project would enable India to control Jhelum River during the winter season;
- Mangla Dam would be adversely affected by construction of Wullar Project;
- The project seems to be a security threat to Pakistan's sovereignty.

The Indian perspective over Wullar Project: India, on the other hand, claims that the project would neither increase the permitted storage capacity nor will interfere with downstream flows. Its purpose is only to improve the navigation over the Jhelum River during lean period (winter months); to connect Baramulla with Srinagar, as it does not violate the norms of the treaty. India also argues that 90 per cent of this project would be beneficial to Pakistan, i.e. it would increase the power generation capacity of Mangla Dam and would increase the efficiency of irrigation network in Pakistan during critical period as well.

On-going discussion over Wullar Project: In 1986 Pakistan referred the Wullar Project dispute to Indus Water Commission, but after one year the Commission recorded its failure to resolve it. Subsequently, India stopped the construction and Pakistan did not take the case in the International Court of Arbitration. From 1986-91, the two sides have held 13 rounds of talks to settle the dispute, but dispute remained unresolved. At 1991, both the parties reached to sign an agreement but the differences could not be resolved due to Pakistan's apprehensions. During the subsequent data exchange process, India agreed to keep 6.2 meters of the barrage ungated with a crest level of 1574.90m (5167 feet), and would forego the storage capacity of 300,000 acre feet. In return, the water level in the Barrage would be allowed to attain the full operational level of 5177.90 acre feet. However, in February 1992, Pakistan added another condition that India should not construct the 390 MW Kishanganga hydropower project, but India refused to accept this condition. Following 18 years of stalemates did not produce any results and the differences in the project persisted. As disputes dominated Indo-Pak talks and discussions at political forefronts in 1999 at Lahore, the Agra Summit of 2001, secretary-level talks of 2011, but not much development has been achieved yet.

The present status of talks over the project manifests that it has been politicized. Though the Indus Water Commission has authority to settle the disputes but assorted political understandings along with political distrust, security issues and growing demand for water and increasing energy needs in two countries are hindrances to reach any consensus.

The Baglihar Project Dispute

The Baglihar project was the major issue between the two countries that went to neutral experts for determining on technical "questions" raised by

Pakistan. The dispute over the Baglihar project emerged in 1999, when Pakistan challenged the design of the project under the Article IX (1)54 of the treaty. Pakistan's objections were related to pondage level, gate spillway, under-sluices, level of intake tunnels, and height of gates and elevation of tunnels.

Pakistan's main concerns were that the project is the violation of the treaty. The gated structure of the project would result in a loss of 7000 to 8000 cusecs of water a day. Further, the project gives India a strategic leverage to manipulate the flow of river during any critical situation.

The project has incurred Pakistan's concerns from economic, strategic and political perspectives. Discussions and the deliberations started only after India provided the required information in 2002, and thereafter, it started the construction of the project which was opposed by Pakistan.

Hence, the issue has stirred intense political debates from both sides. During the discussion, the design of the project remained a major concern between the parties. Pakistan insisted that India should stop working on the project, but India refused to accept it. Consequently, Pakistan sent its "questions" over the project to India under Article IX (1) of the treaty as:

- The project appeared to be capable of raising the water level artificially beyond the full pondage level specified in the design and would contravene the provisions of Paragraph 8 (a) of the treaty;
- The pondage in the operating pool being 37.722 million cubic metres exceeds twice the pondage of water level;
- The site was suitable for an ungated spillway, and therefore, a gated spillway should not have been provided. This was in contravention of Paragraph 8 (e) ;
- The intake for the turbine had not been located at the highest level as required, as referred to in Paragraph 8 (f) to the treaty.

Indian reply to Pakistan's Objections

- the Baglihar was not a violation of the treaty;
- the project was a run-of-the river project;
- the storage called poundage was necessary to meet the fluctuations in the discharge of the turbines;
- the project will not disrupt the flow of the Chenab River and the water will ultimately go to Pakistan;
- India stated that the removal of gates would mean the end of the project.

The "questions" and "differences" over the project imply that one party deemed the project as the violation of the treaty, while the other party assessed the project within the parameters of the treaty. Since Commissioners level talks over the project remained unsuccessful, the World Bank intervened eventually and appointed a neutral expert to resolve the dispute.

The neutral expert, Professor Raymond Lafitte of Switzerland, classified Pakistan's objections while delivering the verdict for minor design changes including the reduction of the dam's height of 1.5 meters. The neutral expert did not question the right of India to construct the project and did not even call the project a "dispute" between the two countries, but considered it as "differences". The neutral expert required India to make some changes but Pakistan was not satisfied with the verdict, as the expert did not consider much of Pakistan's objections.

It is important to note that the neutral expert set a precedence to be followed in future if the need for interpretation of the treaty arises. The expert applied the Vienna Convention on the laws of treaties (1969) and referred to the latest bulletin of the International Commission on Large Dams (ICOLD) rules of science and the state of the art practices.

The need to incorporate state of the art knowledge of science in the interpretation of the treaty was emphasized by Raymond Lafitte. The decision of the court on Baglihar Project was made while using emerging knowledge of hydraulic, environment science, climate change and contemporary research on dams.

The judgment of the court, which is set as precedence and an integral part of the treaty, stated that the rights and obligations of both the parties should be read in light of technical norms and noble standards.

The Baglihar dispute was settled by the third party intervention but relations between two countries again became hostile over the project when water was to be filled in the dam.

According to the provision of the treaty, a minimum flow of 55,000 cusecs has to be maintained above Merala and it should be filled during the period between June 21 and August 31. Pakistan claimed that the filling was not done in the stipulated period. Hence, the filling of the dam has made colossal damage to the country's agriculture sector in downstream areas of the Chenab River. India replied that the filling of the dam was done on time stipulated in the treaty.

Pakistan demanded compensation from India for its losses incurred at the time when the dam was filled. India insisted that it had not violated the treaty and refused Pakistan's claim. Therefore, a lot of discussions were held between the two countries, even pitching top leaderships in both countries. Finally, differences over the filling of Baglihar dam were resolved in 2010 at a meeting of the PICs in the spirit of co- operation and goodwill.

The Kishanganga Project Dispute

The Kishanganga Project is another project being constructed by India over the Kishanganga River at Gurez. The project's power generation capacity is about 330 MW and the height is about 75 meters. It is located about 160 km upstream of Muzaffarabad (Pakistan Administrated Kashmir Capital). The project involves the diversion of Kishanganga (Neelum River in Muzaffarabad) through a 23 km long tunnel into the Madumati Nala, which will empty into the Wullar Lake, through which the Jhelum River flows. Pakistan is of the view that the diversion of the Kishanganga River will reduce the flow of 140,000 million acres feet of water to the Neelum Valley in Pakistan Administrated Kashmir.

In 1992, India officially informed Pakistan about the construction of project, which later raised three objections to the project.

- The first objection raised by Pakistan was that the inter-tributary diversion is barred by the treaty, and the water drawn from a given tributary must be returned to the same river;
- The second is that the existing Pakistani usage must be protected but India's Kishanganga Project will deprive it of 27 per cent of the river's natural flow, thereby inflicting damage to its existing 133,000 hectares of irrigation in the Neelum Valley. Also, it will affect the 900 MW Neelum-Jhelum hydro project on which construction is in progress at Muzaffarabad.
- Lastly, Pakistan criticized the design features of the project that do not meet the criterion of the Indus Water Treaty.

India replied, citing the norms of the treaty, that where a plant is located on a tributary of the Jhelum River around which Pakistan has an agricultural and hydroelectric use, the water released below the plant may be delivered, if necessary, into another tributary but only to the extent that the then existing agricultural use or hydro-electric use by Pakistan on the former tributary would not be adversely affected.

To justify its claim, India stated that inter-tributary diversions in the Jhelum basin are permitted and only "the then existing" agricultural and hydroelectric uses shall be protected.

The construction of the project has created a new issue for heated discussions at different levels after the Baglihar project. The Indus Commission held a number of meetings to console the parties, but due to different approaches, interpretation of and perspectives on the treaty text, the dispute remained unresolved. Essentially, growing needs for water by both the countries and competitive behaviours have affected the discussions at every level.

Pakistani apprehensions over the project: Pakistan further objected to the project on the ground of diversion of water through the tunnel, since:

- The project will have an adverse effect on Neelum-Jhelum link project that Pakistan initiated in 1988.
- Secondly, diversion of the water of the Kishanganga River to Jhelum would ruin the Neelum Valley in Pakistan and also that the project do not confirm to design criteria (a), (c), (e), (f) and (g) mention.
- In Pakistan it is also feared that the project could reduce Pakistan's total water availability from 154 million acre feet (MAF) to about 140 MAF, a shortage of about 8-9 per cent.
- Further, it the project would reduce the energy generation of Neelum Jhelum hydro project by about 16 per cent amounting to an annual loss of Rs. 5 billion at the current rates.
- It is also feared to reduce the flow of water in the River Jhelum by 27 per cent.

Indian perspective on the project: The response of India has always been that the water of the Kishanganga River will ultimately go to Pakistan and there would be no serious damage in lower stream areas of Pakistan administrated Kashmir. Also India's assessment is that the diversion of water through tunnel into the Jhelum would help Pakistan to generate more electricity in Mangla and Neelum Jhelum projects during winter season.

Pakistan has rejected all assessments and appraisals by India regarding the project. However, the dispute has figured on the agenda of talks even at the time and now between the Commissioners.

As the Commission level discussion did not arrive at any settlement, the dispute has been referred to the International Court of Arbitration as instructed in the treaty, because the dispute involves techniques as well as legal issues. Hence, the decision of the International Court of Arbitration about the Kishanganga dispute is awaited.

On-going discussions on the dispute: A series of talks were held between the parties at various levels to resolve "differences" and "dispute" attached to the use of Kishanganga River, but talks remained unresolved and problematic.

Pakistan has frequently criticised the project as the violation of the treaty, and therefore, in April 2006, India offered to modify the project and submitted a revised plan in July 2006. In the revised plan, India agreed to convert the storage and power generation project into a run-of-the-river project and construct poundage in accordance with the treaty. But again Pakistan rejected the plan mentioning that the project still has objectionable aspects. Later

Pakistan communicated these objections to India in a detailed report, while the contention of India has been that the waters will ultimately go to Pakistan. Contemplating the disputes over the use of Indus Basin, it could be concluded that it is the second time in the past ten years that the dispute over the utilization of water is referred to the third party for resolution.

The Kishanganga dispute assumes a greater significance because Pakistan is also trying to construct its own project—the Neelum-Jhelum hydroelectric project—on the Pakistani side of the Neelum River (Kishanganga). The Indus Water Treaty states that the country that completes its project first will secure priority rights to the river.

Hence, both countries are in contest to complete their respective projects as soon as possible without considering the objections and apprehensions of each other. There have been major delays in the construction of the projects on both sides of the border, because of the dispute and the issue of water-sharing between India and Pakistan is spiralling.

There are also some other hydroelectric projects which are seen in the light of controversy between India and Pakistan. These include Dul Hasti, Uri II, Chutak, Nimoo-Bazgo, Dumkhar, Ratle and Sawlakote Project etc. Aforementioned projects, objected to by Pakistan, have added new dimensions to the disputes attached to economic, security and strategic importance, but some are alien to the provisions of the treaty.

In the following table and figure, an attempt has been made to list out the chronology of water-related conflicts in the Indus Basin following the signing of the treaty. At the same time, the table and figure help us to understand the nature and intensity of water conflicts between the two countries and highlight how the two countries are engaged in different types of water-related conflicts.

The figure displays the conflicts over water between the two countries since the signing of the treaty. 80% is about water control, while 20% is about water allocation. Control of water from western rivers has received considerable attention from both the sides. It is because of the construction of the projects on western rivers, Pakistan fears that India is exercising "hydro hegemony" on these projects and it will use these projects as a bargaining tool with Pakistan to settle other related issues. To what extent these interpretations are valid but the growing concerns of the parties leading fierce competition over water.

The outcomes of the on-going disputes have broader implications not only for future water development but also about India-Pakistan relations. The Indus Treaty has served both the countries and stood with the test of time, but the growing economies of both countries and the energy needs are nurturing a different set of challenges. Multiplying problems related to acute water supply have also put on serious burdens on the Indus Basin Rivers. Exploitation of water with the last drops means the violation of the treaty. Under such an adverse situation, the Indus Water Commissioners are also under pressure from respective governments as they have failed to forge any final decision over certain disputes.

Reasons for Differences over Projects

It is usually easier to understand how the "questions," "differences" and "disputes" attached to these projects aroused. To be precise, they appeared on the scene from different approaches to and differing interpretations of various provisions of the main text of the treaty.

Some issues regarding the technicalities of the treaty are not acceptable to both parties. For instance, the Article III (4)75 of the treaty barred India in building any storage on the western rivers, except a limited utilisation of the treaty, and also specifies technical conditions relating to engineering structures and features, such as live storage, dead storage, limits on raising artificially, the water level in the operating pool, poundage levels, crest level of the gates, location of intakes for the turbines, and so on. One party claims to be in full conformity with the criteria laid down in the treaty on these, while the other party says that this is not the case.

The Indus Treaty is a highly technical treaty as compared to other treaties in the region. The dense technicalities allow ample opportunities for differences and have made it difficult to understand for engineers and even to Indus Water Commissioners.

Some experts are of the view that the Indus Water Treaty carried out a surgery of the Indus Basin into two as eastern and western group of rivers. Though both countries are highly dependent on each other for cooperation and development of the basin, but the division of the basin has reduced the level of cooperation between the two countries.

Environmental issues like climate change have not been covered in the treaty. Pakistan, as lower riparian has apprehensions over the projects on the western rivers and considers them as the existential threat to her inhabitants, as stored water can flush out the land and property. Secondly, Pakistan is afraid that these projects will reduce the water flow in critical times, especially during the sowing seasons.

On the other hand, India's concern is to improve its energy efficiencies and economy, for which it is endeavouring to utilise the full power potentialities. Its booming economy, waves of globalization, overwhelming urbanization push India to generate more and more electricity from hydropower projects on Himalayan Rivers. Its peak power demand in the year 2007-08 was 108,886 MW, while the peak power demand met was 90,793 MW; there was a shortage of 18,093 MW or 16.6 percent of peak demand. The projects on western rivers are a crucial part of India's plan to close that gap.

The hydro power sector is also an attractive revenue earner for Himalayan states, which are underdeveloped in the industrial sector as compared to other states. Therefore, the exploitation of hydro power from Himalayan Rivers is the only source to boost their industrial sector. But in reply to Pakistan's apprehensions on western rivers, Indian position is that it is not violating the spirit of the treaty. Secondly, Pakistan's security fears are misconceived as India cannot flood Pakistan without flooding it first.

Bibliography

Akhtar, S.: *Emerging Challenges to Indus Waters Treaty: Issues of Compliance and Transboundary Impacts of Indian hydroprojects On the Western Rivers.* Institute of Regional Studies, Islamabad, Pakistan, 2010.

Ali Ihsan: *Water as an Element of Cooperation and Development in the Middle East*, Ankara, Ayna Publications, 1994.

Ali, S. H.: *Water Politics in South Asia: Technocratic Cooperation and Lasting Security in the Indus Basin and Beyond.* Journal of International Affairs, 2008.

Alka Rani : *Aquatic Plants for the Waste Water Treatment*, Daya, Delhi, 2004.

Allen Carlson, *Unifying China, Integrating with the World: Securing Chinese Sovereignty in the Reform Era*, Stanford: Stanford University Press, 2005.

Allouche, J.: *Water Nationalism: An Explanation of the Past and Present Conflicts in Central Asia, the Middle East and Indian Subcontinent*? University of Geneve, 2005.

Barua, Pradeep: *Gentlemen of the Raj: The Indian Army Officer Corps, 1817–1949*, 2003.

Benjamin, Joseph : *China-Pak Relations : Prospect and Retrospect*, Reference Press, Delhi, 2004.

Bhakar S.R. : *Ground Water Hydrology : Theory and Practice*, Agrotech, Delhi, 2009.

Bhat, T.P. : *India and China : Trade Complementarities and Competitiveness*, Bookwell, Delhi, 2008.

Bhave, P.R. and R. Gupta: *Analysis of Water Distribution Networks*, Narosa, Delhi, 2011.

Biswas Asit K. : *Integrated Water Resources Management in South and South-East Asia,,* Oxford University Press, Delhi, 2001.

Bort, E.: *Boundaries and Identities: The Eastern Frontier of the Asia*, Edinburgh: International Social Sciences Institute, University of Edinburgh, 1996.

Boulnois, Luce: *Silk Road: Monks, Warriors and Merchants on the Silk Road.* Odyssey Publications, 2005.

Bourne, Peter G.: *Water and Sanitation: Economic and Sociological Perspectives* Academic Press. Orlando. 1984.

Brooks, D.: *Water: Local-Level Management*, Ottawa, International Development Research Centre, 2002.

Budge I: *The New Challenge of Direct Democracy*, Oxford, Polity Press, 1996.

Bulliet, Richard W.: *The Camel and the Wheel*. Harvard University Press. 1975.

Charles E. Faupel: *Water Treaty and Civil Rights in Sumter County*, Colorado, Westview Press, 1992.

Chitkara, M.G. : *China-Pak Relations Challenges Before New Millennium*, APH, Delhi, 2001.

Clinton, William J. *A National Security Strategy for a New Century*. Washington, DC: Government Printing Office, 1998.

Conway, D.: *Climate Change and Water Resources in the Nile Basin*, London, University of London, 1993.

Dashti, Naseer: *The Baloch and Balochistan: A Historical Account from the Beginning to the Fall of the Baloch State*, Trafford Publishing, 2012.

Deepak, B R : *India and China : 1904-2004 : A Century of Peace and Conflict*, Manak, Delhi, 2005.

Falkenmark, Malin: *Rural Water Supply and Health: The need for a New Strategy*, Scandinavian Institute of African Studies. Uppsala. 1982.

Felix K. Chang: *'China's Naval Rise and the South China Sea: An Operational Assessment.'* 2012.

Ferentinos L.: *Proceeding of the Sustainable Taro Culture for the Pacific Conference*, Honolulu, HITAHR, 1993.

Forbes, Andrew ; Henley, David: *China's Ancient Tea Horse Road*. Chiang Mai: Cognoscenti Books. 2011.

Frank R.: *The Philippines and the South China Sea Islands: Overview and Documents*. Metro Manila: Foreign Service Institute, 1993.

Friedman, G.: *The Future of War: Power, Technology and American World Dominance in the 21st Century*, N.Y., Random House, 1996.

Friedman, G.: *The Future of War: Power, Technology and Indian Army*, N.Y., Random House, 1996.

Gao, Mobo: *The Battle for China's Past: Mao and the Cultural Revolution*, London, Pluto Press, 2008.

Gleick, Peter H. : *Water "Crisis: A Guide to the World's Fresh Water Resources"*, New York: Oxford University Press, 1933.

Goldrick, James: *No Easy Answers: The Development of the Navies of India, Pakistan, Bangladesh, and Sri Lanka, 1945–1996*. Lancer Publishers, 1997.

Gupta K.R. *: Water Crisis in India*, Atlantic Pub, Delhi, 2008.

Gupta, P. S. and Anirudh Deshpande: *The British Raj and its Indian Navy Forces, 1857–1939*, New Delhi: Oxford University Press, 2002.

Gupta, R. : *Analysis of Water Distribution Networks*, Narosa, Delhi, 2011.

Gurjar, Ram Kumar : *Geography of Water Resources*, Rawat, Delhi, 2008.

Hans J. Morgenthau: *Politics Among Nations: The Struggle for Power and Peace*, New York, Knopf, 1960.

Hansen, Valerie: *The Silk Road: A New History*, Oxford University Press; 2012.

Hoekstra, A. Y. and A. K. Chapagain: *Globalization of Water: Sharing the Planet's Freshwater Resources,* Oxford: Blackwell, 2008

Hoffman, Bruce, *Inside Terrorism,* New York: Columbia University Press, 1998.

Huntington, P. : *The Navy and the State : The Theory and Politics of Civil-Military Relations,* Natraj Pub, Delhi, 2005.

Imtiaz, A.: *State and Foreign Policy: India's Role in South Asia,* New Delhi, Vikas, 1993.

Jackson, Major Donovan: *India's Navy.* Sampson Low. London, 1940.

James Campbell: *Excursions, Adventures and Field-Sports in Ceylon : Its Commercial and Military Importance,* AES, Delhi, 2006.

James J.: *Water Atlas of the United States,* Port Washington, NY, 1973.

Jha, Prem Shankar : *India and China : The Battle Between Soft and Hard Power,* Penguin Books India, Delhi, 2010.

Jha.B.H.: *Diversion of the Brahmaputra: Myth or Reality?* Institute for Defence Studies and Analysis: New Delhi, 2011.

Johnston, Douglas: *The Theory and History of Ocean Boundary Making.* Kingston: McGill-Queen's University Press, 1988.

Juvale, R.P. : *Military Strategy and Diplomacy,* Cyber Tech Publications, Delhi, 2010.

Kruvant, W.J.: *People, Energy, and Pollution,* Cambridge, Ballinger Publishing, 1975.

Kugelman M.: *Water: Asia's New Battleground,* News Security Beat, 2011.

Larsen, Jeanne: *Silk Road: A Novel of Eighth-Century China.* 2009.

Lloyd Myers : *Handbook of Water Harvesting,* Washington D.C.: U.S. Dept. of Agriculture, Agricultural Research Service, 1983

Lo Chi-Kin: *China's Policy Towards Territorial Disputes. The Case of the South China Sea Islands.* London: Routledge, 1989.

Mahajan Gautam *: Evaluation and Development of Ground Water,* APH, Delhi, 2008.

Major Donovan: *Indian Ocean.* Sampson Low. London, 1940.

McGarry, M.G.: *Matching Water Supply Technology to the Needs and Resources of Developing Countries,* United Nations. New York. 1987

Mishra Archana *: Water Harvesting : Ecological and Economic Appraisal,* Authors Press, Delhi, 2006.

Nageswara, Rao K. *: Water Resources Management : Realities and Challenges,* New Century Publication, Delhi, 2006.

Namboodirim, P. : *Intervention in the Indian Ocean,* New Delhi: ABC Publishing House, 1982.

Nayyar, K K : *National Security : Military Aspects,* Rupa, Delhi, 2003.

Neil Frank R.: *The Philippines and the South China Sea Islands: Overview and Documents.* Metro Manila: Foreign Service Institute, 1993.

Nevile, P.: *Lahore: A Sentimental Journey.* New Delhi: Penguin, 1993.

Nissen-Petersen, E. : *Rainwater Catchment Systems for Domestic Supply: Design, Construction and Implementation,* London, U.K.: IT Publications, 1999.

Oudha, Abdul Qadir : *Criminal Law of Islam,* Kitab Bhavan, New Delhi, 1999.

Park Hee Kwon: *The Law of the Sea and Northeast Asia.* The Hague: Kluwer, 2000.

Patrizio Warren: *Developing Participatory and Integrated Watershed Management*, Daya for FAO, Delhi, 2001.

Peter G.: *Water and Sanitation: Economic and Sociological Perspectives* Academic Press. Orlando. 1984.

Peter Lambron Wilson : *Traditional Modes of Contemplation and Action*, University Press, Tehran, 1977.

Postel, Sandra : *Last Oasis: Facing Water Scarcity*, World Water Institute, New York, 1992.

Ram Kumar : *Geography of Water Resources*, Rawat, Delhi, 2008.

Ranjan, A.: *Water Conflicts between India and Pakistan*. Daily Times, Pakistan, 2010.

Rao K. Nageswara *: Water Resources Management : Realities and Challenges*, New Century Publication, Delhi, 2006.

Rosen, P.: *Societies and Military Power: India and its Armies*, Ithaca, Cornell University Press, 1996.

Sam Bateman: *Maritime Change: Issues for Asia.* St. Leonards: Allen & Unwin, 1993.

Samuels, Marwyn: *Contest for the South China Sea.* New York: Methuen, 1982.

Sindhu, Abid Latif: *The Pakistan-India Water War*. Terminal X, Pakistan Observer. 2008.

Singh A K *: Environment and Water Resources Management*, Adhyayan, Delhi, 2006.

Singh, Amarinder : *A Ridge Too Far: War in the Kargil Heights 1999*. Motibagh Palace, Patiala. 2001.

Stephen Bates : *Calming the Waters. Initiatives for Asia Pacific Maritime Cooperation.* Canberra Papers on Strategy and Defence, 1996.

Sumantra Bose, *The Challenge in Kashmir : democracy, self-determination and a just peace*, New Delhi: Sage, 1997.

Sutter. R.G: *Chinese Foreign Relations: Power and Policy Since the Cold War.* Plymouth, Rowman and Littlefield Publishers, 2010.

Sutton, J., *Technology and Defence Market Structure*, MIT Press, Delhi, 1998.

Swain, A.: *Managing water conflict*: *Asia, Africa and the Middle East*. London and New York: Routledge, 2004.

Thubron, C.: *The Silk Road to China*, Hamlyn, 1989.

Upadhyay, Alka Rani : *Aquatic Plants for the Waste Water Treatment*, Daya, Delhi, 2004.

Vallette, J.: *The International Trade in Wastes: A Greenpeace Inventory*, Washington, Greenpeace, 1989.

Vice Admiral Mihir K. Roy: *War in the Indian Ocean*. New Delhi: Lancer Publishers. 1995.

William, K. : *Irrigation Investment Technology, and Management Strategies for Development Studies in Water Policy Management 9*, Boulder, Colo Westview Press, 1986.

Index

L

M

N

P

R

S

T

U

W

❑❑❑